'There are so many colourful characters in Nicholas Foulkes' *Gentlemen and Blackguards* that Dickens would have spread them over six novels' *Mail On Sunday*

'The Queen Mother would have adored Nick Foulkes' book ... terribly engaging stuff' *Spear's*

'Nicholas Foulkes' book is a carefully researched story of money, skulduggery and sporting obsession and will appeal to sportsman and historian alike' *Shooting Gazette*

'Foulkes is a master of the flashing phrase and crafts memorable vignettes of mainly disreputable characters but he is also a shrewd analyst of social change. In his assured telling, the story thunders along with the legs of a dead cert Derby winner' *Daily Express*

'Foulkes' wonderful prose is not only fair; it is also elegant, erudite and – like this book itself – outstandingly entertaining' *Tablet*

'Nick Foulkes' colourful account of gambling in 19th-century England' *GQ*

'Foulkes paints a flamboyant portrait of the society of the day and of a pivotal moment in British racing history' *Good Book Guide*

'The story of their audacious plot and the personalities who unmasked it is beautifully told' *How to Spend It, Financial Times*

'Herein is a rich assembly of underground rogues and aristocratic sporting men, set at the historical crossroads of the Georgian and Victorian eras' *The Sunday Times*

Nicholas Foulkes read English at Hertford College, Oxford, and is the author of numerous books, including two well-received volumes of nineteenth-century history, *Scandalous Society* and *Dancing into Battle*. A former associate editor of the *Evening Standard*'s *ES* magazine, he contributes to a wide range of newspapers and magazines around the world. He is a columnist for *Newsweek* and *Country Life*, a contributing editor to the *Financial Times*' *How to Spend It* magazine and *Vanity Fair*, and is luxury editor of *GQ*. He is co-founder and editor-in-chief of *Finch's Quarterly Review*. In 2007 his contribution to cigar smoking was recognised when he was named Havana Man of the Year. *Gentlemen and Blackguard* was chosen as a Book of the Year by the *Daily Express* and the *Sunday Times* in 2010. He is married with two sons and lives beyond his means in west London.

GENTLEMEN

AND

BLACKGUARDS

or

Gambling Mania and the
Plot to Steal the Derby of 1844

———

NICHOLAS FOULKES

PHOENIX

A PHOENIX PAPERBACK

First published in Great Britain in 2010
by Weidenfeld & Nicolson
This paperback edition published in 2011
by Phoenix,
an imprint of Orion Books Ltd,
Orion House, 5 Upper St Martin's Lane,
London WC2H 9EA

An Hachette UK company

1 3 5 7 9 10 8 6 4 2

ISBN 978-0-7538-2475-7

Typeset by Input Data Services Ltd, Bridgwater, Somerset

Printed and bound in Great Britain by CPI Mackays, Chatham, Kent

The Orion Publishing Group's policy is to use papers that
are natural, renewable and recyclable products and
made from wood grown in sustainable forests. The logging
and manufacturing processes are expected to conform to
the environmental regulations of the country of origin.

www.orionbooks.co.uk

Contents

---

15   A Game of Musical Stables   191

16   The Full Majesty of the Law   204

17   Their Day in Court   216

18   An Eventful Evening   231

19   The Verdict   238

20   Gentlemen Triumphant   245

     Epilogue   257

     Notes   267
     Bibliography   282
     Index   289

List of Illustrations

Acknowledgements

There are a great many people to thank and, as ever, Luigi Bonomi, my talented, tolerant, understanding and highly effective literary agent, has to shoulder much of the blame for *Gentlemen and Blackguards* finally making it into print. However, it would have got nowhere had it not been for the belief and the guidance of Alan Samson, my publisher at Weidenfeld & Nicolson. This is the third book on which I have worked with Alan and if there have been any improvements, which I hope that there have, they are due to his encouragement and perspicacious suggestions as to how I might choose to direct my efforts. At a time when the written word is under threat, it is a joy and a comfort to have such a man on one's side. His team at Weidenfeld has been brilliant; in particular I must thank my editor Bea Hemming for her charm, experience and insight, all of which helped to make working through the manuscript a pleasure. I would also like to express my gratitude to Rebecca Gray for her tireless efforts to publicise this book. I cannot speak highly enough of Laura Fellowes, my brilliant and brilliantly conscientious research assistant, who has lived through this project with me without a single complaint and has worked incredibly hard to help me bring it to life.

Special thanks are due to Tim Cox, who read the manuscript twice and made many useful remarks concerning the history of horse racing in Britain; his Racing Library is a national treasure. Also high on the list of our nation's jewels is the Newmarket Racing Museum, where Alan Grundy was incredibly helpful and from whom I was able to obtain copies of the Jockey Club Enquiry. Anthony Byles's collection of vintage newspaper reports was invaluable when it came to unearthing some particularly piquant details about one of the major characters. Judith Phillips, archivist at the Bowes Museum, was incredibly generous with her time and knowledge when it came to tracking down the *qui tam* letters. Jayne Amat at the Portland Archives at Nottingham University was a model of efficiency. David Oldrey, a doyen of the Turf, was kind enough to plough through the manuscript making many helpful suggestions and even kinder in saying that he enjoyed it; I am so grateful for the time he gave to this book. Tristram Fetherstonhaugh, a gifted friend of mine, was kind enough to take time to come up with the concept for the cover design. Harriet Collins was generous in putting her time and her unique knowledge of Newmarket and its characters at my disposal. I must also thank Sir Mark Prescott for an absolutely splendid summer's day at his exemplary stables; it is always a joy to meet someone who cares so passionately about the traditions of our island. There were many others who also helped in ways too numerous to mention, among them I must mention, the unfailingly helpful staff of the London Library, William Haggas, Charles March, Harry Herbert, Alex Myers, Ralph Lauren, Nick and Giles English, John Ayton, Edward Sahakian, Andrea Riva, Franz La Rosée and Jean Pierre Martel.

Money and its Value

This is a story of men and their pursuit of the excitement afforded by gambling, so it is, perforce, a story of money: the tantalising lure of winning it easily, the fear of losing it all, and the delicious thrill of the moment when these two possibilities hang on the outcome of the turn of a card, the roll of a die, or the speed at which a group of horses cover a stretch of southern English downland on a late spring afternoon. In the 1840s British aristocrats were the most powerful body of men on the planet. They made everything from the fashions to the laws of the world's unchallenged super-power; they accumulated fortunes that are barely imaginable to this day – even in twenty-first-century terms some of the sums involved are impressive, but when adjusted for inflation they are quite breathtaking.

It is hard to convey with mathematical accuracy the exact value of a mid-nineteenth-century fortune in today's terms as the objects valued and prized by one society might be ignored by another. For instance, the affluent early Victorian paterfamilias with three children, jogging along on £1,000 per annum, could expect to spend just £40 – or 4 per cent – of his income on education, a percentage that many affluent twenty-first-century Britons in thrall to private education can only wonder at. In her essay 'Homes and Habits' on the cost of living in *Early Victorian England, 1830–1865*,* Mrs C.S. Peel provides a useful rule of thumb:

Beginning with an income of £150 per annum, the man becomes a

* Ed. G.M. Young, 1934, Oxford University Press.

gentleman, and when his income rises to £250 per annum, his 'wife' becomes his 'Lady'. On £400 a year the family enjoy the services of two maidservants, one horse, and a groom. On £700 they keep one man and three maidservants and two horses. On £1,000 they blossom out into an establishment of three female servants, a coach-man and footman, a chariot or coach, phaeton or other four-wheeled carriage and a pair of horses. On £5,000 a year the establishment has grown to thirteen male and nine female servants, ten horses, a coach, a curricle and a Tilbury, Chaise or gig.

Of course, allowance has to be made for the change in the way of life. Labour-saving devices had yet to be invented, perhaps because labour was cheap – a nursemaid could expect to be paid £10 a year, less than a pound a month, a factor that made the sums squandered on gambling seem even more extravagant. At times the 'servant problem' would make itself felt and staff costs would rise, and as in our own times there were periods of national prosperity and austerity. But Mrs Peel's general conclusion is that 'in early Victorian England a family in good society could live more or less comfortably on £800–£1,000 a year'. While a family might live well for a year on that amount, for the men written about in this book £1,000 (and more often than not, multiples thereof) was considered little more than a reasonable sum to stake on the outcome of a horse race, prize fight, card game, or even a single roll of two ivory dice. In his history of the Jockey Club, *Running Racing* (1997), when describing what jockeys earned for riding in the three great classics of English racing, the Derby, the Oaks and the St Leger in the 1860s, John Tyrrel equates the value of £1 then to £120 in the late 1990s. For want of a better figure I have used this multiplicand to convey some idea, however inexact, of the amounts that were won and lost in the gambling houses, or 'hells', and on the racecourses of early Victorian England.

Introduction

Above the fireplace in my office there is a large print of William Powell Frith's *The Derby Day*. I have owned it for almost twenty years and in amongst the foxing and mottling around its edges it is just possible to pick out the signature of the artist. It is one of my favourite things. I never tire of it. It speaks to me like a visitor from another time.

I can see why the Victorians loved Frith: he depicted their world with the attention to detail and also the panoramic scope of the great novelists of the age. It may be a cliché to say that his narrative canvases are the visual counterpart to the books of Dickens and Thackeray, but then clichés often have a habit of being true.

As I write this, I look up at that image of a vanished age. The dandy, a silk scarf wound round his top hat lolling against a barouche, cigar dangling from his lips, a set of splendid seals hanging from the watch chain on his snowy waistcoat front, casts a supercilious glance at the ragged shoeless girl trying to interest him in her wares; while unseen beneath the carriage wheels, another urchin is reaching out to steal a bottle of champagne. The infant acrobat, lost in dreamy contemplation of the pie and lobster being set out for a picnic lunch, forgets that he is to perform some feat of agility. The thimble-rigger is busy practising his art, inviting bystanders to try their luck and find the pea hidden beneath one of the small cups he moves around a collapsible table, and it seems he has found a victim, as one of the onlookers has a crisp white banknote in his hand. To the left of the picture a row of striped tents promising refreshment and more march off into the distance – you can almost taste the brandy and water, smell the cigar smoke and sense the excitement and expectation. It is a picture that teems with the life of the age.

I have long been fascinated by the event that was the confluence of the varied rivers and tributaries of English life, and it was while researching a book about Count d'Orsay that I came across the story of the 1844 Derby and caught a glimpse of how the culture of gambling in its many manifestations had taken hold of society. It struck me as a great yarn: a tale of rogues and rascals, of subterfuge and chicanery: with duelling, suicide and murder as seasoning. It had the lot: an intricate, audacious plot to 'steal' a fortune, and a cast of characters that, like the best Victorian stories, included everyone from dukes to prize fighters, Corinthians to clerks, moralising prigs to horse dopers, and members of parliament to jockeys. The tide of the narrative swept from grand stately homes to low gambling dens, from the taverns of the day to one of the most ancient courts in the land, via the many racecourses and trainers' yards. It even lapped around the Prime Minister, Sir Robert Peel, whose brother was a key player in the drama.

The more I looked into it, the more engrossed I became in this penumbral world, with its near impenetrable argot and characters so memorable that they seemed to have bathed in the ink of Dickens's pen. In the end it is not so much an account of a horse race, but of a national event and the state of the nation to which it belonged. In a world before Association Football and motorsport, racing was the sport that gripped the nation and the Derby was its ultimate prize. Imagine the thrill of a World Cup Final or the deciding race in a Formula One season and you begin to get a sense of the importance of the event and the sums of money that were at stake. More interesting still was the fact that in the year of 1844 Britain witnessed a paradigm shift in its sense of national morality and its view of itself. In many ways this was the year in which the last embers of the blithe and callous amorality of the Georgian age were extinguished by what have since become known as Victorian values. Above all, I hope you will agree that it is a great story and that I have managed to convey some of its excitement and drama.

Prologue

As he walked into the library of the House of Commons on 25 May 1848, Benjamin Disraeli could be forgiven for feeling rather pleased with himself. Aged forty-three, this former lawyer, stock-market speculator and silver-fork novelist could no longer be called a young man; but at last his political career was gathering momentum. No one, except perhaps he himself, saw in this flashy, opportunistic, over-dressed Westminster fop a future prime minister. However, he was acquiring a reputation as a witty orator whose telling barbs had provided some of the most vivid rhetorical fireworks of the civil war between the protectionists and free-traders over the Corn Laws, effectively destroying the old Tory Party. Passed over for office by Sir Robert Peel, Disraeli had nursed his grudge until he became a lacerating critic of the 'Right Honourable Baronet'.

But it is quite possible that Disraeli would have remained little more than an interesting parliamentary footnote, supplier of amusing soundbites for the political sketch writers and an irritant for the Peelites, had it not been for the tall, severe-looking man he now encountered in the library standing in front of the bookcases, his hand on a book but his mind obviously elsewhere.

Although both men were roughly of the same age – in their mid-forties – they made an odd couple: the macassared dandy and the aloof, auburn-haired aristocrat. Where Disraeli was all poly-chromatic satin and silk, there was an austere patrician elegance about black-clad Lord George Bentinck, the anguished-looking man at the bookshelves. Yet, in spite of the differences that divided them, the two were friends. Although Disraeli would in time become the greater man by far, the most fascinating of the Queen Empress's prime ministers, architect and mythmaker of the Victorian imperium, right now, in 1848, Queen Victoria was still in her twenties and as a younger son of a duke it was Bentinck who was the senior partner in this unlikely double act. After years of political obscurity, during which he had 'attended the house rather as a club than senate', Bentinck had suddenly emerged as the champion of the landed interest, a revanchist nobleman motivated by a violent quasi-chivalric revulsion at what he saw as Peel's breach of honour in repealing the Corn Laws – the import tariffs that had been brought in during 1815 to protect British grain prices had done much over the ensuing years to increase the power and wealth of the landed elite.

Disraeli worshipped Lord George with the intensity of a schoolgirl crush. 'Nature had clothed this vehement spirit with a material form which was in perfect harmony with its noble and commanding character,' he was to write of his idol, caressing his features with honeyed prose:

> He was tall and remarkable for his presence; his countenance almost a model of manly beauty; the face oval, the complexion clear and mantling the forehead lofty and white; the nose aquiline and delicately moulded; the upper lip short. But it was from the dark-brown eye that flashed with piercing scrutiny that all the character of the man came forth: a brilliant glance, not soft, but ardent, acute, imperious, incapable of deception or of being deceived.

Disraeli's affection was doubtless intensified by the coupling of Bentinck's good looks with a background that was about as grand as it was possible to get. Third son of the 4th Duke of Portland, Bentinck was born to the unassailable social position and colossal wealth that Disraeli spent his life working towards. Of Jewish ancestry, Disraeli's father, realising the immanent anti-Semitism of British society, had baptised his children as Anglicans, and Disraeli had secured his financial position only by marrying a rich widow twelve years his senior.

For Disraeli, Bentinck was all that he could have hoped for in a friend and patron. And on his idealised portrait of the man to whom he had already hitched his personal political ambition he hung his own concept of what an aristocrat should be, describing him as 'a whig of 1688' and a champion of 'civil and religious liberty'. However, even Disraeli could not put an entirely positive gloss on Bentinck's 'too rigid tenacity of opinion' and 'quickness of temper', but with a novelist's insight he recognised these short-comings as compensations for a 'too sensitive heart'. And as he walked across the room to his friend, he saw in those expressive brown eyes that this 'too sensitive heart' was suffering cruelly. Disraeli knew that his friend had been fretting about the free-trade leanings of the Select Committee on Sugar and Coffee Planting which had finished hearing evidence a couple of days earlier. But even though Bentinck had been working eighteen-hour days and was keenly interested in the outcome, his distress was of a different, more intense order – 'his countenance was greatly disturbed.'

Before emerging as the surprise political champion of the Protectionists, Bentinck had been known chiefly as an owner of race-horses, a pastime he had pursued with the same monomaniacal, pitiless energy that he now directed against his Free-trade opponents. He had built the finest stud in the country and then sold it on impulse for a giveaway price so that he could immerse himself in the Protectionist cause. However, it was his discarded Turf career and the tantalising prospect of what might have been that was now torturing him so exquisitely. It was the day after the Derby, which had been won by a horse called Surplice on which Lord George had wagered and won handsomely. But money never really mattered much to him; it had only ever been a way of keeping score or, as Disraeli put it rather more picturesquely, 'He counted his thousands after a great race as a victorious general counts his cannon and his prisoners.'[1]

What mortified Lord George was that Surplice had been his own horse. He had bred him, having bought his dam Crucifix, 'one of the scraggiest and most uncompromising foals ever seen',[2] a decade or so earlier. Surplice had gone in the snap sale of his entire stud a couple of years earlier. His whole adult life and hundreds of thousands of pounds (today, tens of millions) had been spent in pursuit of a Derby win, 'that paramount and Olympian stake',[3] and now 'his' horse had won it – except, of course, it was no longer 'his' horse. His distress was particularly piquant as he was even deprived of the satisfaction of seeing the race: he had arrived at Epsom just four minutes[4] after it had finished.

He turned to Disraeli and, giving 'a sort of superb groan', murmured, 'All my life I have been trying for this, and for what have I sacrificed it!' So poignant was his distress that even Disraeli was lost for something to say to comfort him. Taking his friend's silence for a lack of understanding of the gravity and import of the situation, Bentinck reproached him with the words, 'You do not know what the Derby is.'

'Yes I do,' replied Disraeli, 'it is the blue ribbon of the Turf.'

'It is the blue ribbon of the Turf,' said Bentinck slowly, in his curiously squeaky emotion-choked voice, repeating the words as if in search of some solace from them. He then sat down at a table and 'buried himself in a folio of statistics'.[5] But it is hard to believe that his close study of the recommendation for a ten-shilling differential duty to favour sugar produced by Britain's colonies provided the distraction and consolation he needed. Instead, it is likely that his mind wandered back over his Turf career and lingered particularly on his leading role in the extraordinary events of the notorious Derby of 1844, the most crooked and corrupt major race ever run on British soil, a race that marked a nadir in the reputation of British racing and which had been the catalyst for wide-reaching social change. In many ways, what later became known as Victorian values – integrity, fair play and that elusive quality of gentlemanliness – were cooked in the crucible of that tumultuous year.

I

The Blue Ribbon of the Turf

Pompeius before Pharsalia, Harold before Hastings, Napoleon before Waterloo, might afford some striking contrasts to the immediate catastrophe of their fortunes ... and yet the 'before' and 'after' of a first-rate English race, in the degree of its excitement, and sometimes in the tragic emotions of its close, may vie even with these.

Benjamin Disraeli, *Sybil: or, The Two Nations*

Disraeli was perhaps the closest friend that Lord George Bentinck had, and of course Disraeli knew what the Derby was. But could he really know what it meant to a man like Lord George? It is typical of Lord George's arrogance that he thought not. Had he had any doubt about the matter he need only have turned to the opening pages of Disraeli's *Sybil: or, the Two Nations* (1845), a political text disguised as a slightly clunking novel. While the book sets out Disraeli's parliamentary stall as a compassionate Conservative, one deeply interested in the miseries endured by the agricultural and urban working classes, in fiction as in life he is unable to resist the lure of the high life and the book opens with an account of aristocratic betters placing their wagers on the eve of the Derby of 1837.

He was, it seems, only too aware that the Derby was far more than the sum of its parts. Of the race, the few minutes during which a field of about twenty horses thunders around a mile and a half of Surrey downland, he becomes quite lyrical, far more eloquent than poor old Lord George groping for words with which to express his distress. Disraeli writes: 'A few minutes, only a few minutes, and the event that for twelve months has been the pivot of so much calculation, of such subtle combinations, of such deep conspiracies, round which the thought and passion of the sporting world have hung like eagles, will be recorded in the fleeting tables of the past. But what minutes! Count them by sensation, and not by calendars, and each moment is a day and the race a life.' The sense of expectation, the drama of long-cherished hopes dashed or realised, the excitement of the moment all gamblers crave, when events are in train and yet when everything seems possible – it is all here in Disraeli's prose. The modern cliché 'emotional rollercoaster' seems particularly pusillanimous when ranged alongside the parallels drawn by Disraeli: 'Pompeius before Pharsalia, Harold before Hastings, Napoleon before Waterloo', 'the inspired mariner who has just discovered a new world; the sage who has revealed a new planet',[1] are at least in Dizzy's eyes much the same as the 'before' and 'after' of the Derby.

But in his hyperbole the novelist was only articulating the inner experience of the hundreds of thousands attending this horse race, and the many millions more up and down the country who had staked their single shilling or their thousands of guineas on the outcome.

By the 1840s the Derby was a totemic happening, a shared obsession that galvanised and unified the nation. The first annual sporting event truly to capture the national imagination, it was almost a national holiday, and such was the racing fever in the highest circles that even the business of governing the country was suspended. For a period from 1847, on the suggestion of Lord George Bentinck, both Houses of Parliament adjourned for most of the week in which the Derby was run. Lord Palmerston called this holiday 'part of the unwritten law of Parliament'.[2] It was also Palmerston who, trying to commiserate with the notoriously austere Gladstone over some severe disappointment, said, 'Of course you are mortified and disappointed, but your disappointment is nothing to mine, who had a horse with whom I hoped to win the Derby, and we went amiss at the last moment.'[3]

And it was said of another prime minister, the 14th Earl of Derby, that he would 'as soon have won the Derby once, as have been, as he was, Prime Minister of England twice'.[4]*

For many it was not merely the most significant sporting fixture, but the single most important event in the year. People dated events in their lives by it, and years were indexed and identified by the name of the winning horse: for instance, 1830 would have been known as the year of Priam's Derby. 'The "Derby Day" is a sort of era in the lives of most persons, and certain classes are accustomed to date from, or refer events to, the anniversary of its recurrence,' wrote *The Times* in 1844, 'so that, independently of its sporting importance, it has a claim as the terminus a quo or ad quem by which a portion of the community calculate the revolutions of time.'[5]

Of the transformation undergone by the quiet town of Epsom, one commentator wrote, 'It may in this the middle of the nineteenth century, on the morning of the great race, be truly pronounced the national museum of character', adding that 'the main street' of this town of fewer than four thousand year-round inhabitants† 'on this momentous occasion, contains literally, specimens of every rank and calling, every phase and shade of character; and these again, from every county, and most parishes in Great Britain; and fully entitle us to term the display a museum of humanity'.[6]

That great nineteenth-century curator of the national museum of character Charles Dickens wrote up his 1851 visit to Epsom in his magazine *Household Words*, and the day was of course rendered part of nineteenth-century folklore when William Powell Frith painted his epic narrative canvas, simply entitled *The Derby Day*. Exhibited as part of the Royal Academy Summer Exhibition of 1858, the picture required crowd control: a silken rope was insufficient to cope with the throng that surrounded it and instead an iron rail

---

* As it happens, Derby was Prime Minister on three occasions.
† In 1851 the population of Epsom was 3792 (Charles Abdy, *Epsom Past*, p. 39, Phillimore, UK).

was installed to protect it from its admirers. 'My first visit to Epsom was in the May of 1856 – Blink Bonnie's year,' wrote Frith in his memoirs. 'My first Derby had no interest for me as a race, but as giving me the opportunity of studying life and character, it is ever to be gratefully remembered.'[7] But in recording the event Frith was also sentimentalising it: ladies in open barouches sheltering their pale complexions beneath parasols; gentlemen in gleaming top-hats; an occasional apple-cheeked, smocked rustic; even the urchins in the centre foreground look washed, their hair freshly tousled for Mr Frith, giving the impression that they have been borrowed from the drawings of Norman Rockwell rather than the workhouses and slums of Victorian Britain.

This more or less wholesome pageant of mid-nineteenth-century society, making the blue ribbon of the Turf fit the cosy bourgeois template of the family day out, would have seemed very strange to the race's founder, the 12th Earl of Derby, one of the great libertines of the late eighteenth century. Born into a family chiefly known for its patronage of cock-fighting and racing, his father had been thoughtful enough to marry an heiress and then drop dead, leaving his son in possession of a huge fortune while still in his teens. His house in Grosvenor Square, built by the Adams brothers, was a byword for lavish hospitality, and when in 1774 he became engaged to the bewitchingly beautiful daughter of the Duke of Hamilton he set about celebrating the nuptials in the style for which he had become famous.

As well as his townhouse he had just taken a house called The Oaks near the once fashionable spa town of Epsom. Epsom's spring and its foul-tasting purgative waters had been all the rage in the seventeenth century, overtaking Royal Tunbridge Wells in popularity. The place had become the nexus of fashion, crowded with the sedan chairs and carriages of the *haut ton*, as a whole social world grew up around the ritual of taking the waters, a world that included daily races on the Downs. 'Taverns, at that time reputed to be the largest in England, were opened,'[8] and it was one of these, a former ale house called The Oaks, that was turned into a splendid country house where young Lord Stanley, as he was then, celebrated his marriage. By this time the attractions of the spa and the springs had waned, but the races endured and there was cock-fighting too, which suited the young nobleman handsomely. The wedding went off in great style: dancing pavilion by Robert Adam; marital masque, called *The Maid of the Oaks*, directed by Garrick; and the sense of an elaborate *fête champêtre* enhanced by orange trees and haycocks of straw-coloured satin. After such a promising start the marriage, however, foundered; perhaps the earl's fondness for staging cock-fights in the drawing-room had something to do with it. Lady Derby ran off with the Duke of Dorset, leaving her cuckolded husband to his racing and cock-fighting.

During the eighteenth century racing was very different from the fast and thrilling sport it would eventually become. The first year for which anything approaching a full list of races exist was 1727, when out of a total of 332 races the majority (over 80 per cent) were 'plates' or 'purses' put up by the Crown, town, a local dignitary or a racecourse. The other popular method of trying horses was the 'match', a private arrangement where two gentlemen would determine to match their horses against each other over a set distance, typically four miles, on mutually agreed terms. Heat racing was also popular at this time, although this could be confusing on occasion.

The main differences were that the horses were much older and raced over much longer distances than would later be the case; the youngest age for a racehorse was four years old, but the majority of races imposed no age limits, meaning that racehorses were aged six, seven and sometimes older. And the stamina of older horses was required for the long distances: there were just five races under four miles in length, the longest, by contrast, was a taxing eight miles. Gradually, however, there was a move towards a novel form of racing whereby a larger number of horses were entered in a race in which the stake of each entrant was pooled with the rest to provide an attractive prize; these so-called sweepstakes often involved younger horses running at greater speeds over shorter distances.

The most notable of these had been started in Doncaster in 1776 for three-year-olds over two miles. It had been repeated the following year, and by 1778 it was carrying the name of one of its founding subscribers, Lieutenant General Anthony St Leger. That year the roisterers at a house party at The Oaks decided that the following spring they too would hold a sweepstake, for three-year-old fillies to be run over a mile and a half, and that it would be named in honour of their host – or rather his house. Seventeen people subscribed fifty guineas apiece for the first Oaks Stakes and in 1779 a dozen horses started, Lord Derby winning with a horse called Bridget.

The first Oaks was little more than a race among friends, but it had been fun, such fun in fact that they decided to run it again and that a further sweepstake would be added for three-year-old colts and fillies, to be run over a mile.* Racing folklore relates that it was a toss-up as to whether the race would be called the Derby or the Bunbury, after Sir Charles Bunbury. Sir Charles was Britain's first 'dictator of the turf', a role he relished. Bunbury's descendants maintain that the name of the famous Epsom race was decided over dinner with the flip of a coin, the earl giving his name to the eponymous event and Bunbury's horse Diomed winning the first Derby Stakes.

Bunbury had appointed himself president of the nascent Jockey Club, a name that implies far more order than there really was to the group of mainly aristocratic owners who had begun meeting at the Star and Garter in Pall Mall during the middle years of the eighteenth century.† It was run very much as a private club, or clique, and the concept of anything as formal as a governing body for the sport of racing would not have occurred to its members,

---

* The distance was increased four years later to one and a half miles.
† The Jockey Club is first mentioned as meeting at the Star and Garter in 1751 (T.H. Bird, *Admiral Rous and the English Turf*, Puttnam, London, p. 10).

who, though nobly born, were often far from high-minded. Typical of its membership was the 3rd Duke of Grafton, a great-grandson of Charles II and his mistress Barbara Villiers. Born in 1735, Grafton was prime minister by the age of thirty-one but did his best to live down to the standards of a debauched age. Of him Walpole once commented, 'In his Grace's view the world should be postponed to a whore and horse race.'[9] Grafton was an enthusiastic participant in the Derby, winning three times (in 1803, 1809 and 1810).

This, then, was the calibre of man who was attracted to Epsom. And as Britain entered the nineteenth century the temper of the race meeting reflected the rather louche habits of its subscribers: drinking, whoring, cock-fighting, coursing, gambling at hazard and so on. One French visitor to an early Epsom meeting was appalled by the ad hoc nature of this sporting free-for-all:

> Horse racing and cock-fighting are carried on here to a pitch of absolute madness. There are neither lists nor barriers at these races. The horses run in the midst of the crowd, who leave only a space sufficient for them to pass through, at the same time encouraging them by gestures and loud shouts. The victor finds it a difficult matter to disengage himself from the crowd, who congratulate, caress and embrace him with an effusion of heart which it is not easy to form an idea of without having seen it.[10]

Often spectators would get so carried away that they would almost join in the race, shadowing the competitors on their own mounts; and given that the course was only very vaguely marked out, spectators on foot risked injury from the competing horses.

Indeed, the whole of Derby Day was a hazardous event. Thanks to its relative proximity to London, it soon became a magnet for the rogues and criminals of the metropolis. Covering the Derby in 1795, *The Times* reported a catalogue of crime:

> Several carriages were broken to pieces and one Lady had her arm broken. There was much private business done in the swindling way. One black-legged fellow cleared nearly a thousand pounds by the old

trick of an E.O. table.* Another had a faro table and was on the eve of doing business when he was detected with a palmed card; almost the whole of what may be justly styled the 'vagabond gamblers' of London were present. Mr Bowes, half-brother of the Earl of Strathmore, was robbed of a gold watch and a purse containing 30 guineas at Epsom races, on Thursday last. Many other persons shared a similar fate, both on the same evening and Friday. Upwards of 30 carriages were robbed coming from the races.[11]

Although still only a parochial meeting, the Derby was already making its mark as the criminal's playground par excellence. As the century progressed and as the crowds at the Derby grew from thousands to tens of thousands, so the potential for profit by the 'vicious and unprincipled'[12] of all classes (as one contemporary put it) increased.

---

* The letters E and O stood for 'even' and 'odd'; it was a primitive form of roulette with a ball in a spinning wheel and the betters wagering on an even or an odd number coming up.

2

Lord George

His was one of those composite characters, in which opposite qualities, motives, and feelings were so strangely intermingled that nothing but a nice analysis, a very close and impartial inspection of it, can do him justice.

C.F. Greville, *The Greville Memoirs 1814–1860*[1]

There is little doubt that Lord George Bentinck was one of the most spoilt and indulged men in England.

When his father, the irreproachably respectable fourth Duke of Portland, inherited the dukedom in 1809 he also inherited debts of half a million pounds. Through careful and clever management he paid off those debts and in later life was able to enjoy an income of £100,000 a year (it helped, also, that his wife brought a considerable fortune with her). Portland was a racing man, elected to the Jockey Club in 1809 and owner of the 1819 Derby winner, Tiresias. He was committed to the sport in other ways too. As the owner of a considerable expanse of the Heath at Newmarket he invested in making the ground suitable for the exercise of racehorses and bought further parcels of land adjoining the Heath so as to safeguard the gallops. In addition, he loaned the Jockey Club the money to buy the freehold of its Newmarket rooms in 1831. In a very concrete sense he contributed to Newmarket's status as the capital of horse racing. But interestingly, although he bred racehorses he did not care for gambling. To the noise of the Derby crowds he preferred the relative calm of Newmarket, where he had a huge wagon 'fitted up as a movable stand'[2] and watched the races through a powerful telescope. He dressed like the quiet country gentleman he was, in top-boots and stag-skin breeches, the gilt buttons of the Jockey Club gleaming dully on his blue coat.

His third son George inherited his taste for sober clothes. In town – at least when he had not come straight from hunting – Lord George preferred to wear 'a long black frock-coat, a black or very dark blue, double-breasted, velvet waistcoat, and dark trousers, having (in the fashion of that day) straps attached, which passed under his boots. Over his waistcoat he wore a fine long, gold, chain, which went around his neck, and was clasped together on his breast by a gold loop, in which was set a large and very conspicuous turquoise', thought by some to represent the sky blue of his racing colours. 'Round his neck he wore a costly cream-coloured satin scarf of great length, knotted under his chin, and with a gold pin stuck in it. This gold pin (he had two or more of them) contained either a big ruby or a pearl. On his head he invariably wore a tall, new, beaver hat.'[3] By the standards of the day he indeed struck a serious, almost sombre, note with his dress; by contrast, the dandies were still piling on their gaudy double or triple waistcoats and garlanding themselves with chains and rings before squeezing themselves into coats of bottle green. On the racecourse Lord George was his father's son, in appearance at least: 'dressed in buckskin breeches or tight-fitting buckskin trousers – none of your Norway does or West-Riding imitations, but in the hides of his own stags, – with exquisitely-made boots of the true orthodox length, and antique colouring in top; a buff waistcoat, and reddish brown double-breasted coat, ornamented by the button of the Jockey Club; a quiet beaver [hat], placed at neither a right angle nor yet a left, but in the juste milieu of gentlemanly taste, on a well-formed head of auburn hair, with large whiskers of the same colour.'[4]

He passed his childhood at the family seat of Welbeck unencumbered by much in the way of an education. Charles Greville, the prolific diarist who was Bentinck's cousin and sometime racing partner, cannot remember whether Bentinck attended a 'publick school'.[5] His 1971 biographer Michael Seth-Smith says, 'He was sent neither to Eton nor Christ Church';[6] but his racehorse trainer John Kent claims he attended Eton, while the sporting author Sylvanus has him attending both Eton and Oxford. Whatever the truth about his education, it is safe to say that with the exception of his betting book it is doubtful that he ever opened a volume with any pleasure. Even Disraeli was forced to admit of his idol, with ornate understatement, that 'he had not much sustained his literary culture'.[7] As a younger son it was a toss-up between the Army and the Church and accordingly in 1820, aged eighteen, he was gazetted into the 9th Royal Lancers as a cornet.

Indulged at home, he did not take orders at all well, and after a promising start his demeanour deteriorated rapidly. This prompted his direct superior, one Captain Ker, to write to him complaining of 'your inattention to your duty accompanied by a total estrangement from that subordinate & respectful carriage, which marked your entry into the Regiment – your determined opposition to me in every possible way – your avoidance of communication upon points of duty, and in short a fixed disposition to fly in my face upon all occasions'.[8] Lord George sent the letter to his commanding officer, a court of inquiry was convened and Ker was forced to apologise.

Bentinck then left the Army to join the political staff of his uncle, the Foreign Secretary George Canning. But Ker did not let the matter rest. Bentinck wrote from Paris on 21 May:

My dear Father, Captain Ker has thought proper in consequence of the failure of his original attempt to avenge himself upon me early in February last & the rancour that that failure has caused to remain upon his mind to send me a challenge & follow me to Paris to put it in effect. I accepted; & upon his arrival in Paris an attempt at arrangement was made by the friends of both sides but such arrangement not being agreed to it was settled that we should meet at seven o'clock last Friday Evening in the Bois de Boulogne. When we were on the point of taking our ground (both parties having arrived according to appointment) we were interrupted by the Police who exacted from all parties their word of honour not to meet again in France. The next

day the seconds of both parties considering that the affair ought there
to terminate came to a determination not to take any further part in
the affair.[9]

Ker, obviously a very touchy man who felt the injustice of the
matter keenly, claimed that Lord George had alerted the authorities
because he was too afraid to fight the duel. Given the involvement
of the Foreign Secretary and the fact that one of the parties was the
son of a respected duke, HRH the Duke of York, the Commander-
in-Chief, became involved. Captain Ker was forced to retire on
half-pay, later dying of cholera in Paris. It was clearly Ker who
chose to escalate the matter, but the arrogance of Lord George was
what started it and he might have thought twice about 'sneaking'
on Ker to their commanding officer. It was probably in connection
with this incident that Charles Greville, who held the post of Clerk
to the Privy Council, was asked by his uncle the Duke of Portland
to 'go to the Duke of York'.[10]

After Canning's death, for which Bentinck was to blame Peel
and accuse him of as much twenty years later, saying that Peel 'had
chased and hunted Mr Canning to death', Lord George was at a
loose end. He succeeded his brother as Conservative Member of
Parliament for King's Lynn, but what really fired his soul was racing.
Parental influence aside, his first taste of the sport came in 1824
when, aged twenty-two, he rode at Goodwood for the Cocked-Hat
Stakes. It was a particularly thrilling race. He eventually beat 'Lord
George Lennox's bay gelding, Swindon, and three others, after
running two dead heats with Swindon',[11] and the excitement and
the rush of victory would alter the course of his life. Suddenly his
aimless existence had a focus: racing delivered what the Army and
politics had failed to supply, a sense of purpose.

Thereafter 'he attended Goodwood races without intermission'[12]
and, indeed, almost any race meeting he could find. Shortly after
that initial euphoria of winning as a jockey, young Lord George
Bentinck began to take what is euphemistically called 'an interest'
in the horses owned by his cousin Charles Greville. Soon he was

drawn into the engrossing and extremely expensive world of racing.

In the 1820s owning and betting on horses was still an upper-class and aristocratic occupation; it is estimated that the number of racehorse owners in the first two decades of the century did not rise much above five hundred.[13] Racing may have been moving away from the practice of matching a few horses against each other towards races of larger fields such as the Derby, the Oaks and the St Leger, but betting was still something conducted largely between owners. They would typically back a horse at long odds far in advance of a race and, as the race approached, hedge, betting on other horses – in effect, laying against the horse with the object of making a profit if it won, but losing nothing if it did not. There was no betting market as we know it, and the concept of a modern bookmaker taking bets on all the horses in a race did not exist; owners would seek each other out and make wagers between each other, entering them in their betting books.

It has to be borne in mind that the degree of literacy and numeracy required also militated against working-class involvement in betting. It was, by the nature of racehorse ownership and the absence of publicly available information, an exclusive activity. Owners would meet, say, at the Jockey Club's coffee room in Newmarket or at race meetings, or at each other's country houses or in their clubs on St James's Street in London. At the racecourse there would be frantic last-minute betting at the betting post, where the interested parties would form a ring, call out the odds they were prepared to offer, note any takers, then gallop back to see the start of the race or, as some of the more spirited spectators did at the Derby, ride alongside the field. It was a system based on mutual trust and knowledge of the people with whom they were betting. And the system worked well enough when the owners constituted a small, largely aristocratic circle of a few hundred.

Although via the influence of the Jockey Club the phenomenon of racing was growing, the sport was still very much in its infancy. A semblance of regulation was beginning to be felt: for instance, as far back as 1762 some nineteen owners had registered their racing colours, and this list formed a representative cross-section of the racehorse owners, including as it did five dukes, a marquis, five earls, a viscount, a lord, two knights or baronets and two plain misters. In 1773 the Jockey Club sanctioned the publication of a *Racing Calendar* by James Weatherby. The Weatherby family would go on to publish British racing's important works, not least the *Stud Book*, which made its appearance in 1791.

It is fair to say that, on the whole, cheating was accepted as a reality of the sport. There are plenty of stories of eve-of-race break-ins at stables for the purpose of getting at fancied horses; the substances fed to them ranged from two pounds of lead shot, which had fatal results, to opium balls, the effects of which can be imagined. Action tended to be taken only when dishonesty was too blatant to ignore, as happened in 1791 during the celebrated 'Escape Affair'. Escape was a horse owned by the Prince of Wales and ridden by the first nationally famous jockey Sam Chifney. Chifney was a horseman of innate genius, 'an artist with the whip'.[14] Escape was the favourite to win this particular race, so there was surprise when Chifney finished last. Escape was brought out the following day and, given its lacklustre performance, was backed at much more advantageous odds by the Prince and his jockey, this time winning easily, outstripping a field that included two of the horses that had beaten it twenty-four hours earlier. The stewards of the Jockey Club were outraged and after an investigation approached the Prince, informing him that if Chifney raced again for him 'no gentleman would start against him'.[15] The rift was not healed until 1828, when the Prince, now King George IV, gave a dinner for the Jockey Club.

Notwithstanding, the Turf had survived without royal patronage and by the early nineteenth century was a very colourful milieu attracting, and destroying, some of the great fortunes of the age. A famous example was Lord Foley, a noted owner and gambler of the Regency, who was forced to raise almost £1 million (today, £120,000,000) by selling his Worcestershire estate. Indeed, well into the century the sort of man attracted to racing was typically the same rich, aristocratic, reckless spendthrift who had been drawn to the Turf a century earlier. A by no means exceptional example of this sort of man was the 13th Earl of Eglinton (sometimes spelt Eglintoun) who squandered a vast fortune on such indulgences as a full medieval tournament (recorded in Disraeli's novel *Endymion*). Although his horses won many of the classics including the Derby of 1849, the enduring image is of the man who prided himself on his capacity for consuming champagne. One day he was bragging about how much he could drink at the Jockey Club's rooms at Newmarket when Colonel Peel, brother of Sir Robert, mentioned that he knew of someone who might beat him. Peel then introduced his brother-in-law Sir David Baird, who proceeded to match Eglinton bottle for bottle until 'at last Lord Eglinton turned as pale as death, and rose slowly from his chair, exclaiming, "I can do no more"' and went to bed. Thereupon Baird apparently stood up, played three games of billiards, winning two of them, took a nightcap and was out riding shortly after dawn the following day, 'a short black pipe of Cavendish [tobacco] between his lips'. Meanwhile, Eglinton was seen wandering about without his hat 'which he confessed was too heavy for his poor head'.[16] In addition to staging medieval tournaments, backing horses and drinking champagne Lord Eglinton somehow found time to act as Lord Lieutenant of Ireland.

Even more colourful was the eccentric Lord Glasgow who was distinguished by his dogged persistence in breeding from bloodlines that everyone else knew to be useless. He then compounded his error by spending his enormous annual income of £150,000 (£14,400,000) a year making matches (arranging for one of his horses to race against another) and heavy wagers that he almost invariably lost. He changed his trainers almost incessantly and confused matters further by refusing to name the many horses he entered – if pressed, he would register them under names such as 'He isn't worth a name'.[17] Quick to anger, he would shoot horses that disappointed him and yet he devoted his life to them, preferring to drive his own coach and four long after railways covered most of England. A martyr to chronic headaches and back pain, he would try to ease his discomfort by placing a chloroform-soaked handkerchief over his face. He dressed strangely, favouring a bright waistcoat that was many sizes too big and trousers of white nankeen several inches too short, worn over heavy rustic boots that were invariably unlaced. Although eighteenth-century in so many of his traits, this remarkable anachronism of a man survived until 1869. It was Lord Glasgow who once, losing patience with a waiter, threw him out of a window with the immortal line that he should be added to the bill; the waiter sustained a broken arm and Lord Glasgow was charged a fiver. This may seem high-handed and callous today, but the incident illustrates very accurately the relationship that prevailed between aristocrats and menials; while not living in a state of abject vassalage or serfdom, the working classes of the time were separated from their social superiors by an almost unbridgeable chasm, and this was as true in racing as it was when it came to defenestrating recalcitrant waiters.

Eglinton and Glasgow were representative of the aristocratic ownership of the studs. Their birth, wealth and uniquely frivolous outlook on life placed a huge gulf between them and the men who trained and rode for them. The vocabulary of the time is eloquent on the social divide. These men were not skilled professionals but servants; well into the nineteenth century the term used was not 'trainer' but 'training groom', while jockeys were known as 'riding grooms'. The life of these early jockeys was wretched. Slight of build, they were weakened further during the flat-racing season when they could only look on while others ate, and they endured periods of wasting, their wrinkled and sagging features testifying to prolonged bouts of severe fasting. They would take miserable walks of many miles in the heat of summer swathed in heavy clothes, 'scraping the perspiration from their heads and faces with a horn carried for the purpose' sometimes collapsing through exhaustion. The rewards were paltry – 'five guineas if he wins and three if he loses a race'[18] – the gulf between these sums and the fortunes that were wagered providing fecund ground for bribery and malfeasance.

*

This was the curious, colourful, class-conscious world in which the young and good-looking Lord George Bentinck chose to immerse himself entirely for the next two decades. He approached the Turf with the violent energy that was to characterise his attitude to the causes he adopted, funded of course by his family's money. As a creature of impulse and yet monumental inflexibility, the result was that in a very short time he was betting heavily and in the Doncaster St Leger of 1826 he lost a spectacular amount: £27,000 (£3,240,000) was the figure bruited about, but there were those who thought it was much more. His trainer John Kent, for instance, believed that 'from his Lordship subsequently admitting to me that it was "the most disastrous event of his racing career," I feel sure that his loss must have greatly exceeded that sum; and his mother, and sister, Lady Charlotte Bentinck, afterwards Viscountess Ossington, most kindly and generously assisted him to meet it'. Inevitably, his father got to hear of it and, given his own opposition to betting, was 'much troubled and grieved about it'.[19]

Concerned that his son was falling in with a fast crowd, the duke, who had paid £11,000 (£1,320,000) of George's debts, 'extracting a promise that he would not bet any more on the turf,'[20] came up with a plan and bought him an estate in Ayrshire in the hope of distracting him from the Turf. It was a typically indulgent way of demonstrating his displeasure. However, 'the natural instinct could not be suppressed, stimulated as it was by his father's stud, by that of his cousin, Mr Greville (who was his senior by seven years), by his own great attachment to Goodwood, and to his valued friend, the 5th Duke of Richmond' (not to mention the Duke of Richmond's wife, for whom Bentinck had conceived a passion). In other words, Lord George was addicted to racing. While his father thought he was pursuing the quiet life of a Scottish landowner, Lord George had cajoled Richmond into letting him 'share a few horses with him'[21] and very soon he was buying horses and running them in Richmond's name.

One thing led to another, and before long Lord George was also running horses in the names of Charles Greville, Lord Orford, Lord Lichfield, Mr King (a trainer), John Bowe, a Doncaster publican (as well as keeping horses at Goodwood Bentinck maintained a stud at Doncaster) and others besides. Greville takes up the story:

> The Duke, his Father (the most innocent of men), had his curiosity awakened by seeing a great number of horses running in the names of men whom he never saw or heard of. These were all his Son's aliases. He asked a great many questions about these invisible personages, to the great amusement of all the Newmarket world. At last it was evident that he must find out the truth, and I urged George to tell it him at once. With great reluctance and no small apprehension he assented, and mustering up courage he told the Duke that all those horses were his. The intimation was very ill received; the Duke was indignant. He accused him of having violated his word; and he was so angry that he instantly quitted Newmarket and returned to Welbeck. For a long time he would not see George at all; at last the Duchess contrived to pacify him; he resumed his usual habits with his son, and in the end he took an interest in the horses, tacitly acquiesced in the whole thing, and used to take pleasure in seeing them and hearing about them.[22]

But, finally tiring of this subterfuge, the Duke of Richmond had refused to allow Bentinck to run horses in his name any longer, and accordingly Bentinck moved his animals to be trained by the ironically named 'Honest' John Day at Danebury in Hampshire. Day was a talented jockey who had started riding racehorses at the age of ten, before becoming a successful trainer with a highly questionable reputation. A picture of him in later life depicts a florid-featured man. His impressive quiff balanced by splendid whiskers cascading down to his jawline, a flower in his buttonhole and a prominent pin impaling his tie just below a bulky knot, all contrived to give his appearance a meretricious flashiness entirely in keeping with his character: here was a man who would have been pleased to sell you a horse that had had only one careful lady owner.

The Days, father and sons, were a picturesque dynasty of rogues celebrated for their lack of scruples when it came to pulling, doping, nobbling or otherwise making horses 'safe'. They were highly effective and utterly unencumbered by morals, on occasion betraying the owners for whom they worked. While far from alone on the Turf in their dishonesty, it is fair to say that they were among the leaders when it came to fixing a race. Their 'Danebury Confederacy' was a loosely affiliated gang of similarly dubious characters, according to William Day in his *Reminiscences of the Turf* 'whose practices should be rather shunned than followed'.[23] It was with this group that Lord George now identified himself.

If Disraeli was Lord George's political biographer, then he can be said to have had two racing biographers, both of whose fathers trained for him: the hagiographical John Kent of Goodwood, who could find not a harsh word to say about him, and William Day who wrote a bitter score-settling memoir after Bentinck's acrimonious break with his father's stable and his return to Kent at Goodwood. The former remembers every tiny act of kindness; the other recalls each real or imagined slight. What is remarkable is that both books were written towards the end of the century, 1892 and 1886 respectively. That one man preserved an unquestioning admiration for him while the other nursed a grudge for the better part of half a century after Bentinck quit racing certainly testifies to the strength of Lord George's character and the impression he left on those whose lives he touched. But as well as being a strong character, Lord George was a complex one. 'His was one of those composite characters, in which opposite qualities, motives, and feelings were so strangely intermingled,' said the perspicacious Greville, 'that nothing but a nice analysis, a very close and impartial inspection of it, can do him justice.'[24] And when taken together these two accounts by racing men produce a fascinating picture of a complicated, obsessive and driven man, who from the late 1820s devoted himself to mastering the Turf.

One trait that emerges from the chiaroscuro of these two accounts is his stubborn determination. In John Kent's eyes this is a fine quality: he describes him as 'too firm of purpose to be daunted

or turned aside by any disappointment'.[25] Day, however, was exasperated by Bentinck's ever-ravenous appetite for constant victories:
'Success ... had only the effect of making his lordship utterly
impatient of defeat.' Then there was his arrogance. On one occasion
he threatened to withdraw his horse from a race unless 'he had
what he was pleased to term fair odds', in effect holding betters to
ransom until he got the price he wanted. He was also a terrible
snob: Day says that he was known to dislike 'all plebeian owners,
whom, had he but the power, he would have swept off the face of
the earth "in one fell swoop"'.[26] His class-consciousness surfaced
again when he decided to sell his stud – Kent relates approvingly
'how nothing would induce him to sell to set a of bookmakers',
and that 'unless some nobleman, or gentleman of position, or two
or three of them in combination, should arrange to purchase the
stud, and to accept the grave responsibilities involved in forfeits
amounting to about £18,000, he would not sell at all'.[27]

The fact was that Lord George cared little for money for its own
sake. He had grown up with more than enough and felt entitled to
yet more when his own resources proved insufficient to meet his
obligations. For him, money was simply a tool to be used to achieve
victory and, in victory, a useful way of keeping score. He seems to
have had no shame in applying to his family when in need. 'Never
mind the money; my mother will let me have any amount,'[28] he
was wont to say whenever the cost of any undertaking was brooked.
And as well as the money his mother and sister scraped together to
meet his losses on the St Leger in 1826, 'his brothers, Lord Titchfield
and Lord Henry Bentinck, went with him to Drummond's Bank,
and guaranteed him in the sum of £300,000 [£36,000,000] to be
drawn on any time he pleased, this being in addition to what he
could draw on his private account'.[29] This was a stupendous sum
to have at his disposal and he spent it freely, even eccentrically; no
detail was judged so insignificant that it could not be improved
upon by more expenditure. He considered that the best was only
just about good enough for his horses. For a while he believed that
'light-fleshed and delicate animals' should be fed milk and fresh

eggs, and he plunged himself into the minutiae of preparing this unique diet right down to devising a system for ensuring the freshness of the eggs, which prompted the good-natured Duke of Richmond to say, 'You will soon want my farm and poultry-yard, George, to supply your horses with milk and eggs, in addition to filling up my stables.'[30]

On another occasion he had his valet scour London for some giant sponges because he did not think that those being used to bathe an injured horse were sufficiently large and luxurious. 'Go again,' he said petulantly when the servant returned from his errand, 'and search London until you can bring me six sponges half as big again as these.' Some £15 or £16 having been spent on some truly Brobdingnagian specimens, they were sent to Goodwood 'where they were kept as curiosities, being useless for the purpose contemplated by his Lordship, as their size and the weight of water which they held made it almost impossible to handle them'.

As with sponges, so it was with stables and gallops. At Danebury and Goodwood Bentinck spent thousands building, enlarging and improving the stables, and a similar sum tending the quality of the turf (at Danebury it was estimated that he spent £1,500 on bone dust alone). Once when told that the necessary felling of trees and laying of turf to improve and extend the exercise ground at Goodwood would cost at least £3,500, he answered, John Kent tells us: 'If it enables me to win one race I will pay all that', and a hundred men were promptly set to work on the project. He ran his stud on principles that made little economic sense; for instance, he 'would never reduce his expenses by selling a horse'.[31]

When it came to acquiring horses he paid what others regarded as ridiculous money, earning him the sobriquet 'the Rothschild of Tattersall's'.* When he bought Lord Jersey's bay Middleton for £4,000 (£480,000) it was considered an astronomical sum to pay for a racehorse, especially considering that because of a bad leg it never ran again. He entered his horses in all the great races 'partly

---

* Tattersall's was and is the leading equine auctioneer.

to gratify his vanity and partly to deceive the public',[32] and didn't care if the forfeits for scratching horses ran to several thousands at just one meeting. He had anything up to sixty horses in training at any one time, ran three stud farms, yet still wanted more capacity. Once when he pestered the Duke of Richmond to allow him to build more stables, he was met with the retort, 'If you had Chichester barracks you would fill all the stalls.'[33] This allusion to barracks was perhaps apt in that he approached the Turf with all the deadly seriousness of one leading a military campaign. Like Disraeli, Greville uses the simile of a general counting his cannon and prisoners after a battle, 'and his tricks and stratagems he regarded as the tactics and manoeuvres by which success was achieved'.[34]

He executed one of his most spectacular outflanking manoeuvres in 1836. He had a horse called Elis which he fancied for the St Leger and for which he wanted odds of 12–1. Elis was stabled at Goodwood and the nearer the date of the St Leger came, the less likely it seemed that the horse could make the journey to Doncaster in enough time. At the time horses walked between meetings, and the journey from Goodwood to Doncaster would take around a fortnight; moreover, a lengthy journey by road made the likelihood of injury much greater. It was the sheer time it took to make the trip on foot, then recover in time for an engagement, that kept racing in the north and south of England apart. Only when a trainer thought that a horse had a particularly good chance would he send it on a walk of hundreds of miles. (It could be done: for instance, after walking from Malton to Epsom and winning the Oaks on 20 May 1836 the filly Cyprian immediately set off to Newcastle upon Tyne, where on 22 June she won the Northumberland Plate.)

The week before the St Leger Elis was still at Goodwood and those who were laying against the horse believed it was safe to offer long odds. However, they had not reckoned on Lord George's ingenuity. When his trainer told him how a horse had once been transported to a race meeting in a bullock cart, Lord George forthwith visited Herring the coachbuilder on Long Acre in Covent Garden to commission a 'heavy cumbrous vehicle'.[35] The finished article looked rather like a Romany caravan. Lord George had just built the first horse box. His plan was to ship the horse by this specially built mobile stable with its padded interior walls and floor to Doncaster, covering the distance of around 250 miles over three days in stages of roughly eighty miles per day. Ever suspicious, Lord George insisted that only hay or corn from Goodwood was to be fed to the horse en route, and even the sieve used for the feed was from Goodwood.

As the body of the carriage was high off the ground, it needed to be backed up to a bank for the horse to walk into it. Six post-horses were then harnessed to the carriage and off it went, 'the greatest surprise and interest being excited by it in every village and town through which it passed'. Some speculated that it contained a wild animal of great ferocity, others that it was transporting a dangerous felon to trial. The horse arrived at Doncaster, con-founding the local betting ring and allowing the adoring John Kent to state proudly that 'Lord George was a dangerous customer to take liberties with'.[36]

3
Racing Magnate

———

He was now become the Leviathan of the turf; his success had been brilliant, his stud was enormous, and his authority and reputation were prodigiously great.

C.F. Greville on Lord George Bentinck, *The Greville Memoirs 1814–1860*[1]

———

'When I mention that, in 1844, Lord George ran thirty-eight different horses in 182 races at places scattered all over England, and in 1845, thirty-six horses in 190 races, I do not think that a similar record can be quoted about any other patron of the Turf.'[2] John Kent was awestruck at his patron's domination of the sport, to which he applied himself with a maniacal zeal.

Lord George's energy was almost superhuman. Kent recalls one New Year's Day when he had to get up at 5 a.m. so as to meet Bentinck at Winchester station, go with him to inspect his stud at Danebury, travel back to London by train for dinner, then go to see his master at White's Club at 11 p.m. Just shortly before midnight they moved to the office of Weatherby's, publisher of the *Racing Calendar*, where they stayed until two o'clock in the morning nominating the horses Bentinck wanted to enter for races in the coming year. After that they drove over to Harcourt House, his family's splendid London residence, where the two men talked until five o'clock. Breakfast was called for six because he wanted Kent to look over some yearlings that were coming up for auction at Tattersall's paddocks in Willesden. Then, after twenty-eight and three-quarter gruelling hours, spent either on horseback, in a coach, on a train or in meetings with his employer, Kent collapsed into the 8.45 a.m. coach from Piccadilly back home to Sussex.

After this marathon session, Kent blandly observes that 'His Lordship never made any allowance for fatigue, either in himself or in others'.[3] This is all the more remarkable for the fact that Bentinck tended to avoid eating during the day, he felt it made him drowsy and took away his edge (later in life, as the scourge of Sir Robert Peel, he would fast before speaking in the House, to further stoke his ire).

But did he derive any pleasure from his utter immersion in the Turf?

It would appear that the exhilaration that he experienced as a competitive gentleman rider in the 1820s was rapidly replaced by obsession. Bentinck was single-minded in giving himself over to the sport, and developed an almost complete mastery of every aspect of racing. The great nineteenth-century sporting writer the Druid described him as 'the cleverest man that the turf ever had'.[4] Yet at best he was able to derive only a grim satisfaction, rather than pleasure, from his pursuit. What Greville said of him, namely that 'he was now become the Leviathan of the turf; his success had been brilliant, his stud was enormous, and his authority and reputation were prodigiously great' was true enough. But Kent's observation that he made no allowance for fatigue in either himself or in others was characteristic of an ever-growing harshness of character, as gradually every aspect of his life was subsumed by a desire for total domination of the racing world. He allowed nothing to stand in his way and was callous in the extreme, even with those who had done nothing but support him. If his treatment of his mother during her life indicated that he saw her as little more than a cash machine, his reaction to her death is little short of chilling. The Duchess of Portland was thoughtless enough to die at the beginning of Doncaster race week, prompting him to give his trainer the following instructions: 'As my mother will be buried before the races, the event will make no difference to the running of my horses, so take them as before arranged.'[5]

People mattered insofar as they could be useful, and success only goaded him further, forcing him to embark on ever more ambitious undertakings. First it was sufficient to win races, then it became necessary to win races and bets, then it was no longer enough to win races and bets – it became necessary to win and see others lose and suffer, even if it meant that to win huge sums of money he occasionally had to see his own horses lose. Eventually, his vindictiveness reached such a pitch that he stood accused of hurting himself financially in order to thwart an enemy's betting. Accordingly, his own moral universe began to distort and over time a perverse amorality shaped by the unforgiving demands he made of himself took over his life.

By his own confused and murky standards he achieved success; but at what cost? The financial side could be totted up easily enough, from the few pounds spent on unwieldy sponges to the hundreds of thousands that flowed through the pages of his betting book. However, the moral cost was incalculable: cynicism, suspicion and paranoia shadowed every thought and action.

But then, to be fair to Lord George, the life of the sporting 'gentleman' of the time was characterised by institutionalised endemic dishonesty. 'Cheating, in every kind of "sport" is as completely in the common order of things in England, among the highest classes as well as the lowest,' wrote one visitor to Britain in 1828, shortly after Bentinck had begun his career on the Turf. He continued:

> It is no uncommon thing to hear 'gentlemen' boast of it almost openly; and I never found that those who are regarded as 'the most knowing ones' had suffered in their reputation in consequence: – 'au contraire', they pass for cleverer than their neighbours; and you are only now and then warned with a smile to take care what you are about with them. Some of the highest members of the aristocracy are quite notorious for their achievements of this description. I heard from good authority, that the father of a nobleman of sporting celebrity, to whom some one was expressing his solicitude lest his son should be

cheated by a 'Blackleg'. He answered, 'I am much more afraid for the Blacklegs than for my son!'[6]

Perhaps Lord George did not set out with deliberate intentions to behave dishonestly in his dealings on the Turf. But, even setting aside the prevailing moral climate, there were several factors that would have nudged him over the line dividing shrewd games-manship from downright skulduggery. By nature spoilt and used to getting his own way, he would have seen victory, however achieved, as his right. His character, that unique combination of arrogance, boundless energy and self-righteousness, would not have permitted him to fail. Then there was the scar of what he referred to as 'the most disastrous event of my racing life'. The memory of his apocalyptic losses on the St Leger of 1826 was to remain with him for the rest of his days, and explains why he desired to take steps, fair or otherwise, to minimise the likelihood of anything similar happening to him again. It must be remembered that this loss had driven his racing underground, and that having broken his word to his father and raced horses under all manner of other names, later subterfuges would have come more easily. And then there was the company he kept, not least the notorious Days.

It is safe to say that fairly early on in his racing career, in his ceaseless quest to manipulate the betting market he began to resort to practices that were beyond question unethical and dishonest. He is accused of having painted the nostrils of one horse 'inside and out with a mixture of starch, flour, and colouring matter to resemble mucus, before going to exercise' so as to give the impres-sion that the animal was suffering from influenza and thus drive the betting back. He is also said to have devised 'a strangely constructed bridle, having a long porch reaching nearly to the orifice of the gullet, for the purpose of making the horse cough when wearing it'.[7]

In isolation these ruses might seem to have a certain comic charm, but they were in reality minute components in a vast machinery of chicanery and crookedness. During the mid-1840s, by which time Bentinck was seen as a spotless Paladin championing integrity and honesty on the Turf, his cousin Greville was approached by someone once connected with the Days who had kept hundreds of letters written by Lord George during the time his horses were at Danebury. This correspondence, Greville wrote, 'disclosed a systematick course of treachery, falsehood and fraud, which would have been far more than sufficient to destroy any reputation, but which would have fallen with tenfold force upon the great Purist, the supposed type and model of integrity and honour.' Greville was appalled to learn that he, Bentinck's own relative and at that time supposed friend, was mentioned by name as one that should be deliberately deceived about the health of a certain horse. 'Besides this unparalleled tissue of fraud, falsehood and selfishness the secret correspondence divulged many other things, plans and schemes of all sorts; horses who were to be made favourites in order to be betted against – not intended to win; then horses who were to run repeatedly in specified races and get beat, till they were well handicapped in some great race which they were to run to win.'[8] Sadly Greville notes that this dynamite dossier, which went on, inter alia, to link Lord George with the bribing of jockeys, was later destroyed.

But such was Lord George's curious blend of superiority and paranoia that, if he was ever assailed by qualms, he would have suppressed them with the same ruthlessness that never allowed him to express either disappointment or joy at the outcome of his complex racing and betting coups. For him the ends justified the means: amongst other aims, 'he sincerely hoped and tried to break'[9] the largely plebeian betting ring, and was correspondingly scornful of owners who did not follow his reckless example and, in the parlance of the day, plunge deeply. 'I am now on my way home to discharge the weary task of making out my betting-book, in which I have not one winning bet. But I declare I would rather be in this position than in that occupied by my Lord Chesterfield, who has won a paltry £1500 [a mere £180,000] on such a horse!' he remarked with exasperation after the St Leger of 1838, adding sourly, 'If Don

John had been mine I would not have left a card-seller in Doncaster with a shirt to his back.'[10]

Ironically, it was Lord Chesterfield who unwittingly put Bentinck as near as he ever came to realising his cherished ambition of smashing the ring. When Chesterfield's stud was sold, Bentinck picked up the recently foaled filly Crucifix. Crucifix was an extraordinary horse: in 1840 she won the 2000 Guineas, the 1000 Guineas and the Oaks, and it was estimated that he won £100,000 (£12,000,000) in bets on this horse, as well as a five-figure sum in prize money. Many years later Crucifix would also have given Lord George a Derby winner in the shape of Surplice, had he not sold his stud on a whim.

And it was Crucifix that was at the root of his break with the Days at Danebury and his return to Goodwood. In his memoirs William Day records how his father succumbed to a nasty and rare attack of scruples when Bentinck asked him to deceive the touts as to the condition of Crucifix. Bentinck planned to lay against the horse for the coming St Leger, knowing that she had broken down and would be scratched. 'If your lordship insists on this being done, you may take your horse to Goodwood or wherever you please' was the sanctimonious response that 'Honest' John Day is alleged to have made. However, the accepted version of events is that Honest John's other son, William's brother John, who was said to have 'betrayed the secrets of the stable' after a heavy gambling loss, caused the split. As well as being dishonest, John Jr was stupid. He wrote to Lord George that a certain horse, identified in some sources as Crucifix, was doing well – 'I recommend you strongly to back him' – while simultaneously contacting his own commission agent about the same horse instructing him to lay against the animal as 'he is hors de combat, and won't run'.[11] He then put the letters into the wrong envelopes and posted them. Whatever the truth, Day concludes that as a result Bentinck 'devoted the whole of his energy in the latter part of his life to ruin another'.

In his assessment Day is only partly right. It is without doubt that Bentinck sought, hypocritically, to punish the Danebury

Confederacy using his immense wealth as an instrument with which to teach them, as he saw it, a lesson. After a particularly gratifying victory over the Days he once allowed himself the luxury of confiding, *sotto voce*, to the adoring Kent, 'I think I have at last got the better of Danebury.'[12] But William Day is hubristic in thinking that Lord George spent the rest of his life getting back at him and his family. In reality his former trainers were just one small part of an entire universe against which he waged a ceaseless war.

His was not a forgiving nature. He was never one to overlook a slight and let bygones be bygones 'when he had good reason for resenting supposed wrong and injustice inflicted on him'.[13] But that was only the half of it: his behaviour was at times deliberately provocative, almost as if he relied upon the energy and anger these feuds generated to drive his life. His temper was volcanic, and unless he was met with utter compliance or abasement, as he was by his adoring mother and the slavish Kent, he would find reason for a quarrel. 'He was exceedingly self-willed and arrogant, and never could endure contradiction,'[14] commented Charles Greville. Time and time again this arrogance would bring him into conflict with others, whether with his superior officer in the Army, his usually compliant father, his friend the Duke of Richmond, the Days with whom he broke so acrimoniously or his cousin Greville.

His partnership with Greville first foundered in the summer of 1835, over a filly called Preserve that Greville had bought for him. She had won the 1000 Guineas and Lord George had backed her heavily to win the Oaks. However, Greville's instructions to the jockey before the race were overheard by a rival trainer who was able to advise his rider accordingly and win the race. Obviously disappointed at losing, Lord George decided to blame Greville and wrote, according to the latter, 'one of his most elaborate epistles' – he was a voluminous correspondent – 'couched in terms so savage and so virulently abusive' that Greville 'knew not on reading it whether I stood on my head or my heels'. Many years later he would recall: 'His resentment broke out against me with a vehemence and ferocity that perfectly astounded me, and displayed in perfection

the domineering insolence of his character.'[15] There was something
of a rapprochement, but the warmth of their earlier years was gone
and the two fell out again when taking opposing sides in a dispute
about a defaulting better. After that he even stooped to petty
cruelty, humiliating Greville particularly unpleasantly at the Derby
of 1845 when, sitting near him, he gave a merciless running com-
mentary on the accident involving the horse on which Greville had
stood to win the immense sum of £40,000 (£4,800,000). Bentinck
would of course have been perfectly well aware of what was at stake.
'There is a horse on the ground; he is kicking violently; his jockey
lies insensible,' came the reedy, disdainful drawl of Bentinck as he
peered through his telescope (made by Watkins of Charing Cross).
'I don't think he will be able to ride again this season; he has a dark
blue jacket and I believe it is Mr Greville's Alarm.'[16] Moreover, his
arrogance militated against any form of reconciliation. A mutual
friend arranged for the two estranged men to meet at Goodwood
races. Although Greville was willing to renew their friendship,
when Bentinck saw his cousin he thought better of it, blurting out,
'After all, I would rather have nothing to do with the fellow!'[17] It
says much for Greville's restraint that when he came across Lord
George's incriminating letters he confided their contents only to
his diary.

However, on occasion the person he was picking on would fight
back, and in his strange way he seemed to thrive on conflict, even
if it threatened to deprive him of his life.

Among the many colourful characters who populated the sporting
world of late Georgian and early Victorian England was Squire
Osbaldeston, a pugnacious pint-sized Corinthian who at 'five feet
high and in features like a cub fox'[18] could have stepped from the
pages of a novel by R.S. Surtees. He rode hard, played tennis and
cricket, rowed and boxed, could play billiards for a fifty-hour
stretch, used to wager £1,000 (£120,000) on a rubber of whist
and over the course of his life he lost an impressive £200,000
(£24,000,000) on the Turf. His life revolved around country

pursuits, and although he lived for eighty years, from 1786, his autobiography is heroically silent on everything from the Reform Bill to the Crimean War, focusing instead on partridge shoots and prize fights, horses and hounds. Like Lord George he was fiercely proud and immensely stubborn.

His brush with Lord George took place at the Heaton Park races in September of 1835. Coming after the St Leger, Heaton Park was a relatively minor meeting and most of the riders were gentlemen jockeys. However, some were more equal than others and there were two distinct classes: the predominantly aristocratic guests of Lord Wilton (the owner of Heaton Park) and the less august competitors who lodged in the nearby manufacturing town of Manchester. Squire Osbaldeston had worked out that the Heaton Park handicappers made sure to favour Lord Wilton's party and, touchy man that he was, felt he needed to teach them a lesson with a horse called Rush, which he tried at six o'clock one morning on the St Leger course, easily passing the horse he had engaged to ride against him. He was about half a mile from the finish when he spotted two or three touts watching, and immediately pulled his horse up, letting the competing horse pass him and win. Word of this trial leaked back to Lord Wilton and Rush was very favourably handicapped, enabling Osbaldeston to win easily on two con-secutive days. It chanced that Lord Wilton's guests that year included Lord George Bentinck who had bet against Osbaldeston and lost £200. Compared to the ruses that Bentinck employed, Osbaldeston's legerdemain was amateur bordering on innocent. But getting a taste of his own medicine, however mild the dose, did not agree with Bentinck. When a mutual friend approached him on behalf of Osbaldeston for the money he was decidedly frosty, leaving the friend to report back to the squire, 'I think you had better ask him for the money yourself when you see him in the spring.'[19]

As usual Osbaldeston spent the winter hunting and next saw Bentinck at the Spring Meeting in Newmarket. Bentinck's demean-our was not propitious. 'He was standing in the betting yard with his back to the iron railings, looking very black, with a sort of savage smile on his countenance, not uncommon to him,' recalled Osbaldeston, clearly relishing the impending confrontation.

'My lord, I believe you owe me £200 which you lost to me on the Cup at Heaton Park.'

The aristocrat glared down balefully at the plucky little squire, then choosing his words carefully in order to convey the maximum contempt, said, 'I wonder you have the impudence and the assurance to ask me for that money. A greater robbery was never committed by any man on the public; and the Jockey Club think so too; and I have a great mind not to pay you at all.'

Sensing he had struck a nerve, Osbaldeston answered back, 'You must pay me. You don't think, my lord, that this matter will end here. You will hear from me, and I beg you to understand that I consider myself quite as much of a gentleman as either you or any of the Jockey Club although I have not got a title attached to my name.'

'I suppose you can count?' came the weary response.

'Yes, I could at Eton,'[20] answered Osbaldeston, and Bentinck unbuttoned his coat and took a sheaf of notes from his pocket.

However, payment was no longer the object. Osbaldeston now wanted satisfaction. After much difficulty he found someone to second him, and borrowing a pair of Manton pistols he set off to face Lord George at Wormwood Scrubs at six o'clock in the morning. Among Osbaldeston's accomplishments was that of a crack shot – quite possibly the best game shot in the country. When it came to handling a duelling pistol, he was, he said of himself, capable of putting 'ten bullets on the ace of diamonds at thirty feet'. Bentinck had every reason to be worried, and pretty soon Osbaldeston began to sense that his opponent had taken all manner of less than gentlemanly precautions.

Osbaldeston's second was rumoured to be under some obligation to Lord George and on the journey to the Scrubs told him over and over again, 'After Lord George's unjustifiable language to you it is impossible he can try to shoot you and indeed I have very good reason to know that he don't intend it. Under these circumstances it would amount to nearly a case of murder if you killed him, and like shooting at an unarmed antagonist.'[21] Then, once the two combatants were facing each other (Lord George carefully dressed all in black so as not to give his opponent any scrap of white to aim at) and were almost ready to fire, Lord George's second objected to the way the squire had raised his hand and cocked his pistol at the word 'Ready'. He walked over and asked Osbaldeston to face him. Seeing that the Squire was unprepared, he rushed out the words 'Ready, fire!'

Bentinck shot and missed and Osbaldeston, feeling that it would not be correct to shoot to kill, could not bring himself to aim properly. Afterwards he revealed, 'Even if I had been so disposed I could not have shot him, because I am perfectly convinced from the trifling sound and the sensation when the pistol exploded that there was no ball in it.'

Lord George's second later recounted a slightly different story, claiming that the combatants had been instructed to fire on the count of three, that he had left a long pause after 'One' and then said 'two, three' in the same breath, upon which Lord George fired into the air and Squire Osbaldeston put a bullet through Lord George's hat. Both accounts of this farcical meeting end with Bentinck observing, 'Well, Squire, I did not think you were so bad a shot.' To which Osbaldeston growled, 'Perhaps on another occasion the event may come off differently.'[22]

'Dear George, We must thank Heaven, that you have not been hurt,' wrote Bentinck's doting father with relief on hearing that his son had survived; but this letter contains a despairing and frustrated note as well, referring sorrowfully to the strong language exchanged by the two men and implying each was as bad as the other. He finishes with the admonition, 'I hope now, that the event will at least have the good consequence of impressing upon you the necessity of attending to that good rule animum rege qui nisi paret imperat [control your passions; if you do not, they will command you]', adding, surely more in hope than expectation that his son would heed him, how much he admired a friend of his 'who was born with a bad temper & had taught himself to keep it in subjection'.[23] It appeared that this was a lesson that Lord George Bentinck did not care to teach himself.

4

Victorian Dawn

Each knew his place – king, peasant, peer, or priest,
The greatest owned connexion with the least;
From rank to rank the generous feeling ran
And linked society as man to man.

Lord John Manners, 7th Duke of Rutland,
'England's Trust'[1]

In many ways Lord George was a character of Regency England, ready to resort to sharp if not downright unscrupulous measures to achieve his ends. His language was often more eighteenth- than nineteenth-century, his spelling 'just like that of Dr Johnson and Mr Pitt – "publick," "compleat," "tallents," &c'. He was from a time when aristocrats still spoke with a regional accent rather than the polished 'Oxford English' that would become the lingua franca of the ruling class by the end of the century. 'He always used to speak of a "dish of tea", and pronounced Rome "Room," wonder "woonder," and golden "goulden".'[2] And yet he was a Victorian in his reforming zeal. He was the living embodiment of the confusing times in which he lived, one half of him stuck in the all-night gambling and pistols-at-dawn ethos of his father's time, the other a creature of the age of progress and conspicuous improvement.

The conflict in his personality came from trying to resolve these two very different impulses. Greville judges him astutely and fairly, giving him credit for a nobility of spirit that belies the murky practices of his racing and betting:

I will endeavour to do justice to his character, which, paradoxical as it may appear, I do not believe to have been nearly so bad as such facts would warrant in being pronounced. It was in truth a strange compound of inconsistent qualities and opposite impulses, which sometimes drove him into evil, but often urged him into good courses. Undoubtedly the man who *could* act thus must have much that was sordid and selfish in his disposition and could not have been animated with those high and unerring principles which shrink instinctively from flagrant breaches of integrity, good faith and good feeling. His mind was disturbed and debased, and bad habits and evil desires had for a time at least silenced the voice of conscience and honor and made him no better than a rogue. But this was not his natural disposition; I believe that all the time he hated and was ready to wage war with every kind of villainy which he could detect in others, and had not indulgence for any misdeeds but his own. He had made for himself however a certain system of right and wrong, in which he allowed himself a very strange and enormous latitude. He would never have done anything which he thought wrong and which was not consistent with his own ideas; but he had taught himself to believe that such practices as I have described were permissible and all fair at the game he was playing.

But what exactly was the game he was playing? The truth is that Lord George himself probably did not know, but at some stage he began to lose his ability to compartmentalise the action he took on his own account and the action he took against others for doing exactly the same as he himself was doing. Perhaps he tired of the hypocrisy. Certainly Greville thought so; in a postscript added at a later stage to his memoirs he said, 'I am inclined to think that while he was taking to himself the mission of purifying the turf, and punishing or expelling wrongdoers of [all ?] sorts, his own mind became purified and (though I do not know it) I should not wonder if he looked back with shame and contrition to all the schemes, plots, and machinations which, in the ardour of his racing pursuit, he had so cunningly devised.'[3] Or it could be that having no more worlds to conquer, being a mere Leviathan of the Turf was no longer sufficient and he wanted to be racing's saint and saviour.

There was something romantic in the air in Great Britain in the 1830s and 40s. It was an era of social and technical advances: a Reformed parliament, electricity, chloroform and the railways were just some of the innovations that catapulted life forward. But this new age prompted much introspection and a general inquiry came about into what became known as the 'condition-of-England question'. This act of national temperature-taking was a reaction against the laissez-faire, or perhaps more accurately *faire rien*, approach of the preceding age. While Lord George was plunging his hundreds of thousands into his campaign to become dictator of the Turf, the Chartists were agitating for fairer treatment of the working man. On the religious front the Tractarians, so witheringly mocked in many comic novels of the day, were nevertheless hugely popular (by 1850 the Religious Tract Society was able to proclaim a 'present annual circulation of the society's works of about 24 millions'[4]). Pursuing a muscular Christianity, they evinced a conspicuous crusading zeal that took exception to much that Lord George's section of society took for granted: drinking, gambling and the use of the Sabbath for anything other than worship. The typical turfite view of organised religion was amply expressed by the amiable George Payne, who, when spending the weekend at a ducal pile and asked by his hostess, 'Are you not coming to church, Mr Payne?' answered baldly, 'No Duchess I am not', adding as a gracious afterthought, 'not that I see any *harm* in it.'[5]

It was just such attitudes that exercised a small clique of Fellows of Oriel College Oxford. On 14 July 1833 one of them, a kind-faced and usually rather reserved man, climbed into the pulpit of St Mary's Church on Oxford's High Street in front of a congregation of gowned dons. His name was John Keble and he delivered what would become known as the 'National Apostasy' sermon, inveighing against the 'fashionable liberality of this generation' and preaching about the need to put the nation back on a true Christian footing, using fervent prayer and heavily ritualised worship. In later years another Fellow of Oriel College, John Henry Newman, would identify that sermon as the 'start of the religious movement of 1833'.[6] This crusade, begun by the deferential and retiring Keble, would become known as the Oxford Movement. It marked a revival of interest in the Catholic roots of the Church of England. The debate it sparked ensured that during the remainder of the nineteenth century the Church would occupy an increasingly central position in British public and political life, assuming a greater level of social responsibility in the process.

For most people these were hard times, and during the 'hungry forties', as they were known, the Poor Law came to be increasingly regarded as barbaric and unfair. Conditions in the manufacturing towns became a source of national shame as did the exploitation of children, while in the country the rural working class suffered just as cruelly. The opportunistic rising politician Benjamin Disraeli surfed this tide of shifting public opinion and received praise for his novel *Sybil: or, the Two Nations* that contrasted the gambling upper classes with the circumstances of the urban and rural poor.

One of the reactions to this complex combination of scientific progress, economic change and an awakening social conscience was to search for answers to the condition-of-England question in an idealised past. Disraeli, for instance, found himself at the centre of a faintly idiotic group of upper-class idealists known as Young England, who peddled a preposterously regressive political philosophy. Their vision was a Merrie England idyll of benevolent back-to-the-land paternalism that seemed to tap into the Zeitgeist of Walter Scott's novels, the Oxford Movement and the elaborate Gothic architecture of Pugin and Charles Barry. For a while the movement became quite fashionable – Lord Eglinton's celebrated medieval tournament would have been one of the high points of this cultural pantomime (though it ended in bathos, blighted by heavy rain). The key tenet of Young England was articulated in a revealing piece of doggerel by one of its most ardent members, Lord John Manners:

> Each knew his place – king, peasant, peer, priest,
> The greatest owned connexion with the least;
> From rank to rank the generous feeling ran
> And linked society as man to man.

Most memorable is the deathless couplet:

> Let wealth and commerce, laws and learning die,
> But leave us still our old nobility.[7]

It is easy to see how such a mood might have appealed to Lord George: this simplistic, half-baked, quasi-feudal claptrap played right into his personal prejudices. After all, he embodied many of the qualities of the stereotypical British aristocrat: impressive to look at, unapologetically philistine, possessed of a highly developed interest in land and horses, unadorned and plain in his dress. No wonder Disraeli swooned over him.

Moreover, however much he may have played on his bluff openness – 'I don't pretend to know much but I can judge of men and horses'[8] was a favourite line of his – Bentinck was a romantic. There is a sense that he saw something courageous, noble and selfless in the way he waged his wars and certainly by the 1840s his campaigns on the Turf, having been hitherto motivated solely by self-interest, took on a more reforming and zealous complexion. It is quite possible that he thought racing a manly and wholesome pastime, part of the mystical bond that welded all classes of Englishmen into the neo-medieval hierarchy of mutual responsibility eulogised by Young England. Certainly Bentinck's later efforts on behalf of the protectionist cause were freighted with much talk of honour and integrity, and the beginnings of his born-again righteousness concurred with his campaign to clean up the Augean mess that was the early Victorian Turf, a mess to which he had contributed handsomely in his time.

By the 1840s racing seemed to have forfeited any respectability it may have enjoyed and the biggest blow to the sport's reputation was the young Queen Victoria's decision to break up the royal stud at Hampton Court. The stud was started by Henry VIII; the glamorous Tudor monarch had bestowed his patronage on the sport and made matches with his courtiers. Even during the Protectorate, the nucleus of the royal stud had been preserved and Cromwell had enriched the bloodline by importing horses. But since the Escape Affair of 1791 royal interest in racing had been fitful.

George IV certainly liked to wager, and it was widely accepted that he placed bets using various commission agents, among them a Bristol butcher's son named John Gully. But his successor, the sailor king William IV, showed no particular interest in racing. Had it not been for his friendship with the Duke of Richmond he would have quit the Turf entirely when he was hit in the eye by a ginger nut thrown at him at Ascot in the summer of 1832. It was unfortunate for the sport that when Queen Victoria made her first visit to Epsom as monarch, to watch the 1840 Derby, almost everything that could go wrong did go wrong. She and the Prince Consort were greeted with little respect or enthusiasm; the royal couple were reported to have arrived 'slightly agitated'[9] after the police had found it difficult to clear much of a path for them through the crowd. Prince Albert had wanted to see the saddling, which usually took place at a farmhouse called The Warren, but was disappointed when the owner said that 'for religious reasons'[10] he would not be making his property available for this ritual. And then, as the report in *Bell's Life** put it, 'Truth obliges us to state a fact which, we trust, it will never again be our lot as public journalists, to record, namely that the *Queen of England was absolutely in want of a piece of bread.'*[11] Victoria reigned for another sixty-one years but never again went to Epsom races, and even stopped attending Ascot after her husband's death.

Sudden bouts of religious fervour, lapses in catering and crowd control aside, the Derby of 1840 was also a perfect illustration of the low moral standards that had come to typify the Turf. In the

---

* *Bell's Life in London, and Sporting Chronicle* was a weekly sporting paper founded in 1822.

final furlong Will Scott, a noted jockey who was riding Lord Westminster's Launcelot, shouted across to the winning jockey as he pounded past that he would give him £1,000 if he pulled his horse. The winning horse was trained by a colourful character called John Forth, known on the Turf as 'Old Forth' (older than the Derby itself, as a sexagenarian he had won the Derby of 1829 as both trainer and jockey). It was suggested that the horse was four rather than three years old. The controversy surrounding Queen Victoria's first and last Derby deepened five years later when Honest John Day made sensational accusations concerning a plot to bribe his son John (he who had mixed up the envelopes with his contradictory instructions to his commission agent and his client Lord George Bentinck) by a mysterious man called Crommelin, who was disguised with a false moustache and green-lensed glasses. Once again the ill-starred John Jr proved inept at deception when it emerged that far from offering a bribe, Crommelin was meeting him for inside information about the horses in training at Danebury.

While farcical, the whole Day–Crommelin farrago neatly encapsulated the changing social dynamic of the sport. The mere 'training grooms' of a previous generation had risen to positions of commanding importance in the sport. Flashy 'Honest' John Day and his Danebury Confederacy were pre-eminent examples of how the balance of economic power was shifting away from the aristocratic owners. By the 1840s Day was a considerable employer, and when asked how many servants he had working at his Danebury stables he was able to answer, 'About 35 every day sit down for dinner' and that in busy periods, including 'day labourers', the number working at Danebury could reach one hundred.[12] And while the sport's respectability was questionable, there was no denying that it had become increasingly aspirational: success on the Turf was seen as a social passport, particularly among those who made their fortunes in the thriving and illegal field of gaming clubs, the forerunners of modern casinos. 'As soon as a proprietor of an establishment of this nature amasses money enough to appear on the turf, and become known at Tattersall's as a speculator on horse-racing,' noted *Fraser's Magazine* caustically, 'he is dubbed a gentleman.'[13]

Speaking of the fashion among the lower-middle classes for gambling, one solicitor said, 'I think there is a petty ambition in it, that of being thought gentlemen, and wearing a Newmarket coat; appearing for one day as a sporting man, and sinking the clerk, is a great temptation.'[14] It is all too easy to imagine those pale, drab young men at their desks in counting-houses, banking halls and solicitors' offices being seduced by the allure of a rakishly cut coat and the demeanour of the sporting man. And with the serialisation during 1843 and 1844 of *Martin Chuzzlewit*, literature furnished just such an archetype in the form of Bailey Junior, the lowest servant at Mrs Todgers's Commercial Boarding House, who takes a professional step up by working as a tiger* for the fraudulent financier and Ponzi scheme operator Montague Tigg. Bailey is a typical comic Dickens character in his incarnation as a fashionable groom: he learns to pepper his conversation with allusions to racing, horseflesh and Jockey Club members and is described as being dressed 'from head to heel Newmarket'.[15]

While those wan, inky-fingered urban upstarts who followed the racing world, aping its manners and its dress, might have recognised themselves in Dickens's caricature, their hero was an altogether more impressive figure. The owner of an estate in the north of England called Ackworth Park, colliery proprietor and quondam MP for Pontefract, by 1844 John Gully Esq. must have seemed the apotheosis of the prosperous Victorian gentleman. Much later, at the end of the century, his grandson William Gully would become Speaker of the Commons, and in 1905 was made Viscount Selby. However, in 1805 all this lay in the future for the powerfully built, cherubic-faced young man then just into his twenties, who at one o'clock in the afternoon of 8 October ducked under the rope on a

---

* A tiger was a young, extravagantly dressed groom who stood on a small platform at the back of a fashionable cabriolet holding on to a set of straps; when the cab moved at speed the tiger would bounce about and often swing through the air, clinging on to the straps like a miniature Tarzan.

patch of grass near the Sussex village of Hailsham to face Hen Pearce, the 'Game Chicken', the champion prize fighter of Regency England.

It says much for social mobility in England during the nineteenth century that the Gully family's journey to the House of Lords had begun exactly one hundred years before William Gully's elevation to the peerage, in the less than salubrious surroundings of the prize ring. Boxing, the noble art, the 'pugilistic science',[16] exerted a hypnotic influence over the English in the early part of the century. Fisticuffs and its culture pervaded society at every level, from prisons to palaces. Its adherents spoke a slang that was all but incomprehensible to the uninitiated: fights were known as 'mills', fighters were 'professors of the science', money was known as 'blunt', sporting gentlemen called Corinthians and the whole brash, brutal and dangerous world was collectively known as 'the Fancy'. During the Regency, in a world of cock-fighting, hare-coursing, dog-fighting and bull-baiting, these human fighting machines, these 'heroes of the fist'[17] were revered as gods. The fact that a boxing match was technically an 'illegal and riotous assembly' liable to be broken up by 'the attendance of the magistrates, high-constables, petty-constables, and other peace officers, entrusted with the execution of the law'[18] only added to the excitement.

Born in 1783, Gully was the son of a West Country inn-keeper turned butcher, and as a youngster he had demonstrated a natural gift for using his fists, 'soundly thrashing a big bully at Bristol for unfairly setting his dog at a bull they were then baiting. Gully, to his great surprise and delight, afterwards heard that his defeated opponent was a prize-fighter, the terror of the neighbourhood.'[19] However, the Gully family fortunes did not prosper and by his early twenties he was an inmate at the King's Bench debtors' prison.

The regime inside this prison was relatively relaxed. Those who could afford it purchased the 'Freedom of the Rules', whereby they could enjoy the diversions available within a radius of three square miles. Those who could not buy access to the area around the prison, among whom was John Gully, had to make do with the resources within the prison's high walls, where there were dozens of gin shops and a large courtyard in which hatters, tailors, barbers, oyster salesmen and even piano-makers offered their services. As well as shopping opportunities, the yard offered scenes such as the one that unfolded on a spring afternoon in 1805, when Hen(ry) Pearce (sometimes spelt Pierce), punningly known in sporting circles as the Game Chicken, strolled in to visit a youngster who, like him, was from the West Country and about whom he had heard interesting reports.

While incarcerated, Gully had been keeping fit with 'the active amusement of rackets', and the two men 'decided to fill up the chasm in the afternoon's amusement'[20] by engaging in an impromptu sparring session. Although he cannot have realised it, as the plucky youngster squared up to England's champion boxer his life was about to change. Accounts of what happened next vary slightly: some say that one bout was enough to convince the Game Chicken of the worthiness of his young opponent, while another says that 'Pierce used to visit him in gaol, and spar with him for a few hours daily. After having more than an ordinary "set-to", he said coolly: "Gully, fight me. It will make your fortune. I don't know which will win, but I think I may. Still, it is sure to be a very close and exciting thing."'[21]

As if by magic, soon afterwards, Gully found that his debts had been paid by a member of the Fancy called Fletcher Reid, who had been the backer of the great champion Jem Belcher, and he was put into training at Virginia Water for the fight against the Game Chicken. The date of the fight was set for Saturday 20 July, and to avoid drawing the attention of the magistrates it was understood that it would be over by 8 o'clock in the morning. Accordingly the toll-keepers at Hyde Park were kept busy from before first light as the Fancy made its way out to Virginia Water and then a further three miles on to Chobham. There was a delay in starting the fight, concerns being voiced about some highly suspicious movements in the betting that attended the match, and in the midst of these discussions news arrived that the Surrey magistrates were on their way. The whole cavalcade then moved on beyond the borders of Surrey, where the squabbling continued with the result that Gully and Pearce did not fight that day. Instead, 'the amateurs having travelled thirty-two miles from London'[22] had to make do with a scratch bout fought between Tom Cribb, another fighter from the south-west, and one George Nicholls for a purse raised on the spot.

The much vaunted fight between Gully and Pearce eventually took place that autumn on 8 October on the South Downs, a fortnight before that other great battle of 1805, Trafalgar. 'All the admirers of the pugilistic art that could quit the metropolis, set off for Hailsham, a small village situate [sic] between Brighton and Lewes in Sussex. The spectators were immense,' writes Pierce Egan in *Boxiana*, his account of the fight, 'and the Downs literally covered with equestrians and pedestrians, in eager pursuit from the above fashionable watering place, to witness the mighty conflict.'[23] Illegal or not, the fight even enjoyed royal patronage: the Duke of Clarence, later King William IV, was fond of recalling how he had been present on the Downs that day. Perhaps he mentioned it when John Gully Esq. MP was presented to him at a court levee in 1836.

The prize ring in those days was a brutal place. For well over an hour, over the course of between fifty-nine and sixty-four rounds, depending on which account you read (rounds were not of a set length, and ended when one or other of the fighters was knocked down), the two men were locked in what Pearce would later describe as 'the severest battle he ever fought'.[24] The early rounds went in Pearce's favour, with the odds coming down from 3–1 on to 10–2 on by the beginning of round 8, though there was 'considerable science displayed on both sides'.[25] Then Pearce fell for the first time, at which cheers rose for Gully and the air was rent with the cry, 'They are Both Bristol Men!'[26] the West Country having a reputation for fighters. Round 12 saw 'Gully put in a most tremendous blow on the mouth of the Chicken'.

All who saw the fight agreed that the best round by far was

the seventeenth, with the Fancy 'uncommonly interested by the reciprocal manliness displayed'. Pearce was said to be full of 'gaiety and confidence', although probably not after Gully 'put in two severe hits on the Chicken's left eye', resulting in the odds lengthening for the defending champion. The following round saw so much blood gushing from Pearce's mauled face that Gully lost his footing and slipped on the gore-spattered grass. By the twentieth round Pearce's left eye had swollen so much he could no longer see with it, and still the blood poured. However, in the twenty-second Pearce dealt Gully such a blow to the side of his head that the former inmate of the King's Bench vomited, his sputum mixing freely with the blood that was making the ground within the twenty-four-foot ring increasingly treacherous. Pearce continued to improve until the thirty-first round, when Gully 'with great agility, struck over his guard, and nearly closed his right eye'.

But Pearce continued to get the better of the younger man and as the number of rounds fought climbed from the thirties into the forties, Pearce landed punch after telling punch, frequently hitting Gully in the throat, and by the forty-fourth 'Gulley [sic] was literally covered from the torrents [of blood] which flowed from his ear', while 'his head was truly terrific, and had a giant-like appearance from being so terribly swelled, and the effect was singular'. He staggered on for a few more rounds until his 'friends interfered, and positively insisted that he should fight no longer, as the chance was against him'.[27] Given that the Fancy was not known for its sentimentality, one can only wonder at what state Gully was in before his 'friends' persuaded him to concede the fight to the Game Chicken.

Finally, having spent the preceding hour and a quarter knocking the life out of each other, the Game Chicken went to shake the hand of his opponent, obviously with some difficulty – 'neither being hardly able to see out of either eye', as one account has it – and said, 'You're a d—d good fellow; I'm hard put to it to stand. You are the only man that ever stood up to me.' After the fight Pearce conceded that Gully had 'a head for fighting' and added the prophetic words, 'He must be a sharp chap, and get up early, as beats John Gully, I can tell you.'[28]

Gully's prestige amongst the Fancy soared. Barely six months earlier he had been in a debtors' prison and now he was the cynosure of sporting society. He had distinguished himself as a boxer of considerable science, strength and bottom, bravely withstanding over an hour's brutal punishment from the fists of the leading fighter in England as well as landing some cracking punches of his own. This much was impressive indeed, but what made Gully remarkable was what he went on to do with that fame.

While the gentlemen and nobility of the Fancy were happy to consort with the 'heroes of the fist', to back them in fights and even on occasion allow them to travel in their carriages, their attitude was much the same as the owner of a racehorse or a fighting dog might have towards his prize-winning animal. Prize fighters were mascots adopted, then discarded, by a fickle fashionable crowd, who might wish to mimic the manners of coachmen and affect the patois of the sporting taverns, but who in the end believed in the implicit and natural superiority of the higher social order to which they belonged.

Of course, in reality there was not much difference between the worn-out roué, old before his time, and the bloated, boozy prize fighter turned publican. Typical of the former was that mainstay of the Fancy and heavy gambler Colonel Henry Mellish, the proto-typical Regency buck, who had helped arrange the fight between Gully and Pearce. He would bet on anything and was once said to have wagered £40,000 (£4,800,000) on a single throw of the dice. When he had exhausted his fortune he retired to the one farm he had left, married, then died at the age of thirty-six. Of the latter kind there were dozens who kept what were called 'sporting houses'. For years Tom Cribb was the landlord of the Union Arms in Panton Street off the Haymarket, and at one time Smithfield could boast three pubs owned by former fighters: the Plough, the Black Bull and the Bear and Ragged Staff. For a while it looked as though Gully would join this class of man, parlaying his prowess in the ring into the modest prosperity of the celebrity innkeeper. He could be found behind the bar of the Plough, a famous 'sporting house' on Carey Street, and later married 'an exceedingly pretty woman though of the St Giles type of beauty'.[29]

With his brassy wife and his lively pub Gully worked on his boxing and increased his 'science', but, acting against type, he did not indulge in riotous living. Moreover, he appeared to eschew the prize ring and did not actively seek the title Champion of England, which more or less devolved to him on the retirement of the Game Chicken through ill-health. The Chick later died a broken alcoholic. It was at this time that Gully got his first taste of the Turf, walking most of the way to Doncaster to see the St Leger (then accepting a lift for the last leg of his journey from a passing member of the Fancy).

Only in October 1807 did a challenger emerge, a six-foot-two-inch Lancastrian called Bob Gregson. Gregson was bigger and heavier than Gully, with a longer reach, which meant that Gully would have to wait for his opponent to hit him and thus get close enough to stand a chance of hitting him back. Thirty-six rounds saw the fighters reeling 'like two inebriated men, helpless', each barely able to haul himself up off his second's knee, let alone raise his fists. This time Gully emerged victorious, but only just, and his left arm was partially disabled for life. It is significant that the gruelling fight – 'such spectacles were never before witnessed'[30] – took place at Six Mile Bottom near Newmarket, the epicentre of British racing. Although very nearly destroyed by the fight, Gully was taken from the ring into the carriage of a Captain Barclay and was seen the next day on the racecourse.

After that he participated in just one more bout, the following year, a rematch with Gregson, fought in the teeming rain in parkland on a Hertfordshire baronet's estate. In spite of the weather both men stripped and fought just in white breeches and silk stockings, as it was suggested by some that Gregson would attempt to wear spiked shoes. Gully had obviously used the intervening time well, and even though his left arm was still injured he defeated his opponent with relative ease. Then immediately Gully went to the rope and announced that he was retiring from boxing. 'Gully then dressed himself, and was brought to town in Lord Barrymore's barouche. The following morning he was facetiously answering questions respecting the fight and serving his numerous customers at the Plough, in Carey Street.'[31]

In his brief career as a boxer Gully had developed skills and traits that would serve him well when he moved from the blood-soaked turf of the boxing ring to the equally vicious turf of British racing. Although he was prepared to take advantage of it – seen, for instance, in his readiness to accept lifts from aristocratic patrons – Gully had no time for the back-slapping bonhomie of the Fancy and its patronising treatment of boxers as little more than human toys. He was not the man to participate in such stunts as the one got up by Lord Elgin, who arranged for Gregson to pose naked amongst his recently acquired marble bas reliefs from Athens for the amusement of his guests.

A shrewd man, Gully made sure to calculate things carefully, and did what he could to make any given situation favour him. Of his last bout with Gregson it was said that he had gathered information from 'one who pretended to be a friend of Gregson'[32] about the way in which his opponent trained, and learned that he did not guard properly against blows to his left eye. This private information, one might say 'sporting espionage', gave him an obvious advantage over his opponent. Observers of his fighting commented frequently on his mastery of 'the science' and there is in that a clue to the coldly analytical way he went on to amass, by betting on horses, one of the significant fortunes of the age. He was a man to be respected rather than liked, and some went as far as saying that 'he was by no means popular with those who knew him best on the turf'.[33] This distant personality, to put it at its most charitable, was compounded by his taciturnity: he would sit for hours silently smoking a cigar and saying nothing.

Gully was in many ways a man ahead of his time. Much as he may have epitomised the Regency beau idéal – trading blows, stripped to the waist, in silk stockings and white breeches – he moved with the changes. As the century wore on he 'adopted a modern style of dress, and left off his kerseymere breeches and top-boots, for trousers, frock-coat, and blue neck-tie'.[34] And accoutred with his respectable clothes and his remote manner he began his assault on the betting books of his social superiors.

The era when Gully attended his first race meetings saw the rise of a new type of betting man. As plebeian as the owners were patrician, they were called 'blacklegs' or more commonly 'legs', and in time John Gully would become their king. Already by the Derby of 1810 he was betting with a hundred other men on a variety of horses, a procedure known as 'betting round'. As has been seen, racing was still very much an aristocratic closed shop, the five hundred or fewer racehorse owners coming exclusively from the noble and landed class. The number of men who followed racing was not much bigger: the annual *Racing Calendar* had a circulation of less than fifteen hundred. And even by the 1820s the number of betters round (or bookmakers) was, according to one racing historian, 'only a baker's dozen.'[35]

Although they were few, the arrival of men like Gully marked the beginning of an irrevocable change in the nature of betting. Gully's betting books from 1810 to 1825, kept at the Jockey Club rooms in Newmarket, provide a fascinating insight into the birth of modern bookmaking. In the pages of these black pocket books Gully's neat sloping hand records in tidy columns the bet and the amount. In 1810 these bets were counted in tens and the occasional hundred, but by 1825 the pages were inscribed with four-figure sums, often running into dozens of bets for just one race. Moreover, the names listed in Gully's betting books are those of the great Corinthians of the day, including Squire Thornhill and George Payne, the former an immensely fat man, the latter the church-averse ludomaniac who contentedly gambled his way through three fortunes. A few years after starting a career as a blackleg, Gully put himself on an equal footing with his social superiors by becoming a racehorse owner. 'As a turfite he dates his career from 1812,' records the *New Sporting Magazine*, 'when his name first appears in the books as owner of Cardenio.'[36] Thereafter he quickly acquired whole or part ownership of a large number of horses.

There were those who felt that the standing of racing had been diminished by the arrival of Gully and others like him. One sporting writer lamented that 'the art of book-making arose, and henceforward what had been more of a pastime among owners who would back their horses for a rattler when the humour took them, and not shrink from having £5000 to £6000 on a single match, degenerated into a science'.[37] Many saw the legs as parasitical scum, or in the picturesque words of one leg-hater, as a 'drone of Satan's hive'. 'To him, your bone grubber is a fellow infinitely aristocratic. This at least makes his merchandise of honest offal, while the other is a mendicant of vampire carrion.' These 'wager-ghouls' were essentially operating a system of arbitrage, gathering information, exploiting fractional movements in the betting. Having made a bet with the odds to his advantage, 'he is off on the instant, lest the rate of exchange alter, and hedges, with the pull in his favour, with another of the fraternity'.[38] The whole system was hardly less reprehensible than misrepresenting the performance of your horse to deceive other betting men, but its spirit was different. Analytical rather than dashing, it was, in the majority of cases, practised by those who did not keep racehorses and did nothing to support racing, but just lived, and lived well, by treating betting as a financial market. Purists did not see it as at all gentlemanly, but then its practitioners were certainly not gentlemen: 'leg-ism,' commented one disgusted observer of the racing scene in the 1820s, is 'a science of chicanery and fraud'.[39]

That word 'science' again. Gully approached the betting ring much as he had the prize ring: using patient study, knowledge and skulduggery. 'He must be a sharp chap, and get up early, as beats John Gully'[40] was one politely expressed opinion of this impressive figure. But in the less then flattering words of the sardonic Charles Greville, who as an owner of racehorses knew what he was talking about, Gully 'began a system of corruption of trainers, jockeys [sic] and boys which put the secrets of Newmarket at his disposal and in a few years made him rich'.[41] Writing towards the end of the century the racing memoirist William Day said, 'I don't think that Mr Gully would stand very high in the esteem of his countrymen in the present day.'[42] And yet, disreputable though he was, Gully was the most presentable of all the legs.

The arrival of the blacklegs did indeed signal a change in the tenor of racing. Many inns and hotels in country towns associated with racing had added large 'assembly rooms', sometimes on the first floor, jutting out over the entrance. Their presence, still visible in some places today, testifies to the brisk social atmosphere that prevailed during race week: it was a time of liveliness and excitement, a chance for the county families to meet and socialise, as much as for racing men to try their horses. However, at about the time John Gully became heavily involved in Turf speculation this began to change, as one habitué of Doncaster racecourse recalled:

> The parties who came to attend Doncaster races did not merely go upon the course to the race, but they used to bring with them their wives and their daughters to attend the race ball; it was an occasion of county meeting, and when they found the blacklegs and other questionable characters coming in such numbers, mixing with the company in the grand stand, and mixing with the company at the ball, all this has had very naturally, and very properly, the effect of driving away the ladies from the races, and very much diminishing the number of gentlemen who used to come.[43]

And given the character of some of these blacklegs it is easy to understand why the worthies of the county decided to keep their wives and daughters at home. One of Gully's chief conspirators was a character called Harry Hill, who had begun his working life as an 'under-boots at an hotel in Manchester'. He had ambitions beyond shining shoes and decided to go into business on his own account; so, equipped with a table, some thimbles and a few peas, he would hang around racecourses, dextrously swindling the unwary who thought they could detect under which thimble he had put the pea. Even when Hill had made his fortune he made little effort to smarten himself up. In his heyday he was 'always to be seen in the evening at the Coach and Horses, Dover Street, Piccadilly, not in the most select company. He was slovenly in his dress, wearing a faded black suit that appeared to have been made for his grandfather, so ill it fitted him. He was not particular as to cleanliness, and his hard features were too surely an index of the working of his mind. His conversation was licentious and vulgar.'[44]

Then there was Crutch Robinson. 'A more domineering, uncouth being than this sporting cripple could not be encountered,' wrote the uncompromising sporting commentator Sylvanus, 'and to see an old man disabled from the use of his limbs and blanched by time, shouting out his odds, and dealing in the lowest bitter sarcasm and racing slang, either mounted on a four-legged brute as rough as himself, or leaning on his trusty crutch, in the midst of the crushing throng, was an irreverent and revolting sight, even in the motley scene wherein he figured.'[45] As well as his disability, Robinson was characterised by a sinister 'knowing quiet leer' as he 'leant on his crutch, with his back against the outer' – certainly not the inner – 'wall of the Newmarket betting rooms'.[46] It was said that his ugly head carried the details of many scandals concerning drugged favourites and nobbled horses.

Almost as grotesque was 'Facetious' Jemmy Bland, 'an atrocious Leg of the ancient, top-booted, semi-highwayman school'.[47] It was Epsom and its Derby that had convinced Jem Bland to forsake his calling of coachman and take to the Turf, sporting his trademark 'brown body-coat'[48] and '"noble lord" hat', hands thrust into the pockets of his white cords. His 'vulgar dialect' and stentorian voice, which boomed 'acute rough expressions, such as "*niver coomed a-nigh*" and so on, as well as his long nose and white flabby cheeks, made him a man of mark even before he got enough by laying all round, to set up a mansion in Piccadilly'. It was strongly suspected that he and his brother Joe were linked to one of the great racing scandals of the century: the 1811 poisoning of a trough belonging to the trainer Richard Prince, which had resulted in the deaths of four horses and the hanging of a low-level racing tout called Dan Dawson.

Only slightly less unsightly was Ludlow Bond, who, though 'not so coarse in his style' as some legs, had acquired the unsettling sobriquet 'Death on the Pale Horse'[49] when he was seen on the Heath at Newmarket on his grey steed. Men like Ludlow Bond and Crutch Robinson were often seen loitering around Newmarket. They were useful to the aristocratic owners, for whom they would bet on commission when it suited the latter to obscure their betting transactions. Turf morality was more or less an oxymoron, and many saw it as perfectly sensible for an owner to take advantage of privileged information about a horse's health in order to lay against it, knowing it would not run – in other words 'to make wagers against horses, which are disabled with parties who believe them to be well'.[50] The line between the self-interest of an owner wishing to hedge his bet on a horse after it had gone lame and the outright attempt at deception was therefore a very fine one. Moreover, with a system of betting called 'play or pay' in which, even if a horse died, was withdrawn by its owner or fell lame, anyone who had backed the horse would have to pay what they had bet, the incentive was for dishonesty rather than otherwise. The use of a commission agent to place bets would obscure the actions of an owner wanting to take advantage of a particularly sensitive piece of information. Often the aristocratic owners and the working-class legs, betting on their own account, would form tactical alliances born out of mutual interest: for instance, Lord George Bentinck, far from fastidious as he was, made such use of both Gully and Harry Hill. And there was, of course, the widespread assumption that Gully placed bets on commission for George IV.

Increasingly, the legs dictated the tenor of racing life, so much so that in the summer of 1844 the *New Sporting Magazine* was moved to comment sourly: 'By slow but sure degrees for the last fifty years, the ring has been growing into a component part of the system of the British turf. By "the ring" is to be understood, a society formed for the purpose of living – and living in clover – upon the profits to be derived from jobbing in the odds. Very few of its members keep race horses – still fewer support studs; so that their position is that of hucksters of unsubstantial wares upon visionary capital.'[51]

It was by his almost complete mastery of this complicated web of cupidity and self-interest that by 1830, on the eve of his move into public life as a Member of Parliament, John Gully and his partner Ridsdale had been able to pull off such dazzling coups as a win of £35,000 (£4,200,000) on the St Leger and a spectacular £50,000 (£6,000,000) on the Derby.

However, his mastery was not total. In 1827 he had become the owner of a Derby winner, purchasing Mameluke from Lord Jersey, after its win, for the impressive sum of 4,000 guineas. It was the first such amount he had spent on a horse and he intended to get his money's worth, insisting that Lord Jersey keep the sale secret to allow him to place bets for the St Leger. He placed two large ones, of £10,000 (£1,200,000) each, with a man called William Crockford. Crockford knew that Mameluke was a highly strung horse liable to bad temper if the start was delayed, and subsequently fixed the race by arranging for a number of false starts that left Mameluke facing the wrong way when the race began. Gully lost a total of £40,000 (£4,800,000) on that race, half of which was paid to Crockford, who, it seemed, was a sharp chap who got up early enough to beat John Gully.

Gully was punctilious in paying his gambling debts. 'It was not in the nature of Mr Gully to see a creditor near him without paying' was the recollection of one Turf habitué, and when one big winner asked him ironically whether it was 'convenient' to pay, Gully answered, 'Oh! It's always convenient to me', adding with a mirthless smile, 'though it's not always pleasant.'[52] However, he made sure that his big losses were few. With such men on the Turf, the racing way of life, its slang, its dress codes and the tantalising prospects of easy money that it extended to all, created a sustained boom in the sport during the opening decades of the century.

'It must be a matter of sincere congratulation to every possessor of true British sentiments,' wrote James Christie Whyte, author of a *History of the British Turf,* in 1839, 'and consequently every admirer of the field sports so peculiar to our native country, that in spite of all the cant and false religion brought to bear against the amusements of the turf by a numerous class whom in common charity we will call misled fanatics, racing has still gone on increasing in prosperity and the national favour.' The statistics Whyte went on to invoke were impressive. According to him, racing had been on the decline in Britain during the late eighteenth century as a result of the 'wars which were carried on during that period ... Thus in 1800, we find that annual racing meetings were held at only sixty-six towns in England and Wales, five in Scotland, and four in Ireland. In 1816, after the last great peace, we already find them on the increase, the number in that year being eighty-four in England and Wales, nine in Scotland, and eight in Ireland.' He adds with a note of triumph, 'So rapid has been the increase since then, that the number at the present day [1839] is no less than one hundred and thirty-two in England, many consisting of two, and several, more, annual meetings; nine in Wales, nine in Scotland and three in Ireland.'[53] And while the number of races had doubled, the number number of horses in training had trebled.

The increase in races taking place and the spectacular financial rewards began to attract an ever greater number of racing adherents. The standard of information available was also much improved; sporting periodicals were published detailing runners and odds for every forthcoming race. The professional classes and even – *quelle horreur* – tradesmen began to bet. 'There are a great many little Tradesmen that bet,' commented Richard Tattersall, whose eponymous equine auction house was the meeting place of the Turf magnates. 'I have had twenty or thirty letters for people to come into my Room. I do not let any one in now, except upon a reference. I have had many little tradesmen writing to me, and I have written to them that I should not let them in. My advice is, if they have a little money, to keep it; not to engage in betting.

Those are the sort of people who are ruined, they have an itching for it and they go hoping to win £20, or £30 or £50.'[54] This was an era characterised by a get-rich-quick culture. There was an almost erotic charge to the handling of big banknotes, 'the new, brilliant, delicious, tissue fabric of the Bank of England, emblazoned with the sable, unmistakable figures, and delicate fairy-like water-mark of the "large paper"'.[55]

The Turf was not the only means whereby men could enrich themselves with spectacular rapidity. At the same time there was fevered speculation in the railways, which were growing at a rate to match racing. Indeed, these two aspects of life were soon interlinked, railway speculators realising the potential for business offered by conveying racegoers to their day's entertainment. The first 'Derby Special' ran from Nine Elms station, just south of the Thames from Westminster, to Kingston in 1838. Even though racegoers would be faced with a long walk or an overpriced cab ride at the end of their train journey, interest was such that, despite more passengers being crammed into the carriages than was entirely safe, an estimated five thousand people, many of whom had been waiting since dawn, were left behind. The mood turned decidedly ugly, and the crowd rampaged through the station, tearing it apart. Order was only restored by a troop of mounted police.

5

Sporting Paladin

The Greatest Reformer of all abuses connected with the Turf

1843 Doncaster Race Report, quoted in Kent, *Bentinck*, p. 128[1]

It can be imagined how these scenes must have upset Lord George. He now saw the Turf that he had fought so hard, albeit far from cleanly, to dominate under siege from trainloads of clerks in flashy clothes and little tradesmen who were 'itching for it'. He was not going to stand by and let his beloved Turf become a playground for petty swindlers and working-class rogues, or, as the sporting writer Nimrod thundered in 1838, a 'horde of determined depredators'.[2] So from the 1830s onwards, but beginning in earnest at around the time he split with the Days, Bentinck embarked on a serious campaign to 'clean up' the English Turf. The prodigious energy that had hitherto been used in securing victory, via suspect racing stratagems, was now channelled into his crusade to rid the Turf of a multitude of malpractices.

Relying as ever on the indulgence of the Duke of Richmond, he began his duties as racing's self-appointed vigilante at Goodwood, with improvements that were gradually copied and implemented at other courses around the country. Bentinck's was an orderly mind. When he became politically active as leader of the protectionist faction he would insist on total ordering and mastery of all the facts. It was the same with racing: the innovations that he introduced aimed to bring a consistency and transparency to the sport. Starts were notoriously haphazard, and it was not unusual for there to be a dozen or more attempts to begin a race, with starters often being intimidated or bribed. The Derby of 1830 had been blighted by no fewer than fourteen false starts. Bentinck ensured punctuality by fining the clerk of the course ten shillings for every minute a start was delayed. The tidiness he craved was also demonstrated in his decree that jockeys should be clad in 'a silk, velvet or satin jacket, and in boots and breeches'.[3] Up until then a minority of owners had registered racing colours, but they were regarded as optional and many jockeys often rode in the sort of clothes that farm labourers wore.

Racing differed in the way it was practised from course to course. Until Bentinck became one of its most energetic stewards the Jockey Club, while powerful at Newmarket, the 'metropolis of racing',[4] exercised only varying degrees of influence at the other courses up and down the country. His reforms included designated places for the saddling of the horses and a rule requiring their appearance before the grandstand or in the parade ring before a race. He also invented a system of flags for starts, and made it compulsory for the details of the horses and jockeys to be exhibited on a notice board. In many ways Bentinck is responsible for the framework of modern race meetings. It was his indefatigability that pushed through what at the time were regarded as extraordinary measures. When the clerk of Epsom racecourse told him his ideas were impracticable, he coolly replied, 'If the conditions are that the horses must be saddled in Epsom town, never fear but I will enforce them.'[5]

As the years wore on he became more ambitious and, ironically, this aloof aristocrat did much to popularise racing. For example, he was keen on grandstands for which entry could be charged, a portion of which income would be added to the stakes. And all the time his reputation as the fearless servant of honesty and integrity in racing grew; a report on the Doncaster Races of 1843 eulogised his efforts: 'The Corporation had been brought to a just sense of their duties, by the indefatigable Lord George Bentinck, who may with the utmost propriety be styled the greatest reformer of all abuses connected with the Turf.' There was one abuse that obsessed him in particular, and above all else: defaulting. By the 1840s the non-payment of debts incurred on the Turf had reached epidemic proportions. One of the accusations laid against the tradesmen who so keenly anticipated their winnings was that they would bet without any intention of paying up if they lost. Unenforceable by law, the settling of gambling debts was a matter of honour, and honour was something about which Lord George felt strongly – some might argue hypocritically, given the difficulties he had experienced in meeting his own gambling debts on the St Leger of 1826.

During 1842 and 1843 the number of unpaid debts arising from horse-racing bets had leapt to epidemic proportions. Betting had become extremely fashionable, but even those who had come to it only relatively recently noticed an alarming increase in the numbers of 'levanters' (those who avoided their debts). Speaking in 1844, one relative newcomer to the Turf said of defaulting, 'When I began five years ago it was not to anything like the extent it was last year and the year before.'[6] Bentinck began excluding named defaulters from Goodwood, possible because it was the Duke of Richmond's private property and the genial duke usually fell in with his views. This practice was enthusiastically adopted at other racecourses, where men who were known to have unpaid gambling debts were excluded from the enclosures and grandstands. 'The same admirable rule respecting defaulters which worked so well at Goodwood is to be put into force here,' they said at Doncaster, where 'honest men' were exhorted to 'thank Lord George Bentinck for this valuable reform of the Turf; for if that nobleman had not persevered to the utmost, even his powerful influence might have been blighted, and a host of rotten sheep left to infect the constitution of the remaining flock. We are left without sufficient words of praise to the noble Lord for his indefatigable exertions.'[7]

Just how indefatigable those exertions were became clear during what was known as the Gurney affair. Richard Gurney, a better round, or bookmaker, had wagered heavily on the Derby of 1841, and although he had won handsomely his losses were greater still: some £7,650 (almost £1,000,000) was owed to eleven creditors. The Jockey Club assigned three respected figures to superintend the collection and disbursement of the funds. Until such time as they were satisfied, Gurney was to be considered a defaulter. By December, all the debts were said to have been discharged, and the Jockey Club declared that the 'assignees had faithfully and honourably discharged the trust they undertook, under the sanction of the stewards of the Jockey Club'.[8] It clearly hoped that a line had been drawn under the matter. However, it reckoned without the intervention of Bentinck, who owed money to Gurney and now protested vehemently because, he said, some of Gurney's creditors had accepted a compromise payment – five shillings in the pound[9] is the figure mentioned in one source as having been accepted by some. Bentinck claimed that out of the £7,650 owed £3,875 (almost £500,000) remained unpaid, and that any compromise was unfair to those who had paid their debts to Gurney in full. Moreover, he believed that Gurney was lying when he said he was unable to meet his obligations; as Bentinck saw it, he was 'wealthy, but wilful'.[10] It was plainly becoming a matter of principle – and there was little Lord George liked more than a spirited fight over a matter of principle.

Blazing with a convert's zeal, he relished the trouble he was stirring up. He believed that the Jockey Club was ineffectual and made his point clear in a letter to his long-suffering friend the Duke of Richmond, shortly before a lively meeting of the Jockey Club at the Thatched House Tavern on 3 February 1842: 'In regard to the Jockey Club if it proceeds in the course in which it has of late been proceeding, the sooner for the sake of the Turf it is abolished the better. There is no good in such an assembly, in fact it is an absolute nuisance.'[11] Not without justification, he saw the Jockey Club as an incestuous organisation. His newly awakened moral sense recoiled at the notion that members should be able to adjudicate in matters in which they had a financial interest, in effect acting as judge, jury and beneficiary; but then self-interest had been the leitmotif of Jockey Club members for almost a century.

Outvoted at what must have been a tempestuous meeting at the Thatched House Tavern, Bentinck no longer confined his views to his circle but went public with his grievance. On the morning of St Valentine's Day readers of the *Morning Post* were treated to a thirteen-point broadside directed against the Jockey Club by Lord George. He expressed himself in characteristically warm language, leaving no doubt as to his views about the way the matter had been handled: 'arbitrary favouritism as monstrous as it is misplaced', 'intolerable injustice', 'partiality . . . tyranny not to be endured' and 'incompatible with public confidence' were just some of the terms that he bandied about. He closed with the magisterial observation that 'a defaulter of notorious wealth, wanting only honesty and principle to pay his debts of honour, is the last species of defaulter around whom the Jockey Club ought to throw the shield of its partial and paternal protection'.[12]

A better called Thornton who had owed money to Gurney also objected. He sued for the return of his money in the Court of Exchequer, was successful, and made the money over to the charitable school Christ's Hospital. The Jockey Club then branded Thornton a defaulter and wanted to inflict upon him the severe penalty of being 'warned off' Newmarket Heath. However, the only man who could exclude an individual from the Heath was the Duke of Portland, who owned large swathes of it, and this, no doubt under pressure from his son, he refused to do. Thornton then sued the stewards of the Jockey Club for libel and was again successful.

Lord George was plainly unconcerned about any fall in popularity amongst his fellow aristocrats, many of them members of the Jockey Club who tended to allow disputed bets to blow over. Regulations might affect their own conduct on the Turf, where it was in their interest to maintain any advantage they enjoyed due to inside knowledge and their ability to manipulate the betting. He proceeded to adopt what today would be known as a naming-and-shaming policy, and even took his crusade to extirpate defaulting and levanting into the coffee rooms of the clubs of St James's.

One telling vignette reveals much about his cruel, vengeful character, unafraid as he was to strike below the belt if it served his own ends. It concerns the splendidly named Sir St Vincent Cotton, a sporting baronet and a light-hearted, likable man. One of the leading whips in London, he gambled his way through a large fortune and would end up using his skills as a coachman on the Brighton road. A keen roisterer, Sir St Vincent was a familiar presence around the gambling clubs – or hells, as they were known – of St James's. On one occasion, believing himself to have been cheated he smashed up all the furniture, laid out the hell keepers and 'reeled forth with a decanter of brandy, which had escaped the general wreck, in his hand, to seek consolation in the house of a fair friend'. However, when Lord George encountered him he was not in such robust form. Recovering from a serious illness and in need of cheering up, he had appeared in his club one evening, where

[he] had ordered a good dinner, eaten it, and called for the bill. As the waiter was about to deliver it, Lord George Bentinck, who was also dining there, called aloud and in very supercilious tones:

'Waiter, bring me Sir St Vincent Cotton's bill.'

Cotton sat speechless as the extraordinary order was obeyed. George Bentinck read the bill and then returned it, exclaiming aloud:

'Before Sir St Vincent Cotton ordered so expensive a dinner, he ought to have paid his debts.'

Poor Cotton, depressed in Health as he was, probably aware, too, that he had been a defaulter in booking-up for some race, and that he owed George Bentinck money, never said a word.[13]

6

The Gambling Fishmonger

A new star rose upon the horizon in the person of Mr William Crockford; and the old fashioned games of faro, macao, and lansquenet gave place to the all-devouring thirst for the game of hazard.

The Reminiscences and Recollections of Captain Gronow (1892)[1]

Bentinck's vengeful upbraiding of poor convalescent Sir St Vincent Cotton took place in what was arguably the most exclusive London club of the early nineteenth century: Crockford's. An imposing, sepulchral building at the top of St James's Street opposite White's, Crockford's vaunted all the dignity commensurate with the exclusively male world of clubland. But behind its elegant Wyatt façade it operated on entirely different lines: it was a proprietor's club, and whereas at the other establishments gentlemen gambled and lost amongst themselves, at Crockford's they gambled and lost to the eponymous operator. 'One may safely say, without exaggeration, that Crockford won the whole of the ready money of the then existing generation,' commented the Victorian diarist Captain Gronow. 'As is often the case at Lord's Cricket-ground, the great match of the gentlemen of England against the professional players was won by the latter.'[2]

It is one of the amusing ironies of this story that while Gully's father was a butcher, William Crockford was the son of a fishmonger. Just as the West Country seemed able to turn out a disproportionate number of prize fighters, so it appears that the victualling trades of the late eighteenth century bequeathed to the first half of the nineteenth two of its mightiest betting men, who systematically plundered the aristocracy. But whereas Gully concentrated on the Turf, Crockford was a master on the emerald baize of the gaming tables.

Gambling in late Georgian Britain, as has been noted, was a mania amongst the aristocracy, afflicting intelligent and perceptive individuals as well as the intellectually limited and complacent Corinthians of the Fancy. 'Truly,' wrote William Hazlitt, 'the Fancy are not men of imagination. They judge of what has been and cannot conceive of anything that is to be.' And while this might have been true of amiable nincompoops like Colonel Mellish, this accusation could not be levelled at Charles James Fox, scholar and statesman, who was unable to resist a bet or a game of cards.

Bentinck's cousin Charles Greville was another such man, educated, and prominent both socially and politically; had he lived a couple of hundred years later he would have been diagnosed as an addict. Through the many volumes of his diaries his varying fortunes on the Turf, at cards and with dice vie for position with his observations on momentous events in parliament. By his mid-twenties he was already a heavy gambler.

'Ever since the Derby ill fortune has pursued me, and I cannot win anywhere,' he moans on 12 June 1819. 'It is dreadful to depend upon the chance of the dice for almost one's existence. The life it makes me lead is too agitating for I have too much at stake and amusement is the last object I have in view in playing.' He sees himself as powerless in the face of his addiction and feels that his dependence on the dice makes him lead a life that he finds uncomfortable.

> Play is a detestable occupation; it absorbs all our thoughts and renders us unfit for everything else in life. It is hurtful to the mind and destroys the better feelings; it incapacitates us for study and application of every sort; it makes us thoughtful and nervous; and our cheerfulness depends upon the uncertain event of our nightly occupation. How anyone can play who is not in want of money I cannot comprehend;

surely his mind must be strangely framed who requires the stimulus of gambling to heighten his pleasures.

Justifying and excusing his own gambling to himself as the way he makes his living, he nevertheless admits that the pastime is also habit-forming.

> Some indeed may have become attached to gaming from habit, and may not wish to throw off the habit from the difficulty of finding fresh employment for the mind at an advanced period of life. Some may be unfitted by nature or taste for society, and ... for such gaming may have a powerful attraction. The mind is excited; at the gaming-table all men are equal; no superiority of birth, accomplishment, or ability avail here; great noblemen, merchants, orators, jockeys, statesmen,* and idlers are here thrown together in levelling confusion; the only pre-eminence is that of success, the only superiority that of temper. But why does a man play who is blessed with fortune, endowed with understanding, and adorned with accomplishments which might ensure his success in any pursuit which taste or fancy might incite him to follow? It is contrary to reason, but we see such instances every day. The passion of play is not artificial; it must have existed in certain minds from the beginning; at least some must have been so constituted that they yield at once to the attraction, and enter with avidity into the pursuit in which other men can never take the least interest.[3]

This passage is remarkable for its insights into the mind of a man who, though powerless in the face of his addiction, nevertheless understands the unnecessary nervous strain it places upon him and acknowledges its destructive power and mindlessness. Long before scientific knowledge began to explore the notion of genetic pre-disposition, Greville the gambling addict intuitively understood that some men, and women – Georgian society was full of female as well as male gamblers – are susceptible to the virus of gambling while others are immune. He also demonstrates considerable

* It says much about Greville's priorities that jockeys come after orators but before statesmen.

powers of self-deception, excusing his own compulsive gambling as a necessary, money-getting occupation. As the grandson of a duke (his maternal grandfather was the 3rd Duke of Portland), he could hardly be expected to work for a living, and presumably his governmental sinecures, including the post of Clerk to the Privy Council which ultimately made him £5,000 a year, did not enable him to make ends meet.

At the same time as the young Greville was pondering man's eternal weakness for gambling, a hideous, pale, Gollum-complexioned former fishmonger with a Uriah Heep manner and a tendency to mix up his cockney-accented Vs and Ws was profiting from it, and profiting handsomely. William Crockford was a gro-tesque gargoyle of a man. 'His cheeks appeared whitened and flabby through constant night-work. His hands were entirely without knuckles, soft as raw veal, and as white as paper, whilst his large flexible mouth was stuffed with "dead men's bones" – his teeth being all false, and visibly socketed with his darling metal.'[4] Dentistry in those days was rather gruesome: the teeth of the dead were set into the jaws of people like Crockford who had lost their own molars and incisors.

Just as Gully and the legs were changing the nature of betting on horses, so William Crockford was altering the way Society gambled, and invariably lost, away from the racecourse. During the previous century upper-class gaming had been as much a part of Society life as balls and big hair. Fanny Westmacott observed that 'the game of pharoh [sic] has stolen from society much of the fashion of assemblies and balls'. Faro was a relatively simple card game in which players bet on alternate winning and losing cards dealt by the banker. Macao, a game akin to vingt-et-un, was another popular way of losing a fortune in the eighteenth century, as was a card game called lansquenet. Oddly enough, Mrs Westmacott saw a benefit in the popularity of these games: 'It is an advancement that society is hereby grouped into houses every bit as genteel and with better opportunity for the close proximity of suitable ladies and gentlemen.'[5]

Like betting on matches between horses, gambling games in Society were played by the elite, so while the losses could be embarrassing, at times crippling, they remained between members of the ruling class. Crockford's genius was to engineer circumstances to his own profit, that instead of losing money amongst each other they would lose their money to him. The instrument with which he conducted this transfer of funds – one estimate suggests that in a little over a decade he took well over £1 million from the gentlemen and noblemen of England – was a pair of dice. Physically unappealing as he was, Crockford was a phenomenon, a human calculating machine whose arrival marked a new era. As the memoirist Captain Gronow put it: 'In the reign of George IV, a new star rose upon the horizon in the person of Mr William Crockford; and the old fashioned games of faro, macao, and lansquenet gave place to the all-devouring thirst for the game of hazard.'[6]

Hazard was a game played with a pair of dice. In English hazard, one player effectively bets other players that he will throw a number that he nominates from five to nine – a process known as 'calling a main'. Should he throw his main on the first roll, he takes the stakes, this stroke of good luck being known as a 'nick'. However, if, as is more likely, he rolls a different number, he must continue to throw the dice; should he repeat that number, known as the 'chance', he wins; but should he roll his original 'main', he loses. This was the game in its most basic form; but when played in a hell it was subject to all sorts of refinements. English hazard was played in the lower hells where players bet against each other and 'pay a sum to the house, which is called "paying a box," upon throwing in three mains running'.[7] This sum was anything from a couple of shillings to a pound and as many as seven or eight boxes would be paid in an hour.

At the better-funded sort of hells, French hazard was the game. Players pitted themselves against the bank; it was here that the fiendish complexity of the game really worked in the favour of the hell keeper. To the system of main and chance were added various combinations of rolls called 'crabs' (whence the modern game craps derives its name), and if the caster rolled crabs he then passed the box to the next player. As well as the player rolling the dice, other players would gamble on the outcome of ensuing rolls, backing the caster in or out. 'After a chance is thrown to a main, the game assumes a different attitude; odds can then be betted or taken, or even bets laid, for the main or chance to come off first, in the ratio to the number of ways the main or the chance can be thrown,' explained one gambler. Even the way in which the numbers came up could be bet upon: 'When there are *doublets* upon the main or chance, the *event* can be backed to come off with doublets.' As well as the table of odds, the bank had another feature in its favour. 'When aces are thrown to a main, the bank draws all the stakes that back the caster in, and pays double the amount to stakes that back the caster out. But when *deuce ace* are thrown, the bank draws all from the ins, and pays nothing to the outs.' Crucially, while there is only one way to throw aces (each die has to show one pip), there are two ways of rolling deuce ace (die 'A' shows a one, die 'B' a two, and vice versa), arriving at a total of three rolls, and so while the bank might seem to be generous in paying out double and taking in only what stakes are wagered for double one (a single roll), it continues to take money for the other two rolls but pays nothing out. Even before such house advantages as loaded dice, crooked sharpers and drugged wine were introduced into the equation, the bank enjoyed a huge advantage over the players. 'This point in favour of the bank is immense: the riches of the Indies, in a given time, would waste away upon it.'[8]

One of the more charming aspects of the early nineteenth century is the language in which it clothed its vices. Much as half-blind boxers slipping around on a patch of bloody grass were 'heroes of the fist' and jockeys were 'knights of pigskin'; those who like Greville were addicted to the thrilling rattle of the dice in the game of hazard were no mere gamblers, instead they were 'flirting with the elephant's tooth'.[9] A romantic phrase – but there was nothing at all romantic about William Crockford, who would soon earn the sobriquet Father of Hell and Hazard.

*

Born in 1775, Crockford grew up in a fish shop next to Temple Bar. It was not a salubrious beginning. Temple Bar was the gateway that divided the City from the West End, Fleet Street from the Strand, and was known historically for its display of heads on spikes, though the practice of beheading criminals ceased a generation before Crockford was born. Even so, his childhood neighbourhood had little to recommend it: the gutters of nearby Butcher's Row, a slum of Tudor origin, flowed with a mixture of mud, human waste, dung and the blood of freshly slaughtered cattle. The air was thick with the reek of tallow-melting. The Fleet Ditch, London's premier open sewer, also graced the area. Public entertainment came from nearby Newgate in the form of hangings – some five thousand spectators could be accommodated with ease.

And yet within easy walking distance was the West End: the houses of St James's Square, the Palace of St James's, the fashionable coffee houses, the clubs and the aristocratic mansions of Mayfair. In between these two poles were the brothels and low gambling clubs, the so-called copper and silver hells, of the area around Covent Garden. It was on these, the nursery slopes of vice, that Crockford became acquainted with the game that would make his fortune.

Little is known of how he started as a professional gambler. However, gambling soon became a dominant factor in his life and, having hurried to complete his piscine transactions he would rush from his fish shop to the West End without changing his clothes. On one occasion he arrived at a small 'low' gaming-house just off Pall Mall 'with his clothes so covered with fish scales' that the owner told him 'to go away, change his dress and put on something cleaner'.

According to one version of events Crockford's first major coup was to win £1,700 during an all-night session of cribbage at The Grapes tavern in King Street, St James's. His opponent was a butcher, though not John Gully. Another story is that he made his first appreciable sum of money 'taking immense odds upon an "out" horse, which he did upon private information given to him by a jockey, that it was to win'.[10] And using his winnings he bought into a gaming-house at no. 5 King Street, off St James's Street, where in partnership with others he 'put down a bank of £2000'.[11] Crockford's first foray into the gaming world was a rough sort of affair. One of the non-gaming neighbours of 5 King Street complained of being woken late at night by 'scuffling and loud cries of robbery, murder, etc, etc,' and found that the 'quiet of the night is destroyed, particularly in summer time, by the rattling of dice and jingling of money intermingled with the most horrible imprecations, which are plainly heard by all passers by'. The local night-watchmen were among those who saw and heard the nocturnal disturbances on King Street, but they did little about it as they were in the pay of the hellites and were 'well rewarded'[12] for their connivance and occasional assistance in, amongst other tasks, taking angry losers into custody in the watch house.

Running a gambling hell was a dangerous business. As well as the tendency for drunken losers to cut up rough, the activity was illegal and the losers would sometimes threaten to take the proprietors to court – not, usually, with any intention of seeing the proposed action through but more as an act of blackmail in the expectation that the hell owners would arrange a compromise settlement.

As well as a natural facility for figures, Crockford's success can be ascribed to his willingness to think big; he had ambitions beyond running a small operation that bribed local watchmen to take care of troublemakers. During the first two decades of the century Crockford moved to progressively more impressive addresses, although still in partnership with others. At one time he was to be found running a bank at a house on Piccadilly, at another he was part-owner of Watier's, the once select dining club founded by the Prince Regent's eponymous chef. At its peak Watier's was dominated by Beau Brummell and Lord Byron. However, it closed in 1819, and by the time Crockford and a partner called Taylor took over the lease, reopening it for two or three years, Brummell was living in poverty in France while Byron was chasing women and revolutionary causes around Europe. Nevertheless, Watier's was important in understanding Crockford's development: it schooled him in the ways of the social elite, and inspired him to create a luxury hell in which Corinthians could throw away thousands as they flirted with the elephant's tooth.

However, personal social advancement was not on his agenda – far from it. Even though he became ever richer, he never sought to put himself on the level of his increasingly aristocratic patrons. During his thirties and forties he steadily amassed an impressive fortune, supplementing his core business of West End gaming-houses with forays on to the Turf, even for a time operating a gaming hell in Newmarket, where he also kept a farm and a stud. He played on the greed and gullibility of young betters, offering thousands to their tens in the remote chance of a given horse winning the Derby, the Oaks or the St Leger. On settling day he was easy to spot, as Sylvanus explains: he 'generally had some thousands of Bank of England notes pinned to the table before him by the dainty, flexible fingers' rather like the drawers in a modern cash register 'the heavy figures secured by the thumb; the fifties twenties, and tens, under his three longer "prongs" and a sheaf of "fivers" under the guardianship of his little finger'.[13]

The 1820s saw him becoming ever more famous – or rather, infamous – attracting the notice of some of the sterner moralists, who were an increasingly vocal minority. Writing to the editor of *The Times* and signing himself 'Expositor', one correspondent was apoplectic:

Sir, – 'Fishmongers' Hall' or the Crockadile Mart for gudgeons, flatfish, and pigeons* (which additional title that 'Hell' has acquired from the nature of its 'dealings') has recently closed for the season. The opening and closing of this wholesale place of plunder and

---

* 'Flats' and 'pigeons' were neophyte gamblers lured into the hells where they were 'plucked' or 'fleeced'.

robbery, are events which have assumed a degree of importance, not on account of the two or three unprincipled knaves to whom it belongs, and who are collecting by it vast fortunes incalculably fast, but for the rank, character and fortunes of the many who are weak enough to be inveigled and fleeced there. The profits for the last season, over and above expenses, which cannot be less than £100 a-day, are stated to be full £150,000 [£18,000,000].

Expositor's particular concern that those frequenting Crockford's establishment were gentlemen of rank and character was expanded upon:

> These 'Hellites' commenced their career by pandering to the fatal and uncontrollable appetites for gaming of far humbler game than they are now hunting down, whose losses and ruin have enabled them to bedeck this place with every intoxicating fascination and incitement, and to throw out a bait of a large sum of money well hooked, to catch the largest fortunes, which are as sure to be netted as the smaller ones were.

He had a particular warning for the younger, more vulnerable aristocrat:

> Those noblemen and gentlemen, just springing into life and large property, should be ever watchful of themselves, as there are two or three persons of some rank, who themselves have been ruined by similar means, and now condescend to become 'Procurers' to this foul establishment, kept by a 'ci-devant' fishmonger's man, and an ex-waiter to a Faro 'Hell', and who are rewarded for their services in the ratio of the losses sustained by the victims whom they allure to it.

These men, known as 'bonnets', sang their siren song 'dressed out and bedizened with gold ornaments (most probably formerly belonging to unhappy and ruined players)', giving the impression of 'so many jackdaws in borrowed plumes'.[14] Certainly, the sums Crockford took off individual aristocrats were astonishing. When Lord Chesterfield came of age one of the first things he did was to

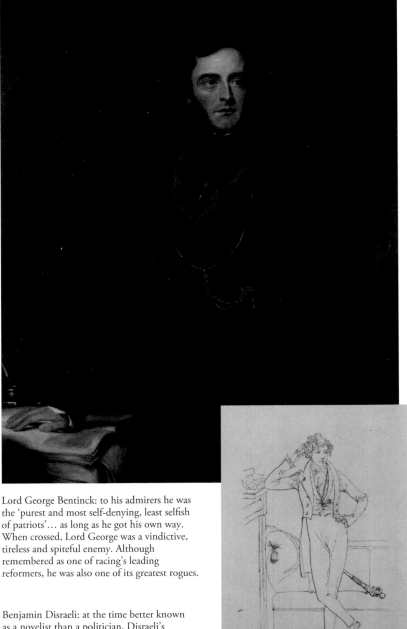

Lord George Bentinck: to his admirers he was the 'purest and most self-denying, least selfish of patriots'… as long as he got his own way. When crossed, Lord George was a vindictive, tireless and spiteful enemy. Although remembered as one of racing's leading reformers, he was also one of its greatest rogues.

Benjamin Disraeli: at the time better known as a novelist than a politician, Disraeli's most boring book was a political life of Lord George Bentinck, but he compensates for the tedium of that tome with a brilliant, breathless portrayal of fashionable London on the night before the Derby in the first chapter of his novel *Sybil*.

Frith's *Derby Day*: quite possibly the most famous image of Victoria's Britain at play in all its gaudy and robust splendour – such was the popularity of the painting that a rail had to be placed in front of it when it went on display at the Royal Academy.

The long-suffering Duke of Richmond, who good-naturedly allowed Bentinck to take over his stables and alter his estate in pursuit of his domination. He even helped push legislation through parliament to protect Bentinck's illegal gambling.

Bentinck showed his gratitude to the Duke of Richmond by falling in love with his Duchess.

John Day: one of racing's most colourful rascals pictured here later in the century. There are earlier images, but none captures his roguishness quite like this one.

Admiral Rous and his friend George Payne: the former would take over from Lord George as dictator of the Turf, the latter gambled his way through three fortunes and merrily avoided the creeping morality of mid-nineteenth-century Britain.

Squire Osbaldeston: 'five feet high and in features like a cub fox', this pint-sized Corinthian seemed to have stepped from the pages of Surtees. Osbaldeston was one of the best shots in Britain – something that lent his duel with Bentinck an added piquancy – and when indoors he could play billiards for a 50-hour stretch.

Charles Greville: Bentinck's cousin and sinecurist par excellence. His candid diaries offer a ringside seat on the great political events of the age and are unflinching when it comes to his own gambling addiction. He and Bentinck were racing partners but the two men quarrelled and Bentinck bore a grudge as only he knew how to.

Colonel Peel, the Prime Minister's brother, found himself at the heart of the Derby scandal. As soldiers go, he was an unusually harmless man rising peacefully through the ranks; any martial prowess he might have possessed was eclipsed by his parallel careers as Member of Parliament, successful racehorse owner and cigar smoker.

The doping of racehorses reached epidemic proportions in the early nineteenth century. The horse here seems to be getting off relatively lightly: they were fed anything from a few pounds of lead shot to opium balls. Those found guilty of poisoning horses on occasion risked the death penalty.

A VIEW of the FIGHT BETWEEN
GULLY AND GREGSON

They fought in St John Sebright's Park near Market Street Herts on May 10 1808 when Gully beat his antagonist there was a great crowd of Spectators

| A | Gully |
| B | Jos Ward his second |

C	Gregson
D	Harry Lee his second
E	The Umpire

John Gully: one of the founders of modern bookmaking and a perfect example of the social mobility that was possible in nineteenth-century England. A failed butcher from Bristol, his fists and his betting book took him from debtors' prison to the Palace of Westminster. He twice fought Bob Gregson, a towering Lancastrian whose physique was so fine that Lord Elgin had him pose naked among the bas reliefs he had brought back from Athens for the amusement of his guests.

Drawn & Engraved by Robt Cruikshank

GREEDY OLD **NICKFORD** EATING OYSTERS

Leaving the poor Devils from minor Hells in a Starving condition

William Crockford: Uriah Heep in manner and Gollum in appearance, the former fishmonger was the casino king of Victorian Britain – yet, as these images attest, contemporary satirists never let him forget his piscine origins. He operated on a progressively grander scale throughout his career, but however lavish his establishments, they were inevitably known as Fishmongers' Hall, a punning reference to the headquarters of the City Livery Company.

In the lower gambling hells, customers on a losing streak would often cut up rough, and burly doormen were used as much to eject troublemakers as to keep out the forces of what passed for law and order.

Crockford's eponymous club at the top of St James's Street was at the centre of fashionable life in London and the place where a great many aristocrats were separated from their fortunes.

pay him the £100,000 (£12,000,000) he owed him. The wonderfully named Sackville Tufton, the 9th Lord Thanet, in the company of Lord Granville, 'Mr Ball Hughes and two other gentlemen', is said to have lost 'the enormous sum of one hundred thousand pounds' during 'a sitting of twenty-four hours'.[15]

What made Crockford's success remarkable was that the 1820s actually saw a crackdown on hells. 'We this day publish the reports of two trials, which, so far as they go, ought to be viewed with no little satisfaction,' crowed the leader page of *The Times* a trifle sanctimoniously on 28 October 1822.

> They are of the nature of vermin-hunting; and the noxious animals have not escaped their pursuers. Some of those miscreants against whom we have lately been employed in rousing the public vigilance and the arm of justice, viz., the keepers of common gaming-tables, have been attacked in a way which it is possible that they will feel more severely than any police prosecutions – they have had actions brought against them in the Court of King's Bench, and have been forced to disgorge, in one or two instances, a portion of their spoil.[16]

One of the premises in question was no. 5 King Street, where Crockford had started his career as a hell keeper. These prosecutions had been made using an obscure law, what *The Times* called 'a salutary statute, 9th Anne'. The paper went on to list a further twenty-one hells in Piccadilly, Jermyn Street, Bury Street, King Street, Bennett Street, St James's Street, Pickering Place, Cleveland Row, Oxendon Street and Leicester Street: 'Here, then, is work for a whole winter. Private vengeance has, we learn, been the moving power in most of the recent prosecutions; if so, the police has still a large arrear to bring up.'

The foundation of the Metropolitan Police was still seven years into the future, but already in the autumn of 1822 the magistrates of Bow Street 'expressed their determination to exercise to their fullest extent the powers which a recent statute [the Vagrant Act] has vested in them, in order if possible, to put a stop to the ruinous system of gambling which has of late been carried on with such impunity in and about St James's'.[17] Just as the science of 'leg-ism' was making itself felt on the Turf, so the scourge of the gaming hells was infesting the West End of London. These were different from the 'silver hells' around the Strand that Crockford had frequented when he was still a fishmonger, 'where persons could risk their shillings and half-crowns'.[18] At the evidence given against the keepers of a hell at no. 75 St James's Street the court heard how 'the house was handsomely kept' and the furniture 'was of the most splendid kind'.[19] Hospitality was in keeping with the surroundings: 'wine, spirits, and refreshments were plentifully served, free of expense' – with predictable results: one gambler was so drunk that he was unable to play hazard and obligingly the hell keeper 'played for him, and betted against him'.[20]

After years of turning a blind eye and a deaf ear to the complaints of irritated residents high-profile action was at last taken, albeit on the information of a disgruntled gambler, when no. 33 Pall Mall was raided at three-thirty one afternoon towards the end of October that year. The raid, which included elements of farce and drama, was more or less typical of a number carried out at that time.

It was usual for gamers to have to pass through two doors to get to the hazard and card tables or the roulette wheels: a front door guarded by a burly porter, then a further door with a shutter that could be opened for another check to be made. Realising this, the Bow Street officers brought a ladder, and while two of them waited down below the rest entered a first-floor room and, *The Times* reported, finding it empty

> rushed on to two doors at the extremity of the apartment. But before they could reach the staircase the Cerberus of the establishment, whose station was on the landing place of the first floor, immediately between the two doors, had heard them coming, and sprang up stairs to give the alarm to those in the second floor where 'the business' was going on. Morris [one of the raiding officers] was close behind him and had nearly caught him by the leg, but he succeeded in reaching

the play-room, into which he entered, and closed the door against the officers. He had previously rung a large bell violently, and all was confusion now in the room. The officers were stopped for a few moments at the door by the united strength of some of those within; and they heard money rattling, scrapers, balls, and other implements of play being removed, chairs falling, and players swearing. At length they burst in the door, and two or three of the party within escaped in the confusion to the stairs; but one of them with a small box in his hand was secured by Smith and Baker and the box was found to contain seven dozen and a half silver counters, £2 12s in silver coin, and £7 10s in gold.

Further searches revealed two men hiding, huddled in a cupboard. Another two managed to get on to the roof and 'ran along the parapets of the adjoining houses', one of them forced his way into a garret window of number 31, and another tried to make his escape through the trapdoor in the roof of a neighbouring house but was dragged out by one of the raiding officers.

It was the second time in six weeks that this particular hell had been raided and the officers noticed that further precautions had been taken in the interim: the rear windows had been 'heavily barred, and at the top of the first floor stairs was a door nearly three inches thick, strongly cased with iron, and fastened inside with three stout bolts and a heavy iron bar'. Correspondingly, the officers decided to make a more thorough job of dismantling the place. Instead of contenting themselves with removing the portable items, they resolved, in the words of one of the raiding officers, 'to tear the thing up root and branch'. Calling in carpenters, they had the heavy fixed gaming tables removed, chopped up and placed on a wagon, which was also stacked with the high chairs used by the croupiers and even the lights that hung over the gaming tables. Then off they trundled exultantly to Bow Street. The sense of Roman triumph about the affair was compounded by the treatment of the prisoners, who were kept for a short while at the Bunch of Grapes in Bow Street and then led out for questioning at 7 p.m. A crowd of spectators 'formed an avenue from one door to the other for the prisoners to pass, and amused themselves with cracking sundry jokes upon them, and reminding them of the pleasures of the *treading mill*'.[21]

While such raids were high profile and attracted the attention of the newspapers and the population, they were not particularly effective in tackling the problem. Although dramatic, the raid on 33 Pall Mall had netted less than £10 in cash and a few nondescript gamblers. The informant, an officer of the King's German Legion on half-pay, admitted that although the Israel Jackson who had been seized in the raid was the proprietor, he doubted that he actually put down the bank himself. Moreover, the resilience of the hellites was evident – the house had been raided only six weeks earlier and yet had managed to reopen with improved fortifications.

Prosecutions became more difficult to obtain, relying as they did on an informer coming forward, whom the hell keepers would either bribe or intimidate. 'As they net thousands a night,' noted Expositor bitterly, 'a few hundreds or even thousands can be well spared to smother a few actions and prosecutions, which are very rarely instituted against them; and never but by ruined men, who are easily quieted by a small consideration.'[22] Nevertheless, from twenty-two hells in London in 1821, the number dropped to fifteen in 1824,[23] though thereafter they began to increase slightly. When the Metropolitan Police was founded the hell keepers simply bribed officers for information about any prosecutions that might be brought and raids that might be planned. One enterprising hellite even went as far as distributing cards which read: 'Note, the house is insured against all legal interruptions, and the players are *guaranteed* to be as free from interruption as they are at their own homes.'[24]

Indeed by the 1830s a system of corruption, intimidation and tightened security in the hells, along with a fear among police officers that they would be entrapped into unlawful entry and then prosecuted – it was rumoured that the hellites had established a fund to be used to fight legal actions – minimised the chance of a hell being closed down. Between 1839 and 1844 a mere seven were raided and, as in the 1820s, they were likely to reopen (the total of seven raids in six years includes one hell raided twice. Furthermore, the penalties were not severe by the standards of the day: a fine or a few months' imprisonment was the worst that convicted hell keepers and their employees could expect.

The raids failed to tackle the very crux of what campaigners like Expositor felt to be the real problem: namely, the thousands lost every week to William Crockford. Crockford was alluded to in the *Times* leader of 28 October 1822: 'The proprietors of one [hell] which was formerly Watier's club House, made at a certain period, as we are told, upwards of £100,000 in one twelvemonth.' And yet he appeared untouchable. By 1824 he was said to have spent almost £40,000 fitting out what was the 'most splendid house interiorly and exteriorly in all the neighbourhood'. However, even this glittering incarnation of 'Fishmongers' Hall,'[25] as Expositor called it, was but a shack when compared to the ultimate hell, the great 'Pandemonium',[26] a term employed in its Miltonian sense as the home of all demons and the capital of Hell.

Proof that Crockford had 'arrived' came in 1827 with the publication of a most extraordinary book called *Crockford's, or Life in the West* by one Henry Luttrell. Although ostensibly a work of fiction that could be described, very loosely, as an epistolary novel, it was in effect a lengthy rant and public warning, in two volumes, as to the perils that awaited young men in the gambling hells of London – in particular, the threat to both public morality and private fortunes posed by Mr Crockford. The narrative leaves something to be desired: for instance, the connection between gambling and the emancipation of Catholics, a subject that takes up most of the first chapter, is never quite made apparent. But the scenes of gambling life it describes are vivid. And the accounts of the various underhand methods of separating well-born young men from their inherited fortunes are as compelling today as they were in 1827.

With a voyeuristic eye for detail, this book opens up a rich and engrossing world. It brings alive the slang and customs of a long-vanished milieu where 'Greeks', seasoned habitués of the gaming world, talked of how best to 'land a flat' or a 'flounder' and debated the best way to catch a 'gull' (an unsuspecting neophyte), while the job of a 'sharper' or a 'bonnet' was to appear to win and look prosperous, 'dressed out in the first style of fashion, with expensive military cloaks, and bedizened with diamond rings, gold watches and snuff boxes, all of which belong to the establishment, and are lent out for the occasion'. Six hundred pages long, it gives insights into dozens of ruses. It describes the way cheats manipulated specially made playing cards, the low ones 'convex at the side, and concave at the top and bottom, the high cards concave at the sides and convex at the top and bottom'.[27] It told how unscrupulous billiard players used balls of varying weights; and how almost every imaginable game of chance, even those with seemingly innocent names such as roly-poly, could be, and invariably were, rigged.

The book was a *succès de scandale*, quickly running to three editions. It enraged the hell proprietors. When, *The Times* reported on 11 June 1829, during the Derby meeting a man who wandered into a gaming room in Epsom was mistaken for the author, cries of '"Turn him out – turn him out," intermingled with the most horrible imprecations, instantly resounded from all parts of the room. Upon this a person connected with the play-table, struck the table violently with a bludgeon, and exclaimed with an appalling oath, "Then murder shall be committed tonight."' Fearing for his life, the man ran into the road, followed by a gang of fifteen to twenty enraged ruffians including the man with the bludgeon, who caught him a glancing blow on his shoulder – whereupon he was rushed by the mob, who made 'for his costly watch and seals, and also for a valuable cloak which hung over his arm'.[28]

The notoriety that the book attracted was certainly compounded by events at the upper end of St James's Street, where Crockford owned some properties. These he had demolished in order to build the *ne plus ultra* of gambling hells. He engaged the fashionable architect Benjamin Wyatt, and financed in part by the money he took off Gully after the 1827 St Leger, his monumental dream began to take shape. It is a tidy irony that, before working for Crockford, Wyatt had held the post of Surveyor of Westminster Abbey. Having worked for the purveyors of Heaven, he was now, quite literally, building a hell.

Wyatt was responsible for numerous fashionable projects around Georgian London, including the Drury Lane Theatre, the Duke of York's Column and Londonderry House. From the outset it was clear that this new building was going to be at least as substantial as anything else he had designed.

> During the progress of this superb building, St James's Street presented a most confused and extraordinary appearance. Nearly the whole upper end ... from Bennett Street to Piccadilly was in a state of excavation for the arrangement of pipes, forming and perfecting drains etc., but principally for the object of making a most capacious ice-house. Great was the alarm that such extensive underground operations would endanger the foundations of the adjoining and neighbouring houses, and this alarm, as things turned out, was not without cause; for, while the work of excavation was proceeding, one entire side of the Guards' Clubhouse (situate [sic] at the northern adjoining end of Mr Crockford's premises) fell in with a fearful crash, leaving the complete interior of the house, with the beds and furniture of the different apartments, in rather a ludicrous state of exposure and in a most perilous position.[29]

Work went on round the clock: 'The nocturnal operations of the numerous workmen by torchlight gave to the scene an extraordinary appearance, causing it to resemble more the locality of a manufacturing district than the main fashionable lounge of London, and the chief thoroughfare to the palace of the sovereign,' *Bentley's Miscellany* reported. What was even more remarkable was that there was no secret as to the purpose of the building: 'The magnitude of the project, and the known and somewhat unpopular purpose for which it was intended, caused great and general excitement, and gave rise to daily moral comment and sarcastic witticism in most of the journals and periodicals of the day.'[30] And while his dream hell was being built, Crockford continued business at premises further down St James's Street, at a site which he subsequently failed to make profitable as an early department store called the St James's Bazaar.

At the beginning of the century he had been skulking around the backstreets of St James's running small banks of a few hundred pounds. Now, far from disguising his operation, Crockford seemed to be flaunting the illegal basis of his fortune. While in manners and dress he was always careful to appear the inferior of those whom he fleeced, the very flagrancy and boldness with which he carried on his business spoke eloquently and loudly of his mastery over them. The years 1827, 1828 and 1829 were said to be the most successful enjoyed by Crockford. The splendour of the new establishment right opposite White's which opened at the beginning of 1828 was remarked on by everyone: 'The population of London thronged to its exterior survey under much greater excitement than was apparent on the late opening of the splendid and stupendous national structure, the Royal Exchange.'[31]

If the exterior was impressive, the interior was spectacular: Doric and Ionic columns, splendid sperm-oil powered chandeliers, a domed ceiling 'perforated with luminous panels of stained glass', a 'State drawing-room' got up in the 'most florid' Louis XIV style with decorative panels executed in the style of Watteau. 'Royalty can scarcely be conceived to vie with the style and consummate splendour of this magnificent chamber'[32] and, 'No one, I believe, not even those accustomed to visit the mansions of the aristocracy, ever entered the saloon for the first time, without being dazzled with the splendour which surrounded him'[33] typify the encomiums lavished on the place.

The new Crockford's prefigured many of the polyglot decorative tendencies of the later years of the century, but there was also still evidence of its roots in an earlier age: the large subterranean ice-house that had contributed to the collapse of the Guards' Club was in fact 'a small circular cockpit' with, it was rumoured, 'a bolt-hole' leading to 'an adjacent and convenient spot in the direction of Piccadilly'.[34] Also underground were the extensive cellars. They ran for 285 feet beneath St James's Street and were said to hold 300,000 bottles of wine as well as 'innumerable hogsheads'.[35] They were superintended by one of Crockford's sons – during his rise to the pinnacle of metropolitan gaming Crockford had married a woman described as the governess to a lady of quality, and had fathered fourteen children (one source claims that he kicked out his first wife and married his children's nursemaid).

As well as being an opulent farrago of decorative schemes, Crockford's was a gourmet's Elysium. To match the encyclopaedic wine list there was a kitchen ruled by Eustache Ude, the culinary master of the era. Ude's appointment on the impressive salary of £1,200 per annum and with a deputy on £500 had been amongst the marvels discussed in the press in the excitement that preceded the club's opening. Ude's father had worked in Louis XVI's kitchen, and Ude himself had cooked for Madame Letitia Bonaparte before coming to England in the service of the sybaritic Earl of Sefton for the handsome sum of 300 guineas a year. But it was at Crockford's that Eustache Ude achieved his immense fame. Dinner was served from 4.30 p.m. until six, and his famous menus were as rich as the décor. Most celebrated was his dish of mackerel roes, created while he was working for Lord Sefton, which involved the roes being covered in clarified butter and baked, then dusted with salt, smothered in velouté, thick cream and then a little more butter for good measure. Another favourite was the *Boudin de cerises à la Bentinck*, a cherry pudding that Ude had created for the normally ascetic Lord George.

Ude was a theatrical individual who seems to have conformed to the stereotypical British view of the temperamental French chef. He was not above chiding his clients if he felt they failed to appreciate his art. The most famous disagreement concerned a dish of red mullet priced at two shillings and served with a sauce for which Ude charged sixpence. One day a member refused to pay the sixpence, at which insult the chef bellowed, 'The imbecile must think that red mullets come out of the sea with my sauce in their pockets.'[36]

The members were as choice as the food, the wines and the décor. '[They] ... included all the celebrities of England, from the Duke of Wellington to the youngest Ensign of the Guards,' rhapsodises Captain Gronow in his diary, 'and at the gay and festive board, which was constantly replenished from midnight to early dawn, the most brilliant sallies of wit, the most agreeable conversation, the most interesting anecdotes, interspersed with grave political discussions and acute logical reasoning on every conceivable subject, proceeded from the soldiers, scholars, statesmen, poets and men of pleasure.'[37]

The place was the apogee of fashion, and attracted anyone with pretensions to social standing. As well as the revered Wellington there were Waterloo amputees the Marquess of Anglesey and Lord Raglan. The dandies, led by Count d'Orsay, included the likes of Grantley Berkeley, who would wear two or three brightly coloured satin waistcoats and three or four equally vivid silk neckcloths at once, and 'Golden' (on account of his riches) Ball Hughes, who was said to be the only man capable of carrying off a white waistcoat in the morning. The Turf was, of course, well represented. Fashionable novelists Edward Bulwer Lytton and Disraeli were often seen there. Many members were MPs: notable among them was Thomas Slingsby Duncombe, the radical member for Finsbury.

The younger habitués, numerous high-born, high-spirited hooligans, would sally forth from Crockford's late at night and embark on an orgy of drunken pranks: beating up nightwatchmen and stealing door knockers and shop signs were chief among the wholesome pastimes enjoyed by the young gentlemen and noblemen of the day.

And right at the heart of it all were the members who interested Crockford most: the plutocrats such as Lord Sefton, said to be the biggest of the many big losers who walked up the steps and into the magnificent vestibule of 50 St James's during the years 1828–44.

The splendour, the columns, the glittering chandeliers, the quarter of a million and more bottles of wine, the artery-clogging mackerel roes, the witty, well-dressed members all had a purpose, a twofold purpose: they would camouflage the true aim of the club and simultaneously serve as a lure.

Crockford's was, then, just as its creator had intended, a fashionable club, which meant that *le tout Londres* (or at least that male part of the city that was rich, well born or stylish) wanted to join. With a committee of gentlemen and noblemen deciding who should be elected and who not, Crockford could claim that this was essentially a private club like, say, White's and Boodles across the road, or Brooks's a few doors down, which had nothing in common with the low gambling hells where he had started out. Also, the desirability of Crockford's membership ensured that there was a ready stream of prominent and successful men curious to be admitted to the club to sample its food and see its splendid rooms. The expensively decorated Saloon, or State Drawing-Room, was in reality a hook baited by the French chef. But it did not catch everyone. 'Those of the members who have set their faces against gambling, very seldom partake of these suppers,' wrote one visitor to Crockford's in the 1830s. 'They have a coffee-room down stairs, where they can order any refreshment they please, which is furnished to them at reasonable prices, as in other clubs.' And in a way these members were useful too, adding a veneer of respectability. However, the proprietor made sure that enough people did eat and drink well in that glittering Saloon, for 'nightly observation has taught Mr Crockford that the transition from the supper in the saloon to the hazard room, is as natural as is the transition from the latter to ruin'.[38]

In contrast to the splendour elsewhere, the engine room of this great pirate's ship of a building was a comparatively small and handsomely, rather than lavishly, furnished room whose main feature was the hazard table, 'of oval shape, well stuffed and covered with fine frieze cloth marked with yellow lines denoting the different departments of speculation. Round these compartments are double lines, similarly marked for the odds or proportions between what is technically known as the *main* and *chance*. In the centre on each side are indented positions for the croupiers or persons engaged at the table in calling the main and the chance, regulating the stakes and paying and receiving money.'[39] Everything was just so: the lights suspended above the table, three pairs of new ivory dice at a guinea a pair[40] every evening, and the odds carefully embroidered into the baize around which the players sat. All this added to the aura of expectation and excitement as eleven o'clock struck and play began.

In a corner of the room was another important item of furniture, a small writing desk at which Crockford sat all the time play was in progress and from which he dispensed loans and advanced players further funds to lose at the famous oval table. In addition, as he 'never handles a card or throws a die personally', there was a 'groom-porter' (croupier) called Page who sat on 'an elevated chair at the centre of the table, facing Mr Crockford'. His job was to supervise play using what one visitor described as a 'miniature representation of a hay-rake' to pull in money won or push money towards anyone else who won. Although play began at 11 p.m. and the club shut three hours later, anyone remaining inside the club at that point did not have to leave. It was usual for people to play until four or five in the morning, one group so 'spellbound by the game at which they had been playing, that they never rose off their seats from the time they sat down at eleven or twelve at night, until eight in the morning'. In order to keep distraction to a minimum there was a small supper room adjoining the hazard room 'for none but those who play at hazard'.

The mystery of such a flagrant flouting of the laws was in part explained by this observation of James Grant's:

On the ground-floor, detached from the reading-room, there is another apartment, smaller than that upstairs, for playing hazard. This lower room is used during the parliamentary recess, the number of gamblers in town being then much less; or should it be wanted during the time the houses are sitting, owing to an unusual muster of the gamblers, it is then thrown open. The one upstairs is always shut during the legislative recess.[41]

It was simply not worth Crockford's while to run his operation at full tilt when the Houses of Parliament were not in session, and it was the presence in his club, night after night, of the social and political leaders of the country that put it above the law. Whereas other, lower, hells had to buy off their accusers, Crockford no longer needed to. 'As for Crockford's, you might as well talk of shutting up Westminster Abbey, as of closing down that club.' His members were not just above the law. As Members of Parliament they made the law; and, after a hard day running the country, they would stroll or drive over to St James's Street and cheerfully flout it until dawn seeped through the shuttered windows.

'I think it may be said of Crockford and his club-house – we must, I suppose, sink the "hell," as the great Pandemonium of the play-world appears in the Court Guide among the clubs – that they are above all Greek, above all Roman, fame and also above English law – a fact by no means difficult to account for, when we consider that one-half the legislators of the country are "members of Crockford's".' Writing in *Fraser's Magazine*, the sports journalist Nimrod goes on to explain it with an orotund classical flourish:

Why did not Cicero pursue the affair of Catiline's conspiracy to its fullest extent in the city of Rome? The reason is evident. Finding out, by a list given him of the names of some of his accomplices, that several of the greatest and most powerful families in Rome were engaged in the plot, he judged it imprudent to push the matter further at home, and contented himself with pursuing Catiline with his vengeance in a distant land. Thus will Crockford and his hazard table remain unmolested in London.[42]

7

Legal Matters

'Qui tam pro domino rege sequitur quam pro se ipso in hoc parte sequitur'*

After Lord George Bentinck's death in 1848, Disraeli wrote the political biography of his friend. It is surely Disraeli's dullest book, dealing as it does in the minutiae of the protectionist movement and its doomed struggle against the repeal of the Corn Laws. Lord George 'had sat for eighteen years in parliament' doing little and saying less. He conformed perfectly to the stereotype of the pre-Reform MP: refusing governmental appointments so that he could concentrate on his racing and hunting, turning up late at night in the House of Commons, having got up at six, taken the train out of London, enjoyed a day's hunting and then returned 'clad in a white greatcoat which softened, but did not conceal, the scarlet hunting coat'.

But to say of himself, as he did in that self-consciously antiquated English of which he was fond, that he 'sat in eight parliaments without having taken part in any great debate' is slightly disingenuous. While the rest of the Reformed parliament might have written him off as an anachronistic dilettante, there was one group of MPs who were in no doubt as to the range of his influence and the ferocious power and energy with which he could pursue a cause. 'Although he took no part in debate,' writes Disraeli, 'and attended

* 'He who sues on behalf of the king sues as well as for himself.'

the house rather as a club than a senate, he possessed a great and peculiar influence in it. He was viewed with interest and often extraordinary regard by every sporting man in the house. With almost all of these he was acquainted; some of them, on either side, were his intimate companions and confederates.'[1] Just how much power he wielded and how far he was to go in protecting his own interests became apparent at the beginning of the eventful year of 1844.

Bentinck's mutation from cheating racehorse owner to purifying Paladin was characterised by a personal campaign to rid the Turf of levanters and defaulters, those who had no intention of paying their debts if they lost their bets. He was inclined to be merciless in hunting down and excluding defaulters from the racecourses, and his enthusiasm can only have been stoked by the fact that the winner had no right in law to reclaim the debt. The betting market was also further muddied by a class of gambler, often younger men, who, while they did not set out to swindle, got in too deep and bet beyond their means. Richard Tattersall was among those who felt that a legal obligation might help discourage 'deep' play:

> I am convinced, from what I see of betting, as to young men, it would be the saving of thousands, because young gentlemen who bet, and cannot afford to pay, compromise with those betting men, to pay hereafter, and go on upon the chance of winning again. If you could get the money out of them by process of law it would prevent half the betting that now takes place, which would be a great thing and save thousands from ruin.[2]

Racing was simply too widely followed, by too many men of questionable means and even more dubious motives, for the continuance of the honour-based system that had largely succeeded until now. While Young England could dream of a society locked into time-honoured patterns of mutual respect, the reality of the early Victorian Turf had very little in common either with that or with the oppressive, dark-mahogany-coloured morality that would in time become associated with the still young Queen Victoria.

As has been seen, the links between the world of the illegal gambling hells and the racing world were closer than many wished them to be. As both a bookmaker and a hellite Crockford was the most notorious example. But there were plenty of less exalted individuals who migrated from the sordid hells to the more glamorous and aspirational racecourses, bringing with them their low ethics, backstreet morals and fraudulent schemes. Typical was a bookmaker called James Wood, described as 'a defaulter on the turf, a swindler, and utterly unfit to associate with any honest man'.[3] Scion of a criminal dynasty – his father was a known hell keeper on Bury Street, St James's – and a defaulter, Wood was one of the predators who swarmed over the Turf in the 1840s. In advance of the Derby of 1841, the race that had given rise to the Gurney affair, Wood came up with a con trick which he practised on a man called Hawker, opening a fictitious book on his behalf and taking long odds against a horse called Coronation, mentioning well-known figures on the Turf as the other parties to the wagers. Unfortunately for Wood, 1841 was Coronation's year and he found himself out to Hawker by some £2,640. Wood was declared a defaulter, although given that Hawker had a similar reputation it is not clear whether, had the result been different, Hawker would have paid anyway. It appears that in the end the two men reached an accommodation, Hawker being let off a debt of £1,200 incurred while playing roulette at Wood senior's hell.

However, Bentinck was not interested in any complicated compromise that might have been reached between Wood's father and Hawker. The bully in him identified here someone he could make an example of. As he saw it, 'this was a case a thousand times worse than that of any ordinary defaulter',[4] and he set out to crucify Wood. As a bookmaker, Wood depended for a living on attending races, and yet suddenly, at grandstands everywhere from Liverpool to Goodwood, he found that he was no longer welcome. Moreover, his rejection was handled with minimum discretion: wherever possible he was manhandled from the place even if he pleaded to be allowed to leave quietly. Such thoroughness and vindictive cruelty were, of course, the trademarks of Lord George Bentinck who, either personally or through his friends, hounded Wood off every major course in the kingdom. At one Doncaster meeting Lord George was seen in conversation with a policeman, who then went and turned Wood out. At Goodwood the Duke of Richmond's solicitor evicted him, and he was seen trudging dejectedly away from the course.

It was the Liverpool races of 1843, though, that were the most humiliating for Wood: here, in his capacity as a steward, Bentinck convened a kangaroo court. Wood was called out from the enclosure for which he had purchased a ticket, and brought before Bentinck and his fellow stewards 'in front of the stand and in the open air'. In full view of the public Bentinck acquainted his colleagues with his opinion of Wood. 'The result was, we unanimously ordered him to be turned off the stand, and to have his ticket taken from him. He begged to be allowed to go out quietly, but we insisted on his being taken out in charge of a policeman, and his ticket taken from him. I said as senior steward, that we were determined to mark our sense of his offence,' Bentinck would later recall with self-righteous satisfaction, adding smugly, 'I am not aware that he made any attempt to return.'[5]

It is easy to see the division in class terms. Moreover, it was a clash of value systems. In his way Wood had squared the matter with Hawker: he had attempted to cheat him, had been discovered, and then set his losses against Hawker's losses at an illegal gambling den owned by his father. Even a Turf grandee of the calibre of the religion-fearing George Payne, whose name Wood had fraudulently used, was inclined to look the other way. When Wood apologised to him he simply said, 'You have paid me all you owe, and you had better say nothing to me about that affair. The more you speak of it the more villainous and rascally it appears to me.' But it was not enough to deter him from betting with Wood. Wood felt sufficiently aggrieved to take legal proceedings against the policeman who had evicted him from the stand at Doncaster, striking him with a stick and offering him 'other indignities', but not a refund. The jury was told that the policeman, Leadbitter, 'was no doubt the instrument of other more influential parties'.[6]

Bentinck's merciless pursuit of Wood was perceived as a threat to the hellites. It was a signal of the escalating tension between the aristocratic cabal of racehorse owners and the plebeian crowd of legs and hellites, the latter perceived by the former as parasites. If Bentinck were to be allowed to succeed in his campaign to break Wood, where else would his crusade take him? Who would be his next target? So, while waiting for Wood's case to come to court the hellites hit back at the nobility. They hit hard, and they hit them where it hurt: in the purse.

Their instrument of choice was an unusual one – the law. They employed a little-used statute to bring what were called *qui tam* actions. 'Those who bring Qui Tam actions have a double chance. If they win, all right; if they lose, bring their action and recover double; thus winning by losing,' explained Richard Tattersall bluntly. 'If such a system is suffered no man is safe. There are many men now living in their country houses who owe thousands, which if they were honest men they could pay; but no law can make them and they laugh at you.'[7] '*Qui tam*' were the first two words of a statute dating from the time of Queen Anne, which had been brought in to curb excessive gambling. It provided for the recovery of any bet in excess of £10, plus treble that amount as a fine. Its significance was that it enabled the suit to be brought by a 'common informer'.

Lord George had been making life increasingly difficult for swindling betters. But the hail of *qui tam* actions, eventually numbering thirty-four in all, that would rain down on the high-rolling patrons of the British racing scene in the winter of 1843–4 showed that the former were not afraid to retaliate, using a highly effective piece of antiquated legislation that had languished on the statute books for generations. Lord George Bentinck was particularly affected, some six writs being issued against him. Among other prominent racehorse owners involved were Colonel Jonathan Peel, brother of the Prime Minister Sir Robert, Charles Greville and Lord Eglinton.

At first Lord George was inclined to ignore the resurgence of the statute as a nuisance. However, the action brought against him by a petty criminal called Charles Henry Russell, who had strong connections with the underworld of illegal gambling houses and had been implicated in the theft of almost £3,000 from one such club belonging to a relative, showed no sign of going away. Given that Lord George was one of the deepest 'plungers' on the Turf he stood to lose 'upwards of £100,000' (£12,000,000),[8] and he was not alone: 'No fewer than twenty-one actions involving penalties to the extent of half a million had been brought,'[9] recorded *Hansard* on 5 February 1844.

Most accounts of this intriguing battle take the line that the statute was a rusty piece of legislation twisted in a manner that was never intended, involving a group of upper-class sportsmen, the prime minister's brother included, acting in ignorance of the law and falling prey to unscrupulous attack. However, this was far from being the case, for this same legislation was from time to time used against hell keepers. Its most recent and high-profile success had been in 1842 against an infamous hellite called Bond who had once been talked of as the only serious rival to Crockford. It is interesting to speculate whether, given his influential patrons, Crockford might have had a hand in the case being brought against him. But whoever was behind it, the result was conclusive – Bond had been put out of business and fled the country. As Bentinck noted ruefully in a letter to the noted turfite John Bowes, 'The success of the action against Bond is what has set all the fellows ago to attack us.'[10]

Certainly no callow neophyte when it came to the ways of the gambling world, Bentinck was sure that behind Charles Russell, the ostensible plaintiff, were one or more of the many men who had at some point been upset by his own irascible behaviour on the Turf – in particular, those targeted during his recent, some would argue hypocritical, campaign to reform the racing world by vigorously pursuing, punishing and excluding those who did not pay their gaming debts. About Charles Russell, Bentinck was remarkably well informed – thanks, most likely, to the unappealing Harry Hill, Gully's former henchman, who acted as Bentinck's commissioner and spy in the low taverns where the legs and down-market hell keepers gossiped over their brandy-and-water and cigars. Bentinck discovered that 'Russell the informer I believe keeps a Hell called the "The Strangers" and is himself a Turf Defaulter having cut and run at Wolverhampton'.[11]

The action had in fact been prepared by the plaintiff's brother, a shadowy solicitor operating on the fringes of the law called James Russell, whose father and uncle had been hell keepers. James Russell himself was working for an even more nebulous figure.

He had been leaving his office at around noon one day when he was stopped by a stranger and 'asked if Mr Russell was at home'. Having established Russell's identity, the stranger then asked if he had a few minutes to discuss a point of law. Mentioning the *qui tam* action that had put Bond out of business, the man wanted to know 'whether a Qui Tam could be brought against a Person for winning money by betting upon a Horse Race'. Russell answered that he 'really was not certain about it', but that he was dimly aware of a 'penalty for winning at a Horse Race'. However, he would need to do some research into it and research would cost money. As a frequenter of gaming-houses and a Turf better himself Russell was always in need of money. '[The stranger] then asked me if I had any objection to bring the Actions against several parties who were in the habit of betting large sums of money. At that time I did not know who the person was.' When questioned about it later, though, Russell admitted that he thought he had seen him at Hampton races, but that he was not inclined to be too selective about his clients, especially those such as the one before him who was happy to pay 'the fee for preparing the case'.

For a moment, when he looked down the list and saw the names of many people he knew, Russell was assaulted by a few scruples. As well as noblemen and Members of Parliament, the list included a well-known gaming-house keeper plus a couple of the shifty characters known as commission agents who placed bets on behalf of those who preferred to remain anonymous. 'I said I knew several Parties who have been betting large sums of money; and in case I was on terms of intimacy with them I should be sorry to do so great an injury to them.'

'If you do not choose to do so I shall take it to some one else,' came the uncompromising response from the stranger, who added a further veil of mystery to the proceedings, saying, 'It is not me that is going to bring these actions; it is a friend of mine who is anxious to put an end to the System.'

Keen to be paid, yet anxious not to get his hands too dirty in what was clearly a vindictive action motivated by a desire to 'punish' some very prominent people, he had hit upon the scheme of using his own brother as the plaintiff. Since he had 'picked up some very bad acquaintances' through hanging around London's illicit gambling scene, 'I knew his character was already so tainted that merely bringing these actions could not in any way injure him.' Charming, yet true. Charles Russell had been implicated in the theft of cash and securities worth £2,900 (£348,000) from the Berkeley Club, a hell part-owned by his uncle. James knew his brother's reputation for toughness was justified; he was someone who could not be compromised or tampered with, especially as he was to gain half of the penalty should any of these actions prove successful.

Their business almost concluded, the mysterious stranger added: 'You having determined to bring these actions, and having arranged it, for your management I should tell you the party for whom you are to bring these actions wishes never to be known in these transactions.' Russell was on his own – although later he did let slip the tantalising detail that the Mr Big behind this elaborate sting was 'a person I have seen repeatedly about Town. A gentlemanly-looking man and one whom I have seen at Tattersall's.' As well as being seen at London's premier equine auctioneers, Russell added, he bore a resemblance to a certain member of the House of Lords.[12]

There was undoubtedly a class element to this struggle. Some of the most powerful men in the country, including the brother of the Prime Minister, were facing potentially ruinous and at best humiliating legal action from a wily and resourceful section of the capital's criminal underworld. Their assailants had clearly gone to considerable lengths to ensure success, assembling a crack legal team in which the Russells were mere 'men of straw'.[13] 'I grieve to say that the "Infernal Alliance" have been beforehand with you and have already retained the Solicitor General,'[14] wrote Bentinck to John Bowes.

Bowes, the son of Lord Strathmore, who would have inherited his father's title had his parents taken the precaution of being married at the time of his birth, was one of the leading patrons of the early Victorian Turf. He had received a *qui tam* writ relating to the Derby of 1843 for which Bentinck's horse Gaper had been fancied, and he was in touch with Lord George to see what could be done. Lord George wrote back to him on 8 November that year, and what he had to say was hardly encouraging. 'At first I and my solicitors were alike disposed to hold these threats very cheap and to look upon them as idle attempts to extort money – but I am sorry to say that upon examining the matter more closely they have entirely changed their note and think it a very serious matter. There is no doubt the vagabonds have the law on their side and our only chance of defeating them is by their failing in their proofs or by our throwing them over upon some technicality.' Bentinck was in no doubt that an 'unholy gang of Hellkeepers' were the 'the fellows really moving in this matter'.[15]

A letter written a few days later to Sir William Gregory – heavy speculator on the Turf, classical scholar, liberal-minded Conservative MP and sporter of a pair of truly magnificent sideburns – found Bentinck similarly grave, but not hopeless. 'Though I have no apprehension that these rascally informers will succeed in their suits, I cannot consider them otherwise than as serious,' he wrote. He had 'no doubt but that betting on horse-races comes within the meaning of the Act. It is vain, therefore, to disguise from ourselves that these vagabonds have *prima facie* the law on their side. On ours we have the difficulty of proof, and the indisposition of juries to give them a verdict. Even if the verdict went against us, such a decision would, I feel sure, be reversed on appeal to the House of Lords.'

Bentinck had good reason for writing in a more optimistic tone than he might have felt as he knew himself somewhat alone in the matter. Bowes was in Paris and had not the slightest intention of returning and being served with an action, while Gregory was in Dublin. Bentinck tried to entice him over: 'For all practical purposes you are as safe in coming over from Ireland now as you would be if you postponed their serving you with a writ until Parliament meets.' Should this reassurance not get Gregory to come to England, he was not above trying to frighten him into action. 'From the heavy commission you executed for Bowes you stand in greater hazard than anybody.'[16] One day before the Derby of 1843, Bowes, who would win a remarkable total of four Derbys, had come to Gregory's house at 'an unconscionably early hour of the morning'.[17] He had Sir William roused from sleep to tell him that he had just run a trial with his horse Cotherstone and his trainer John Scott believed he would win the Derby. Bowes apologised for waking Gregory but explained that he wanted him to place £1,000 to win on the horse before news of the trial leaked out. Cotherstone duly won the Derby and Gregory collected £21,000 (£2,520,000) for Bowes. At the time this had been wonderful news, but now ...

Gregory was taking no risks and certainly did not feel safe on the other side of the Irish Sea. He announced in a letter written from Dublin on 15 November that as soon as a recently purchased horse arrived safely in Ireland he would

at once retreat on Galway where I do not imagine any man would be sufficiently insane as to put his life in jeopardy by serving a writ. In these fastnesses I shall be secure from Saxon pettifogging and chicanery till the commencement of the session when I presume some declaratory act will be at once carried to render null all penalties recovered under this obsolete statute. Under any circumstances whether as defendant or witness any appearance would be most awkward, and on leaving Ireland I shall at once and quietly proceed to France, there to remain till this tyranny be overpast.

In the meantime, leaving nothing to chance, he wrote to a friend asking him to 'put about my intention to return immediately to London, this will prevent the writ reaching me in this city and make them less anxious for my capture'.[18]

Nor were Bowes and Gregory the only upper-class betters to decide that a swift departure from England for a continental holiday of undetermined length was necessary – even if, in the case of Lord Harry Vane, son of the Duke of Cleveland, 'his absence from London would deprive him of the means of completing his Derby book'. Writing to Bowes in Paris, Vane asked if there was anything 'you wish me to bring over in case I visit Paris'. Betting still went on but it was conducted more carefully, Vane reassuring Bowes that his name would 'not transpire or appear in my [betting] book at present except by an initial'.[19]

Such precautions and paranoia were not misplaced. At the beginning of December, despairing of finding Bowes in London, James Russell embarked on a detective mission. He traipsed around Bowes's various London and country addresses to serve him with more writs, prompting a friend of Bowes to write, 'It is a thing quite unprecedented in experience for an attorney to undertake a journey to Durham to serve a writ the great expense of which must inevitably fall upon him or his client whatever may be the result of the action.'[20] Whether in their houses or their castles it appeared that the aristocratic plungers were not safe from the Russells' writs.

While his contemporaries fled the country, Lord George Bentinck was unafraid to remain in London and to coordinate some kind of action against this unwelcome assault on the gentlemen of the Turf. From his country seat in Galway Gregory was able to write to Bowes, 'Since my return here my mind has regained its former tranquillity, it is soothed by the lawyers' consolations on the one hand, whilst its mettle is kept up by the angry denunciations of Lord George on the other.' He felt sufficiently complacent to add, 'The rogues are I guess in a pretty considerable tarnation fix, and the crusade against their hells will perhaps open to their expanded eyes, the impolicy of their undertaking – I trust you are one of the subscribers to the Society for the Suppression of Hells.' He added jocosely, 'What a blessing it will be for the poor whores, whores must be in, when Hells are out.'[21]

However, in London Lord George was feeling anything but jocular. His wily opponents were spreading rumours and disinformation so as to obscure their plans. In a letter to Bowes he urged him to subscribe to a sweepstake in Lord Maidstone's name. 'I think you must add your name to it,' he wrote, piling on the emotional blackmail, 'to console Maidstone for going to <u>Newgate</u> <u>which he must do</u> to save you from conviction at the hands of the "Infernals" – I imagine they rely entirely upon Maidstone's evidence to convict in your case for which reason they have not served him with a writ, – in order that he may have no excuse for not answering the questions the "<u>Infernals</u>" will put to him.'[22]

Moreover, Bentinck was awaiting judgement in a case of his own that he had brought against a Mr Connop who had refused to pay his subscription to a sweepstake that Lord George had won. In suing Connop he was citing another obscure piece of legislation, this one dating from the reign of Charles II. He felt that this would give some indication as to how the legal establishment were viewing the blizzard of *qui tam* actions. Merciless as the scourge of the Turf defaulters, Bentinck was now experiencing the consequences of his campaign. His personal quest to purify the Turf had had unexpected and unpleasant results, but from the fascinating correspondence that now flew between these frightened aristocrats there seems to have been little recognition that, to a large extent, it was Lord

George's actions that had brought about this uncomfortable situation. A *Sunday Times* reporter later told Bentinck that a defaulter called Weatherby had pledged revenge against Bentinck in particular, in retaliation against the exclusion of defaulters from racecourses.

Not for the first time his energetic, headstrong and precipitate nature had got him into trouble. It is entirely in keeping with the character of the man that, believing right on his side, he had pursued his enemies with such vindictiveness that they had fought back viciously. No one was denying that defaulters were an expensive nuisance and an embarrassment. But by the amoral laissez-faire standards of the sporting world at that time most of the Fancy would have regarded such men as an occupational hazard, especially as many themselves enjoyed reputations that were far from spotless. In their defence some of the defaulters would argue that it was they who were being 'defrauded by the unfair practices of the Gentlemen of the Turf in withdrawing their horses'.[23]

The issue here was the system of betting known as 'play or pay' that characterised 'all the bets upon the great races, such as the Derby, the Oaks, and the St Leger of Doncaster'. As has been seen, this system allowed that 'whether the horse is dead, or whether he is lame, or whether he is withdrawn by the owner, the persons who have backed him, if he does not run, must pay what they lose'. Even in the racing world, where almost every tactic was tolerated, play-or-pay betting was regarded as an iniquitous system; as one unusually high-minded turfite put it, 'The withdrawal of horses is opening a door to what is improper.'[24] In other words, it was an invitation to unscrupulous owners to withdraw perfectly fit horses if it helped their betting books. And so huge were the individual sums involved that it was not unknown for heavy betters to offer inflated prices for fancied horses shortly before certain races, then to remove them from the running.

Bentinck was just such an owner. He served his interests before all others, and he was not a man to question his own motives and behaviour when he could impugn someone else's. Futhermore, it was impossible to overestimate Bentinck's own capacity for revenge, especially when his highly developed sense of righteousness was pricked. Reformed parliament or not, he and his class still ran Britain. As the year drew towards its close the flurry of correspondence between worried aristocrats in London, Ireland and France and from their various stately homes around the British Isles saw a consensus gradually crystallising: the hell keepers would be made to pay. As Vane wrote with unintended irony to Bowes, 'The projected and threatened crusade against the Hells has made the proprietors of those establishments reflect that those who live in glass houses should not throw stones.'

In Vane's letter as in many others, 'Lord G. B.' is depicted as the leader of what was called in this correspondence 'our "Society for the Suppression of Hellkeeping"'.[25] In Lord George the defaulters had an adversary who, for all the high-minded rhetoric he would later fling in Sir Robert Peel's face about breaches of trust, was not above fighting dirty if the occasion demanded it. Disraeli was to identify one of his defining characteristics as 'the fierceness of his hates and prejudices',[26] and it was this fierceness that had now come to the fore. 'I have registered a vow in heaven to take signal vengeance upon these scoundrels and please God to favour my pursuits of these said devils,' he wrote to Bowes. He was particularly outraged when he heard that the Russells, uncle and nephew, had been so presumptuous as to spend an hour and a half prowling in front of one of the clubs on St James's Street – Crockford's, as irony would have it – and then had dared to go into the vestibule in search of someone on whom they wanted to serve a writ.

The way Lord George saw it was that, if these 'devils' were trying to use the law to get at him and his racing friends, then the law would have to be changed. From early November 1843 he had been of the opinion that 'our first endeavour must be to procrastinate as much as possible in the hope of getting the trials postponed beyond the meeting of Parliament, when we must see if we cannot get an Act passed at once staying the proceedings and permanently altering the Law'. Accordingly, it was of 'vital importance ... by hook or by crook' to delay the actions coming to trial. But this audacious plan to change the law so as to protect himself and his racing cronies against massive financial loss did not run altogether smoothly, as a frustrated letter written to Bowes in mid-December recounts. 'There is no use now in your playing at hide and seek any longer – therefore I think you would be more good if you were to come over to England [to] agitate for a repeal of the law – I am sorry to say I hear Lord Palmerston expressed a doubt whether Parliament could be induced to pass such a law and that Roebuck* has declared that he will oppose it to the uttermost.'[27]

Towards the end of the month William Hutt MP waded into the debate. Hutt had been tutor to John Bowes when he was a boy and had married his mother. He wrote to his stepson saying, 'Whether Roebuck or any other person were to oppose I do not think there would be any effective opposition to a Bill for altering the law without any reference to the parties against whom proceedings had been commenced. But having had some experience in this matter I should recommend that immediately on the meeting of Parliament a Bill be introduced into the Lords for altering the law and <u>containing a clause</u> staying all pending suits.'[28]

Bentinck, however, was still finding it hard going. Ever impatient, he had taken the matter to the rather priggish Home Secretary Sir James Graham and had not received the welcome he had hoped for.

With respect to getting a bill things do not look so pleasant at present. Nothing is settled and upon my going to Sir James Graham on Saturday last my interview was far from satisfactory; – he said that in the first place it was a very delicate matter for the Government to touch; – that anything like protection to betting on horse-racing would be quite sure to rouse up indignation and opposition of all the Saints in both Houses of Parliament and especially of the Bishops in the Lords; – that before he could even meddle with the matter a

* John Roebuck, radical MP for Bath, known as 'Tear-Em' Roebuck because of the vehemence with which he defended his independent political views.

formal representation must be made to him either by the Jockey Club
or from a large body of the great supporters of the Turf of both parties
[Whigs and Tories] praying for the interference of the Government
to stay proceedings and to alter the law; this done he will bring the
matter under the consideration of the Government and take the
opinion of the Cabinet upon it . . .

In short, Bentinck was being given the brush-off. It can only be
imagined how he seethed as the Home Secretary droned sen-
tentiously on, maintaining that there 'could be no just ground for
interference by Parliament' until some action had been decided
against Bentinck or one of his friends. This was too much for
Bentinck, who exploded – this was 'locking the door after the steed
was stolen' – to which Graham answered dogmatically that legal
opinion must be sought, a formal 'memorial', or petition, must be
drawn up, that this memorial must be duly signed by leading
members of the Turf and then, only then, would he 'lay the matter
before Sir Robert Peel'.

Bentinck felt overwhelmed and alone. 'These conferences of
great lawyers are fearfully expensive. At present I am the only
member of the Turf moving in the matter and I quite tremble at
the thoughts of my solicitor's bill,' he whinged in a letter to Bowes
on the penultimate day of the year. 'At the same time I do so well
know the selfishness of mankind and above all of that portion of it
which constitutes the Jockey Club that I am quite sure that unless
some previous arrangement is made they as a body will leave the
whole business and expense upon those who fight the battle.'[29]
Lord George did not seem to be looking forward to a particularly
happy New Year. But in a few days he was back on form. The New
Year had brought some welcome news: his old friend the Duke of
Richmond had ridden to his rescue and was going to bring a bill
before the House of Lords. To Bowes on 10 January he wrote
jubilantly: 'It seems by universal consent of all the world that the
Duke of Richmond is the fittest and the most influential man to
bring it forward.'[30] Nonetheless, there were those, Hutt among

them, who wished that Bentinck would keep a lower profile. 'I only hope that he will not now look upon this undertaking as too easy and too certain of success. I feel confident that he runs some risk of trouble, tho' perhaps little of defeat in the House of Commons. He must not talk about legalizing betting. It is quite enough to make it not penal.'[31]

'Our Bill is to be bold, manly, and straightforward, staying proceedings under the Queen Anne statute without costs, and legalising betting on horse-races, foot-races, sailing matches, cricket matches, coursing and all other manly and wholesome, sports,' Bentinck wrote to William Gregory, still lying low in Ireland, chiding him for his cowardice. 'I cannot, therefore, see the necessity of you and Bowes skulking, you in Ireland and Bowes in Paris. You would both be of much more use here canvassing for support to our Bill, which thus far, but for me, would have been left to its fate. As yet no satisfactory arrangement has been made as to the great expense already incurred, and as to how it is to be met.'[32]

It is difficult to know whether Lord George was taken in by his own 'manly and wholesome' humbug. Even putting the most charitable complexion on events, this sort of self-serving manipulation of the legislature could hardly be regarded as consistent with the public face of probity and honour that Lord George would choose to present during the Corn Law crisis in 1846, when he said, 'If we are a proud aristocracy, we are proud of our honour, inasmuch as we never have been guilty, and never can be guilty of double-dealing with the farmers of England – of swindling our opponents, deceiving our friends, or betraying our constituents.'[33]

But this noble oratory proclaiming the honour of his class remained in the future. As 1843 merged into 1844, Bentinck was conscious that time was running out. The more he looked into it, the more he worried that there was 'no safety but in an Act of Parliament – and therefore no time must be lost in agitating both sides of the House to procure the passing of a new Law on the subject'.[34] As well as his famed fixity of purpose Lord George was exhibiting one of his less desirable traits – his supreme arrogance. A spoilt man, used to getting his own way, what Bentinck set his mind to he usually achieved, even if it meant changing the law of the land.

8

Parliamentary Hypocrites

'All that was proposed to be done was to relieve from the operation of a law which was constantly in operation certain powerful individuals, who, of all others, were the least entitled to plead ignorance of its existence inasmuch as they themselves as Legislators assisted in the framing of the laws.'

Milner Gibson MP, reported in *Hansard*, 14 February 1844 [1]

The Duke of Richmond was indeed the perfect person to push such a law through on Bentinck's behalf. Respected, influential and a wounded veteran of the Peninsular War, compared to Bentinck he was a relatively uncontroversial figure. There is the sense that the overbearing Lord George bullied the duke; although he paid his way at Goodwood he also treated the place much as if he owned it. Moreover, it was widely believed that he was madly in love with the duchess, although it appears that the affair, if indeed it can be called that, was platonic and never consummated. He was once warned by Greville, when the two men were on a more friendly footing, that his feelings were so obvious that he was exposing himself and her to scandal and gossip. Bentinck wrote back, 'confessed his sentiments without disguise' but while unable to 'sacrifice feelings which made the whole interest of his existence', he said, 'he had no reason to believe his feelings were reciprocated by her'.[2]

Addressing the House of Lords in early February 1844, His Grace protested that

he did not bet himself, and he objected to a great deal of the betting which took place on the turf at present. Indeed, he believed that, if the system of betting was not checked, the turf would soon be deserted. His bill was intended to protect other manly sports. At present no one could play a game of cricket where the loser paid the expenses of the ground without rendering himself liable to a qui tam action. He happened to be one of those who wished to encourage manly sports; he thought them of great importance, and that they had been of late too much discouraged.

In fact, warming to his theme he fervently hoped that 'in all future enclosure bills' there would be provision to 'set aside a portion of land near the large towns, to which the people might resort for manly amusement. It was better that they should do so than go to the beer-shops, where they became sullen and discontented.'

The genial duke may well have been an early proponent of the benevolent paternalism that came to be associated with Victorian England, but nobody was really convinced by his wish to move the urban working class out of the beer shops and on to the playing fields. Nor does it seem that he was in much doubt as to why the legislation was being proposed; perhaps he felt it was his duty to say that 'he hoped their Lordships would adopt at once a measure which would defeat the attempts of a set of scoundrels who had been turned off the turf during the last year for not paying the bets which they had lost'.[3] It was perhaps to save everyone the bother of enduring this charade that Lord Brougham, the Lord Chancellor, suggested that the 'noble Duke withdraw the bill for the present, and introduce one which should have the effect of quashing the qui tam actions already brought upon the existing statutes'.

And so three days later, on 8 February, Lord Brougham, 'in the absence of the Duke of Richmond, moved their Lordships to give a second reading to "A Bill to discontinue certain Actions under the provisions of several statutes for the prevention of excessive Gaming, and to prevent for the future the bringing of such Action"'. Brougham went on to explain that the bill had been 'rendered necessary in consequence of a number of qui tam actions which had been brought by certain parties, out of spite, because they had been excluded from associating with the respectable gentlemen who had formed themselves into clubs, where arrangements were made for carrying on horse races'. Just in case their lordships were in any doubt as to the nature of the business they were dealing with, those bringing the actions were 'disreputable individuals', 'inveterate gamblers', while those with whom their lordships were invited to identify were 'men of the highest rank and the most respectable character in this country', 'noblemen and gentlemen' who, if Lord Brougham were to be believed, involved themselves in horse racing only as far as it 'encouraged the breeding of horses'. However, even the most well disposed of those listening to Lord Brougham might have permitted themselves a wry smile when he added that 'many of them never betted at all'. Presumably if they never betted, then they would have nothing to fear.

Granted, the individuals behind these actions were motivated by nothing other than a desire for vengeance and cupidity, but they were hardly less attractive than those against whom they were employing their piece of arcane legislation. This had not escaped the spiritual leaders who sat in the House of Lords. The Bishop of London said that the whole business 'partook of the nature of modifying the existing laws on behalf of the rich, at the expence [sic] of the poor'. The bishop was concerned that the bill before them might seem to sanction betting rather than restrict it, and he pointed out that 'the beer-houses which had been of late years opened', presumably the same ones that were such a cause of concern to the Duke of Richmond, 'had led to a great increase of betting among the poor'.

Lord Brougham did his best to make all the right noises. He agreed that 'they ought not to have even the appearance of favouring the rich', and then ventured the spectacularly patronising opinion that 'gambling had much more fatal consequences, and was far more injurious to morals among the inferior classes than among the superior classes'. This was not just legislating 'on behalf of the rich, at the expence of the poor' – rather, it was legislating on class grounds. It would appear that even in the age of railways, electricity and a Reformed parliament Lord Brougham spoke for many in the Upper House, as only the Bishop of Exeter raised a note of disagreement. He made a reasonable point: in light of the duke's assertion that, while maintaining one of the best known and best run racecourses in the country, he 'did not bet at all', 'this proved that betting was not necessary to the manly sport of horse-racing. The noble Duke enjoyed it without the additional excitement of betting. How then could Parliament be called upon to protect betting as being necessary to this manly sport, as the bill calls it?'

The Bishop of Exeter was on a roll. Next, he brought a nice point of law to the attention of their lordships: namely, that 'if the loss did not, under one act, exceed £100 and under the other, £10, the informer could not bring an action. It was only excessive gambling that the law restrained.' And given that Lord Brougham had just mentioned the serious consequences of gambling, particularly for the lower orders, then surely there was a duty to restrict heavy betting. Just 'three individuals were charged to such an amount, that the penalties nearly reached the sum of £300,000 (£36,000,000)'. He then asked even 'the most ardent pursuer of horse-racing in their Lordships' House, whether this was not excessive gaming'.[4] But the objections of the Bishop of Exeter seemed positively mild when compared to some of the outrage expressed in the House of Commons. The bill's most vociferous critic was Milner Gibson, MP for Manchester, one of the constituencies created by the Reform Act and exactly the sort of place where the Duke of Richmond would have liked to see the working men (who still did not have the vote) forsake the ale house for the playing field.

The bill was the perfect weapon for the fiery Gibson, who demanded a proper explanation for this proposal to 'enact an ex post facto law to relieve those who had violated the law, to give protection to those who had violated the spirit and the words of an act of Parliament, and to withdraw protection from those who obeyed it'. His point was that 'the House should pledge itself to revise the gaming laws before it discontinued these actions. It had given the country no pledge that it would not continue these penalties. All that was proposed to be done was to relieve from the operation of a law which was constantly in operation certain powerful individuals, who, of all others, were the least entitled to plead ignorance of its existence inasmuch as they themselves as Legislators assisted in the framing of the laws.'[5]

Clearly not one of the nobility – and probably not considered much of a gentleman by the likes of Lord George Bentinck who was relying on the swift passage of this piece of legislation to save him from a costly court case – Gibson went on to contend that 'to call this bill, as it had been called in another place, "The horseracing and manly sports bill," was neither more nor less than to mislead the public'.[6] He mocked the proceedings in the Upper House, insisting that 'those who supported this bill in the other House of Parliament must have been jesting when they called the bill at present before the House a "manly and wholesome pastime bill"'.[7]

There was much more in this vein, received with cries of 'Hear!'[8] and gales of laughter at the obvious discomfort on the government benches. Gibson's blows kept hitting home. 'It was believed in the country,' he went on, 'that the spirit of Legislation in Parliament was to legislate for themselves and that there was no activity in either house, unless something took place, which affected the interests of the Members themselves.'[9] Cries of 'Name!'[10] attended his expression of regret 'that he did not see present some Gentlemen who seemed to arrogate to themselves the exclusive guardianship of the religion and morality of the country. It was a remarkable coincidence,' he continued, 'that they should be absent on an occasion when their services were so much required, especially when their opinions might be in opposition to those of the Gentlemen by whom they were surrounded.' A pity, because 'the country ought to have noticed how Gentlemen voted on this question'. He concluded 'by moving as an amendment, that a Select Committee be appointed to inquire into the existing statutes against gaming of every kind'. As he sat down the House erupted, rendering the next speaker barely audible.

William Hutt MP had been correct in predicting a rough ride for the bill in the House of Commons; and worse was to come when Captain F.F. Berkeley got to his feet and asked the House to 'pause before legislating with respect to gambling transactions, lest, by implication, it might be supposed that the House was about to protect these transactions'. He then launched into a blistering attack. 'Of all the gambling transactions of the present day there were none, in his opinion, more mischievous, more dishonest, or in which there was great cheating than those connected with the present system of horse racing. It was a system of book-making which engendered most of the evils, he said, adding that "it was a very common saying among those connected with the turf that unless a man went on the turf determined to be a rogue he must be a fool".'[11]

Against this unstoppable tide of rhetoric, voices such as that of Colonel Peel against whom a *qui tam* action had been brought, bleating that he 'was prepared to state, that the parties against whom these actions were brought were perfectly unconscious of having transgressed', sounded almost comically out of step with the mood of the House. However, the prize for fatuousness must go to Captain the Hon. Henry Rous, second son of the Earl of Stradbroke, who would come to dominate the Turf later in the century. It was the height of the Derby betting season – 'the absorbing interest attending a heavy betting Derby extends from September until May, if not longer,'[12] one sporting writer informs us – and Rous felt compelled to argue for an extension of a proposed amnesty for the sake of 'a great many Gentlemen now making books upon the Derby'. Rous felt that 'if they were to be prevented from betting after the 1st of March, a great injury would be done them. For many of them who had only "got on," or bet against, perhaps twenty horses, would not be able to get round by betting against others; and would thus have to stand to be shot at'. In conclusion, he said that 'the rich were obliged to keep horses for the amusement of those who could not keep them themselves. As to any harm that was done to the morals by mixing in horse racing it was all humbug. On the contrary, it did a great deal of good, in making friends, and concentrating interests, and comparing opinions as to which horse would win.'[13]

As it happened, the House was more inclined to agree with the gallant captain than with the excitable Mr Gibson. The *qui tam* actions would be suspended pending the findings of the Select Committee that would be appointed to look into the question of gaming in Britain. Lord George Bentinck must have felt hugely relieved, or more accurately, given his well-developed sense of his own rectitude, thoroughly vindicated. But while there might have been immediate relief for those who had feared ruinous *qui tam* actions, the real result of the lively debate in parliament had been to open up the murky world of mid-nineteenth-century gambling to scrutiny. Bentinck surely did not know what he had set in train, or how events would unfold over the rest of that eventful year of 1844, which would see gambling identified as one of the greatest threats to national well-being.

For the moment, the House had taken notice of the voluble Mr Gibson and his exhortation that it 'pledge itself to revise the gaming laws'. He had pressed hard for a committee to look into the matter, as 'it would show how far the Members of that House were in earnest, and whether they desired to abolish the penalties upon every description of gambling, whether on sports or cards, or only upon those descriptions in which their own class was concerned'.[14]

The general tone was summed up by another MP who 'thought the people of England had just cause to complain of the conduct of this House in wasting so much time in an attempt to screen certain noble Lords and Gentlemen who had been guilty of committing a breach of the law'. He then asked: 'How can you expect the poor to be moral and orderly, when the rich set such examples?'[15] Clearly the issue was seen not as one of legality but rather of morality, and it would seem that at the beginning of 1844, parliament considered it had a duty to determine public morality. What emerges from comparing the frenzied correspondence of late 1843 and the backroom machinations to change the law in order to benefit a few rich men who had fallen foul of an old law, alongside the spirited debates in the Houses of Parliament, is the gulf between the myopic view of those turfites who could see the question only in terms of legal technicalities to be exploited in their battle to thwart the 'Infernals', and the broader concerns of an increasingly numerous and vocal proportion of society for whom gambling of all sorts was a social ill.

9

The Giant Evil

Shun the gambler – whether in the family or in the world; however insidious may be his professions, however polished and fascinating his manners, shun him as a living moral pestilence, and as one, who, already burning with the fiercest passions of hell, would drag you down to its darkness and despair.

Revd T. Archer, *Gaming and Its Consequences*

If gaming, then, brethren, is viewed in its influence upon the social state, it will be found most destructive. It ruins the morals of a people, destroys the fame and character of those, who from station should be the ornaments of the state; it prepares and trains a mass of villany [sic] and crime – ready for any extremity and ready to be let loose at all times upon society.

It was Wednesday evening, 11 April 1838, and at the Wells Street Chapel just off Oxford Street in London the Revd T. Archer was in full spate. As many of the 'ornaments of the state' gathered at Crockford's in anticipation of a good dinner and some high-stakes hazard, the good reverend thundered from the pulpit about the evils of gaming and its deleterious consequences. In a bravura performance, his language larded with the threat of earthly ruin and eternal damnation, the Revd Archer pulled no punches. This was not, he had warned at the beginning of his sermon, a subject to be 'regarded as one of partial or temporary interest' but rather 'intimately connected with social stability'.

'Let but the habit of gaming pervade a people – not only its higher orders, the *ornaments* of society, but in its middle class, whose intelligence and virtue constitute its defence – and no matter how ample its resources, how balanced and venerable its constitution, how impregnable and sure its bulwarks, there is at work in its very core that which exhausts its energies and prostrates its independence.' O to have been in the congregation that evening as the minister took his flock on a tour through gambling's infamous history, from classical antiquity to modern-day London where gambling's 'temples are glaring before the eye' and 'its emissaries are ever on the watch for victims and prey'.

'How, then, is this giant evil to be put down?' It is easy to imagine him pausing magniloquently between each rhetorical question. 'How is this outrage on morals and feeling to be abated?' If his congregation hoped that the newly established Metropolitan Police Force, whose truncheon-wielding officers in their leatherreinforced top-hats were still a novel sight on the streets of the capital, would save them, they would be sadly disillusioned. The law, explained the reverend, 'will not be enforced by interested parties whose evidence may be bought and sold, and cannot be enforced upon the private scenes of gambling without a system of *espionage*, which the genius' – it is unsure whether this word was spoken with irony or respect – 'of our constitution repudiates'. 'Is nothing, then, to be done, to repress this monstrous evil – nothing ultimately to destroy it?' The entire chapel, now hanging on his every word and hoping for the hand of God to deliver them from this 'moral contagion', listened intently. 'It can be repressed and destroyed only through moral agency. It must be preached, and prayed and frowned down.' Yes, that's right. Crockford and his ilk were to be preached, prayed and frowned out of business.

Archer was coming at the issue from a somewhat different direction from Captain Gronow and his Crockford cronies. But it is interesting to note how many of the reverend's observations on the 'splendour of the scene' and 'the wines which fire his brain' were shared with the likes of Gronow, who enjoyed dropping into Crockford's for a dose of moral contagion and were pleased to fire their brains with one of the quarter-million or so bottles of wine in the cellars.

Archer aimed to put the fear of God into his 'young friends'. 'Taste not the cup,' he urged them, 'refuse it with loathing abhorrence, remembering that, if you take it into your hand, it will steal over your soul and stupefy your sensibilities.' His impassioned survey of a ruined society in which the parent 'sacrifices his children's happiness' and 'the son robs his parents' was roundly inclusive. No one, from the tradesmen 'who (I fear) too much frequent the low houses of play', to 'one-half of the nobility', to even 'royal gamblers who have demeaned themselves to a level with licentious courtiers', was safe.

At the end of this sustained tirade he took his leave of his congregation, in particular of the young men, with the imploration that they 'shun, shun that vice. Shun it in its first assaults; and shun it with the conviction, that it ends in utter and hopeless ruin. And shun the gambler – whether in the family or in the world; however insidious may be his professions, however polished and fascinating his manners, shun him as a living moral pestilence, and as one, who, already burning with the fiercest passions of hell, would drag you down to its darkness and despair.'

Were the Revd Archer's sermon to appear in the pages of a novel by Dickens it would come across as a hilarious histrionic caricature. But its presence in a volume of *Christian Instruction Society Lectures* 'to young men and others' is straight-faced. And unintentionally amusing though it may be today, it was indicative of a growing public concern. Gaming was no longer the idle diversion of a few hundred aristocrats but was coming to be seen as a serious social ill alongside drinking – it was at this time that the temperance movement was gaining momentum. When Archer delivered his sermon Victoria had not yet been a year on the throne. The moral climate of the nation had yet to change from the permissive society of the Regency and the rambunctious reign of William IV with his numerous Fitzclarence bastard children. But the moral minority, among whom Archer clearly counted himself, was becoming more vocal. Public opinion was gradually turning away from a lazy tolerance and acceptance of gaming. Archer had said of gambling, 'It prepares the mind for every kind of deed of wickedness',[1] and this was no empty rhetorical device. He went on to remind his congregation of a number of high-profile scandals and crimes that had been linked to the world of gaming.

The Derby of 1836 had been of note not because of the victory of Lord Jersey's bay Middleton, subsequently sold to Lord George Bentinck for a steep £4,000, but because of a much darker affair.

> This year there has been a miserable catastrophe [wrote Greville of the Derby in his diary]. Berkeley Craven deliberately shot himself after losing more than he could pay. It is the first instance of a man of rank and station in society making such an exit. He had originally a large landed estate, strictly entailed, got into difficulties, was obliged to go abroad, compromised with his creditors and returned, fell into fresh difficulties, involved himself inextricably in betting, and went on with a determination to shoot himself if his speculations failed, and so he did. He was very popular, had been extremely handsome in his youth, and was a fellow of infinite humour and good-humour.[2]

Although Craven was unable to pay his losing bets on the Derby, it was said that 'the Oaks would have brought him entirely round, had his nerve sufficed to suffer him to wait the result of the latter race'. But 'this martyr to turf gambling' had had enough. Nevertheless, he demonstrated his good humour to the last, 'chatting and *laughing* with his party during their boisterous drive to town', all the time knowing that he would end his life on his return to London, shooting himself 'in his own drawing-room'.[3]

A couple of months before this tragedy, Greville had been approached by a friend who told him that Henry de Ros, the premier baron of England, had been cheating at cards. The rumours continued to circulate during the summer, doing the rounds of the clubs and fashionable drawing-rooms; Greville records the subject being brought up at breakfast with the Duchess of Buccleuch. By the end of the season, though, the scandal had not spilled out into the public domain and it was hoped that de Ros would leave the country and that the affair would blow over. But a report in *The Satirist* made the matter public and the story came to dominate fashionable life during the winter of 1836–7. Even the Duke of Wellington weighed into the debate, coming down strongly on the side of de Ros who 'continued vehemently and solemnly to assert his innocence'.[4]

But as the accusations mounted, de Ros was forced to action. In February of 1837 he took one of his accusers to court.

> The Court of King's Bench was occupied the whole of yesterday with the trial of the action for libel brought by Lord De Ros against Mr Cumming, who had accused his lordship of cheating at cards. The trial excited great interest; and among the distinguished persons present were Lords Lyndhurst, Alvanley, and Wharncliffe. It was charged against Lord De Ros, that at the whist table he frequently contrived to have a violent fit of coughing when his deal came, which obliged him to put his hands under the table; and then it always happened that he turned up an honour; and that the aces and kings in the packs Lord De Ros played with, were frequently marked, slightly but perceptibly, with the thumb-nail. Many gentlemen swore to their having been cheated by these tricks; and some refused to play with Lord De Ros; though others did not shun him after his cheating had been discovered – they sent him anonymous notes of warning, and hoped that he had left off cheating. The play of these gentlemen was very high sometimes; and one of them, Mr Brook Greville, admitted, that he had made £35,000 (£4,200,000) by play; another, Captain Alexander, said, that he was a 'better man by £10,000 (£1,200,000) for card-playing.

In spite of an attempt to get an expert medical witness to prove that de Ros had 'a stiffness in his finger-joints, which prevents him from playing tricks with cards', the evidence against him was overwhelming. 'There never was a clearer case against any delinquent; and the jury only took fifteen minutes to determine upon their verdict.'⁵

Sensational though these two cases of upper-class depravity were, for sheer lurid prurience, nothing outdid what quickly became known as the case of the Gambling House Murderers, which had held the attention of the nation throughout the autumn of 1823. So salacious was the case that it was compared to the Cato Street conspiracy, in that 'they each broke alike upon the dull uniformity of civil life and awakened the drowsy sensations of the world into feelings of horror', as *The Times* put it. The case had the ingredients of a grisly melodrama: a discarded pistol found matted with hair, blood and 'a portion of the brain of a human being'; a half-naked body dragged from a pond, its throat cut 'nearly from one ear to the other'; a gunshot wound to the right cheek, a hole in the left temple where the pistol had been forced into the man's skull and 'penetrated both hemispheres of the brain'; a suspect – John Thurtell – arrested with blood-soaked clothes, who had apparently told a friend that the blood 'came on his face and into his mouth in such quantities that he was nearly choked' and who, it emerged, had been in bed with another man when he had been taken into custody.

The victim was a man called Weare, who had been in the habit of carrying '£1,000 to £2,000' which he put 'in an old pocket book and generally placed next to his skin beneath his shirt'. As to the reason for his carrying such huge amounts of cash, it emerged that he had a half-share in a gambling house on Pall Mall. He had been the victim of a contract killing after attempting to bring off a complex double-crossing that involved an attempt to bring criminal proceedings against some people with whom he had connived in relieving a 'flat' or 'pigeon' of some £7,000. As the investigation was broadened other characters were added to this infamous cast, including a professional singer and a man who obtained large quantities of wines and spirits under the influence of which it was said 'no woman whom he wished to possess could escape him'. While incarcerated in the King's Bench Prison for debt this man was said to have 'debauched the wife and daughter of the person

with whom he lived there'. There were numerous supporting
players: sundry habitués of billiard rooms, 'females of loose character', and more dead including a murdered Polish officer, and a
captain who had beaten this motley bunch to it and committed
suicide, presumably preferring that fate to shooting, bludgeoning
and tracheotomy.

Speculation was fevered, even the respectable *Times* mentioning
in a leader article that 'the wretched men now under confinement
for the murder of Weare, had formed an association and taken
houses in different parts of the town – near the Thames, in Cannon-
Row, and Manchester-buildings – for the express purpose of inveig-
ling their victims, and committing a series of assassinations'. After
warning its readership as to the dangerous proximity of blood-
choked homosexual sociopaths and fraudulent sex-maniac wine
merchants, the *Times* leader writer launched into a rhetorical climax
of which the Revd Archer would have been proud. 'For whence
was it that they became acquainted with each other? In honest
company? In respectable houses? Oh, no: in the midnight haunts
of vice and villainy.' It was the newspaper's fervent hope that 'the
gambling-houses may receive a severe shock by the late dreadful
occurrence, and all the subsequent discoveries or suspicions. These
are the seminaries of self-murder and assassination.' For *The Times*
it was clear that 'It was the gambling-house that murdered Weare;
and when his murderers shall approach to their frightful and un-
pitied end, it will be to the gambling-house that they will look back
as the birth-place of their crime, and the office from whence issues
the warrant for their execution.'

The case was a national sensation. The section of a hedge through
which the corpse had been dragged disappeared, 'cut away piece-
meal by the persons who have visited the spot'. The cottage where
Thurtell and his accomplices had met became a tourist attraction,
entrance priced at one shilling. Some claimed that the unnatural
smell in the parlour resembled 'that which proceeds from a corpse
in a state of decomposition'.[6] It was noted that the Marchioness of
Salisbury was among the visitors.

The murders entered national folklore. They became part of the catechism of shame recited by later moralists, illustrating the depraved depths to which men would sink once they had fallen into these 'seminaries of self-murder and assassination'. In *Crockford's, or Life in the West* Weare's name is linked with that of Page, the groomporter (croupier) at Crockford's. Also in *Life in the West* is to be found the remarkable allegation that Thurtell offered to murder eight men who were harassing the gaming-houses, threatening court cases in the hope of extorting money. Apparently Thurtell had been happy to have the funds placed in escrow 'subject to the performance of the undertaking'.[7] Given that much of what is stated as fact in this work can be verified, the statement can be taken reasonably seriously.

This allegation of mass murder for sale in the gambling world was eagerly repeated by sundry anti-gambling crusaders, including the impassioned Revd Archer himself. Indeed by the time Archer was preaching, the death toll associated with just one gaming-house on St James's Street was twenty suicides per annum – he had culled this 'statistic' from James Grant's sensational analysis of the London gaming scene in his book *The Great Metropolis*, published in 1837. Grant's tone is almost as hectoring as that of the Revd Archer. He was particularly upset that gambling was corroding class barriers: 'Our nobility have no scruples in admitting such characters to their houses, on a footing of friendship! Nay, the daughter of one of these gambling proprietors, was some years since married to a Peer of the realm!'

Grant's observations also describe the growing spectre of middleclass gambling. Expressing the commonly held view that the nobility was setting a bad example, he cited the establishment of a second class of gaming-house, pitched just below the Crockford's level, aimed at what the hellites called 'Cits' – 'city merchants, and city clerks in situations of confidence'. Those clerks, again, itching for it. For the hell keepers the Cits represented a relatively new and lucrative field to exploit. 'The city merchants resolve on becoming gamblers under the impression that the making of a fortune by selling chests of tea, or measuring yards of lace, is not only a slow and tedious process, but a very vulgar one,' Grant wrote. 'To do it by gambling is much more expeditious – so they think till they try – and infinitely more fashionable.' The twin lures of social advancement and easy money quickly made were often cited as motives for entering the gaming-houses.

And below those hells aimed at the Cits was a third class of house 'chiefly visited by noblemen's and gentlemen's servants, and shopmen with small salaries'.[8] But even here it was noted that there was an aspirational edge to the gambling: it was stated in evidence given before the Select Committee on Gaming that many of the 'shop persons' were seen to 'dress very smartly and go into the better houses'. But so small were their salaries that they were soon eaten up by gambling, and the shopmen turned to crime. In evidence given to the Select Committee the shopkeepers of St James's stated that proceeds from the series of robberies in the area '[go] into gambling houses', and that moreover these robberies were committed by their employees. The governors of two of the largest prisons in London seemed to corroborate this, explaining that in respect of 'all the cases of better instructed people that have gone through those gaols, whenever they have questioned them as to the commencement of their crimes, it has been from gambling'. And as well as the primary use of these funds at the gaming tables there was another 'inducement to robbery ... if a servant or shopman can scrape together £200 or £300, by the agency of the keepers of these houses he has the opportunity of lending out his money to the losers at 60 per cent'.[9]

But even aside from the loan-sharking and the robberies, the primary impact of the vogue for gaming on what was perceived as the most vulnerable class was considerable. It was estimated that £1,500,000 (£180,000,000)[10] a year was wagered and lost by servants of noblemen and gentlemen alone. However, this sum, taken from hundreds of small-time gamblers over the course of twelve months, was as nothing to the vast amounts staked at Crockford's. On a single evening it was 'positively stated' that 'the enormous sum of nearly £1,000,000 (£120,000,000) was turned over, from the time play commenced till it concluded – a period of eight hours'.

But while Crockford's was a glaring example of the age's most besetting vice, it may also have been, ironically, the safest place to gamble. Unlike at almost every other establishment, the dice were not loaded and the atmosphere was civilised. It was a decorous contrast to the less salubrious establishments where the proprietors would get their victims blind-drunk – at times so drunk that they required someone to place bets for them and would be so far gone as to be betting against themselves. Of course, given that half of the nobility and much of the legislature were members there was little chance of Crockford's getting raided, and Grant even advances the theory that some nobles provided financial backing for Crockford's. 'The club was formed on the principle of not allowing any two members, or any two strangers, to play at hazard together, because it was deemed unbecoming in noblemen and gentlemen to run the risk of breaking in on the friendship assumed to exist between them, by gaining money from each other.' In order to preserve their scruples 'it was therefore resolved that an establishment should be opened in which all the members might play against the proprietor, who not being of their own class, but simply a tradesman, they could cheerfully fleece'.[11] Grant suggests that the infamous Marquess of Hertford, Thackeray's Marquess of Steyne, was involved in financing Crockford's, but adds that by the late 1830s he had retired.

Even though Hertford was a terrible roué, this is still a serious charge. An indication of its gravity can be seen in the reaction of the radical MP for Finsbury and Crockford's member Thomas Slingsby Duncombe, one of the great ornaments of early Victorian politics. He had been described in *Fraser's Magazine* as 'a distinguished supporter of the gambling-house, the brothel and every haunt of vice'[12] – but it was not this that Duncombe objected to so much as the allegation that he was a partner in Crockford's. He felt compelled to challenge the magazine's eponymous proprietor

Hugh Fraser to a duel, and the *Morning Chronicle* commented that youthful indiscretions were one thing, but that to suggest Duncombe 'decoys men to Crockford's hell to be plundered, and has an interest in the profits of the concern' was simply outrageous; 'Never was a fouler calumny uttered.'[13]

Whether Duncombe shared in them or not, the profits to be had from running a high-class hell were astronomical. And Crockford was not the only one to become rich: at one time the Bond brothers (one of whom had fallen victim to *qui tam* action in 1842) were seen as serious rivals to the one-time fishmonger, while the author of *Crockford's, or Life in the West* claimed that some of the hellites were 'now worth two or three hundred thousand pounds, all made in the space of nine or ten years'.[14] There were plenty of stories of gaming-house keepers who had grown rich and retired as gentlemen, to own country houses and maintain strings of racehorses. On the Turf they were able to meet as equals members of the class that they had robbed.

It is difficult today to understand the strength of paternalistic feeling in early Victorian society. But with the law seen as virtually powerless to act against this growing social problem, an increasingly vocal constituency looked to their social superiors to make a stand. When viewed against this background, it may be easier to understand the growing disapproval of what many saw as the transparent hypocrisy of the 'Manly Sports Bill'. To much of the population it must have seemed that Lord George Bentinck's vigorous campaign against defaulters on the Turf was a mere semantic quibble, and that something rather more sweeping needed to be done about this social, moral and financial problem. It was in this climate of discontent that the Select Committee on Gaming was ordered by the Houses of Parliament to launch its investigation, with evidence heard by both the House of Commons and the House of Lords.

10

Gambling in the Dock

———

'I think the great pleasure of living in a free country is, the being allowed
to bet upon any subject you please.'

Captain Rous, before the Select Committee on Gaming, 3 April 1844[1]

———

Before the Select Committee could begin peering into the Stygian
gloom of the gambling world, parliament needed to enact another
bill, to be called the Gambling Transactions Witnesses Indemnity
Bill. The object of this was to 'afford indemnity to the witnesses
called upon to give evidence before the committee'. Only a matter
of days after it was set up the committee ran into problems, finding
it 'impossible to make a searching inquiry into gambling without
the examination of persons implicated in transactions for which
they were liable to prosecution'.[2]

In moving the second reading of this bill to remove the threat
of legal action against those called to give evidence, the good old
Duke of Richmond once again professed his strongly held revulsion
for the 'excessive system of gaming' that was corroding the nation.
He added the rather pious hope that the Select Committee would
remove the prejudice against the Manly Sports Bill

as a protection to the rich and not to the poor, and he regretted that
truth obliged him to state that there was more gambling amongst the
lower than the higher classes. He hoped they would be able to procure
such evidence before the Committee as would enable them to legislate
efficiently on the subject, and to prevent gambling so far as it could
be prevented by legislation among all classes.[3]

On 21 February a committee of MPs was nominated, including prominent figures such as Milner Gibson, the MP for Manchester who had already held the Tory government up to ridicule over the gaming bill, and Colonel Peel. Partisan tensions in the committee would soon become apparent when Gibson was accused of using it to build himself a reputation – 'being desirous of becoming a prominent man somehow or other', he was motivated by 'the love of popularity, notoriety, or celebrity' even though he 'did not understand anything of the subject then under the consideration of the House'.[4] By contrast, much of the rest of the committee was packed with staunch turfites who had a vested interest in protecting betting on horses. One estimate reckoned the more sporting members of the Select Committee had 101 outstanding wagers between them. Moreover, they stood open to accusations of vindictiveness against the disaffected hellites and defaulters who were thought to be behind the *qui tam* actions. This committee would hear evidence until the early summer and publish its findings on 20 May, just two days before the Derby, by which time the Lords too would have established a committee to look into the matter.

The combined reports, minutes of evidence, findings, appendices and so forth would eventually run to many hundreds of pages and would provide a comprehensive panorama of gambling in early Victorian England. Over the course of several months an intriguing cast of characters was paraded before the committee: racehorse trainers, betting men, policemen, lawyers, sporting journalists and even a stray cheesemonger.

Concern was rising about what was seen in some quarters as a chronic social ill. And yet ranged against this was the genuinely and dearly held tenet that betting was one of the most cherished rights of an Englishman. It is possible to see the tide of history on the turn: views and opinions associated with Georgian England were voiced alongside the morally interventionist aspirations of those who felt it their public duty to improve and protect the morals of the population, especially the more vulnerable, lower orders of society. It was this dichotomy that characterised a considerable portion of the evidence given before the Select Committee, and the sense is of a set of double standards emerging that allowed the rich and powerful to act as they pleased while restricting the actions of the poor. Today such a view might seem patronising; then, it exemplified the spirit of paternalism that would come to typify the era.

It soon became clear to the committee that 'wagering is still deeply rooted in the habits of the nation, and the practical imposition of pecuniary Penalties for Wagers would be so repugnant to the general feelings of the people, that such penalties would scarcely ever be enforced, or, if enforced, would be looked upon as an arbitrary interference with the freedom of private life'.[5]

However, the nature of gambling was changing, as the Hon. Frederick Byng – or Poodle Byng, as he was known on account of his curly hair – magistrate and former churchwarden in St James's, explained. According to him the time when faro banks and gaming tables were kept in private houses and clubs was long gone. The only memories he had of this were from his younger days: 'I think I may add, that formerly in the clubs, the gambling was confined to a very high rate, and to a very few people. I could have named all the gamblers in my early days in the clubs. No person coming into a room where hazard was carried on would have been permitted to play for a small coin and therefore he left it.' In recent years, he went on, there had been a marked increase in the number of specialised gaming clubs aimed at various sections of the general population. 'Many years ago the few gambling houses which existed were low places frequented only by persons of bad character; now these establishments are conducted in a very different style.' Characteristic of these more self-consciously upmarket operations was an atmosphere of exclusivity, prejudice and snobbery: 'for instance, the Berkeley Club would not let a Jew into it; nor a common fellow that has hardly a shoe to his foot'.

As a consequence of this assumed exclusivity, these new hells were often described as 'respectable', they changed the nature of the West End considerably. Byng's point was that the gambling scene used to consist of a small number of rich men losing money amongst themselves, its impact negligible. But the new rash of gaudily appointed gambling houses was spreading almost unchecked and there were real fears of an associated crime wave. One factor was the distorting effect of the hell keepers' money on local property owners and leaseholders, who would sublet one or two rooms to gamblers for as much as 12 guineas a week; by contrast, an entire unfurnished house could be rented in the affluent suburb of Holland Park for 7 to 10 guineas.

The Commissioner of the Metropolitan Police Richard Mayne corroborated what Byng had to say. When pressed as to how many hells his force had closed down between 1839 and 1844 he was only able to say that seven had been raided, little more than one a year. Mayne was able to furnish the committee with a list of fifteen West End addresses that he knew for certain were operating as gambling hells, but this was only a small proportion of the total: he admitted that there were other houses under suspicion, not including the 'many houses where there is play carried on, such as at billiard-tables, and many cigar-shops, and even some public-houses'.

The committee was understandably keen to learn why, if Mayne knew which addresses were operating as illegal gambling clubs, he was unable to close them down. The Commissioner then set out the obstacles that he had to negotiate before a raid could take place. First, two neighbouring householders would need to swear on oath that an address was being 'kept or used as a coming gaming-house'. Even this first step was rarely achieved, as householders were reluctant to appear as informers, fearing 'that it would make them marked objects in the neighbourhood'. There was the real fear that the organised hell keepers would exact retribution on them. Should the police get lucky and two householders be willing to go on oath, they would next need to apply to a magistrate for a warrant, giving ample warning to the hell keepers. Moreover, keepers took elaborate precautions regarding security: as well as burly porters and stout bars on the windows, some hells had as many as five sets of doors, accessed only by coded knocks.

Furthermore, they were careful about the people they admitted, using amongst other things an 'examining room, as it is called, to see that you are a proper person to be admitted up stairs'. So either the police would have to attempt to infiltrate the gambling house in disguise, or by the time they broke through using the gamblers would have been alerted and all traces of illegal gaming would have been cleared away.

It was a frustrating situation that Mayne faced; as he said, 'I have frequently desired the superintendent to do all in his power to get persons to make the necessary affidavits and he has told me that he has been unable to proceed.'

The lot of the police in 1844 vis-à-vis gambling hells was not a happy one, Superintendent Thomas Baker commented in great frustration in a letter to the Select Committee. Baker professed himself 'extremely anxious that something more should be done respecting the gaming-houses to put them down, which are the cause of so many young men's ruin'. He went on to enumerate

[the] difficulties I have to contend with before an entry can be effected, from the reluctance of the housekeepers to make the required affidavits, from not wishing to have their names brought forward in such matters: also from the great difficulty in gaining an entrance to a gaming-house from their extreme caution and watchfulness, besides the strength of their doors and fastenings, which gives them ample time to remove any implement they have of gaming from the premises; their vigilance is such that it is impossible to obtain an entry for the purpose of seeing play, unless treachery is used with some of the players, which is attended by danger and great expense. On the slightest alarm, the cloths, which are thrown loose over a common table, &c, are in a moment removed and secreted about the persons of the keepers &c; and as the present law stands, the police are not empowered to search them at all: there are no complaints by the housekeepers respecting the gaming-houses, and in every instance of putting them down, the police have been obliged almost to compel them to go to the police court to swear to the necessary affidavits;

such has been their reluctance. As the present law stands before I can enter a gaming-house with safety, I am obliged to go through the following forms: 1st, to make such inquiry as to have no doubt that gaming is carried on in a house; 2d, to make a report of the circumstances to the commissioners; 3d, to show the said report to the housekeepers residing in the parish and neighbourhood where the house is situated, and the offence carried on, for them to make the necessary affidavits; 4th, to prepare affidavits for the housekeepers to sign, in the presence of the magistrates; 5th, to make a report of the same to the commissioners when sworn to; 6th, to make out the commissioners' warrant for me and the police under my control to enter; 7th to endeavour, if possible, to get an officer in disguise into the gaming-house to witness play being carried on previous to my entry, which is the most difficult task to encounter, as no one is admitted unless brought there by a Bonnet [a gambler who lured the neophytes] or a play-man as a pigeon, or freshman [uninitiated players] commonly known as Punters or Flats.

The struggle was a Sisyphean one, and hardly helped by the notoriety that had attended a gaming-house raid at no. 34 St James's Street the previous year, during which the hell keeper's son had fallen to his death trying to escape from the police over the rooftops. When Superintendent Baker appeared in front of the committee in person he left them in no doubt that the war against the gambling hells was being lost. Far from pursuing them, he feared that he was now the target of hell keepers all over the West End. There had been threats on his life, and at the very least he feared that they would use the law against him: 'If I broke into a house and found neither gaming implements nor persons at play, I should be liable to an action for breaking into a house, almost as a common felon.' Whenever he left his station house and headed westwards he was followed. 'Having been engaged in this duty year after year, I have a great deal to contend with night and day respecting these gamblers, that it has almost worn me out,' he commented wearily.

Byng was in no doubt as to whom to blame for this state of

affairs. 'I think the increase of gambling houses is entirely the offspring of Crockford's. The facility to everybody to gamble at Crockford's has led to the establishment of other gambling-houses fitted up in a superior style, and attractive to gentlemen, who never would have thought of going into them formerly.' The characteristically forceful Captain Rous went even further in identifying the culprit, touching on a possible solution for dealing with the problem: 'So far as regards my opinion, I wish Crockford's had been burnt down many years ago.'

In one of the most unusual sessions, William Crockford himself was brought in front of the committee. Here at last, if the evidence presented to the committee was to be believed, was the architect of the nation's ruin, the man who had done so much to create a climate of debased morality that threatened the well-being of the country. However, rather than the evil genius they were expecting, what the members of the committee saw before them on 28 March 1844 was a somewhat frail, unappealing and uncooperative septuagenarian. While the name of Crockford's had entered the national vocabulary as a synonym for decadence and depravity, the reality was that Crockford himself had ceased to be the proprietor in 1840. His resignation had shocked fashionable society, but the club carried on, and it was unclear whether he was still involved in a less formal capacity. Having questioned him, the committee was no better informed in the light of his evidence – although he was older and nearing the end of his life, he was still as suspicious as ever.

When asked about his occupation he answered, 'I have no occupation generally speaking; I am concerned in mines and other things.' Asked about the rules of admission to the club, he was similarly unenlightening. 'It was a private club; not a thing done in public at all; it was amongst private gentlemen. I should wish to decline answering that question.'

However, this answer was a model of frankness compared to the response he gave to the largely rhetorical question: 'There was a lot of play carried on at the club, was there not?'

'There may have been so; but I do not feel myself at liberty to answer that question, to divulge the pursuits of private gentlemen. Situated as I was I do not feel myself at liberty to do so.'

He was then asked to withdraw while the committee consulted among themselves. Called back into the room, he was read the Act that indemnified witnesses against prosecution and asked if he still wished to decline giving an answer about the club. To which he answered, 'Yes, certainly I should beg to decline it.' Thereafter he continued to dodge the questions put to him, parrying the committee's probes with an 'Upon my word I do not know', or 'I do not feel myself at liberty to go any further with the question', or 'I do not come here to give my private history and character; I must decline it'.

After the following exchange the committee lost patience with him.

'Are you aware of there being in St James's Street and the adjoining streets a great number of gambling houses?'

'I do not know; I never go in the evening into St James's Street.'

The committee even failed to secure his acknowledgement of many a young man's ruin by gambling. 'Many people will say they have been ruined by gambling who have been ruined by keeping women, and having a box at the Opera and other things of that kind, but they lay it all on gambling.' Only in his last answer did he show a spark of the old Crockford acuity – when asked if there were any provisions to deter levanters at hazard, the whip-fast answer came back: 'If the Honourable Member were the frequenter of a hazard-table he would know that they played for ready money.'

What must have made sitting on this committee by turns infuriating and highly amusing was the sheer diversity of characters who came before it. Directly after Crockford's decidedly economical performance, the stage was filled by Captain Rous, who more than compensated for his predecessor's evasiveness. Whereas Crockford had all but refused to acknowledge gambling's existence, and certainly declined to offer his opinion on it, Rous was only too happy to express a variety of splendidly revanchist views on the matter. He declared histrionically, 'If you legislate against betting you would make this country not fit for a gentleman to live in; you will go on and make laws against the way in which a man walks ... I think the great pleasure of living in a free country is, the being allowed to bet upon any subject you please.'

Captain the Hon. Henry Rous would succeed Lord George Bentinck as the most important – some would say the most dictatorial – figure in Victorian racing. His long period of influence was marked by a voluminous correspondence (some private, some carried on in the pages of the newspapers) and by a bombastic manner that made 'his lightest pronouncements almost judgements'.[7]

Elected to the Jockey Club in 1821 and serving as its senior steward for a second term at the time of his death in 1877, he was a skilled handicapper of horses, an able administrator and as blinkered in his views as the horses he cared so deeply about. Rous was a monomaniac who viewed the entire human condition through the lens of horse racing. For him horse racing was the ultimate panacea and as much a force for good in society as was muscular Christianity or temperance for others. Of class divisions in Britain he once wrote, 'There is at least one amusement in which all classes participate, one point of contact between all parties, and one source of enjoyment to individuals of every rank – namely horse-racing.'[8] In this heartfelt expression of what he believed to be a universal truth there is as much lyricism as in the poetry of the Young England movement. There is little doubt that he genuinely did view betting as one of the inalienable rights of an Englishman.

Even in the dry minutes recording the evidence given long ago in the spring of 1844, it is possible to detect the vigour and impatience of his answers. As he saw it, government had no business interfering in betting on horses: 'The feeling on the turf is, that there is no wish on the part of gentlemen connected with the turf that bets should be legalized, that they should be recoverable by law: they are considered as points of honour between persons, and if a man does not choose to pay there is no other penalty beyond the contempt which naturally falls to his lot.'[9]

Having expostulated at some length on how legislature oughtn't to touch betting, and how such an involvement would 'be the worst thing that could happen', he was asked what should be done about gambling booths on racecourses. To this he gave an equally impassioned and almost totally contradictory answer: 'I would abolish them, and propose the heaviest punishment that the Legislature' – presumably the same body that would do well to keep its nose out of betting – 'could inflict, and especially on race-courses; and not only would I abolish booths, but I would have the strictest penalties against gaming tables, and every species of gambling, on a race-course' – every species of gambling except, that is, gambling on the outcome of a horse race.

Far from being obsessed with equality, this was a time characterised by the growing sense of obligation incumbent on the ruling class to legislate on behalf of the sections of society that were considered incapable of looking after themselves. This view expressed itself from the streets of London to the colonies, whether exporting copies of the scriptures to the heathen parts of the Empire – by the early 1840s the British and Foreign Bible Society was distributing almost a million copies a year – or stopping 'mechanics' and clerks from laying a bet. And although he believed that parliament should leave betting on horses well alone, Rous was clear about where its obligations lay when it came to gambling hells, whether in the West End of London or under canvas on the country's racecourses.

> I think that in respect to society commercially, the great harm happens to clerks belonging to men of business; but I think with respect to a rich man, it does not signify whether he loses his money as long as the money is distributed among the public. I wish that the merchants and tradesmen of this city should be protected. When a man has made his money, why should I care what a rich man does with his own;

but these common gambling-houses affect the credit and debauch the clerks and persons who are employed in the merchants' houses and bankers' houses. I think those men ought to be protected. The poor should be protected, but I would let a rich man ruin himself if he pleases.

The Commissioner of the City of London police force, Daniel Harvey, spoke for many when he told the committee: 'I think it is a matter of little importance to hear and to know that men of large fortune have transferred from one to the other £100,000 (£12,000,000); but I think it is a very undesirable thing that mechanics and persons engaged in industrious pursuits should be crowding around thimble tables, and going into gambling booths and losing their money. I think the moral and social inconveniences would be much greater from the latter.' But he was not blind to the fact that the example of the men of large fortune would inspire the less well heeled: 'I admit that the existence of the one palliates, and perhaps justifies the conduct of the other, and hence the undesirableness of both.' What the committee heard time after time was that working-class gambling was inextricably linked to crime and a general breakdown in social order. Ancillary gambling at racecourses, on simple games of chance in temporary booths and tents erected at race meetings, was singled out as being a prominent component of this social ill.

The picture that emerged revealed what amounted to an entire industry. One visitor to Doncaster, home of the St Leger, was shocked at the number of houses, some forty or fifty, where gambling was openly advertised. 'At the same time upon the race-course the thimble men were in hundreds with their tables, as well as by the roadsides on every approach to Doncaster, playing and cheating the people out of their money as fast as they could induce them to play.' The thimble-riggers with their trays of cups, under which they challenged punters to locate the elusive pea, were more than a mere nuisance. As a body they could turn vicious if threatened, as happened at Doncaster in 1829 when the police fought a pitched

battle with thimble men who 'had assembled with their sticks, and
bid defiance to the police, who were actually afraid to attack them.
Lord Milton, the present Lord Fitzwilliam, Mr Beckett Denison,
and half a dozen other gentlemen on horseback, came to the aid of
the police; they galloped at the thimble men, and by a regular
charge dispersed them.' One of the committee was heard to ask,
'The thimble-rig people do not seem to be in good repute?'

The view taken on the thimble-and-pea people varied from
course to course. Some, like Goodwood, excluded them rigorously,
seizing and breaking their tables; Egham tolerated them and at
times took a fee from the chief thimble man; while at Epsom the
thimble-riggers were each charged between five shillings and half a
sovereign in exchange for a ticket that they displayed in their hats
or on their tables.

But the real source of revenue on racecourses was the small city
of tented gaming booths that were in effect mobile gambling hells,
offering hazard, roulette, 'E.O.' (even odd also known as roly-poly,
a simplified form of roulette) and other games. Among other ways
in which visitors could chance their money were such delights as
rouge et noir, a game played with six packs of cards around a table
'covered with a woollen cloth, divided into four compartments,
two of which are red and two black, at opposite angles'. Players put
their money on either red or black, the cards were dealt and the
croupier counted out the pips until thirty-one was reached or
exceeded; this number he then declared for black, the process was
repeated for red, and the total closest to thirty-one was declared
the winner. The house would take half the money on the table in
the event of both colours having thirty-one. As well as the near-
limitless scope for cheating, booth operators would also rely on
'swindling confederates' to allay suspicion by playing the part of
bona fide gamblers, 'apparently losing their own money, and affecting to curse the fickle jade Fortune'.[10]

Crockford's, or Life in the West describes the following popular
game. 'Une, deux, cinque' was 'played with an ivory ball, about the
size of a plum dumpling'. This dumpling featured

forty-eight small round flat spots, twenty-four black, sixteen red, and eight blue. The points in favour of the bank, upon what is considered the fair ball, are, three bars to black, two to red, and one to blue – six points out of forty-eight. If the black turns up and is backed an even amount is paid to the stake; if the red, twice the stake; and if the blue, five times the stake, excepting when the bars of either colour come up, when the stakes are lost upon the losing colours, and nothing is paid upon the winning one.[11]

Invariably the gaming-booth operators kept a second or 'double' ball, so called because it had double the number of bars; when a promising 'flat' came into view, the 'fair ball' would be dextrously substituted for the double one.

But the opportunity to be cheated was only part of what these booths had to offer. Such was their notoriety and so infamous were they as haunts of villainy, vice and violence that their perils were an accepted part of the lore of the time. Those who went in were lucky if the worst that happened to them was that they emerged penniless. Stories of assault and robbery were axiomatic. Typical was the fate of the Derby Day racegoer who was 'knocked down in a booth, where gaming was going on, and after being plundered of hat, purse, and gold watch, was left on the Downs in a state of insensibility from the effects of barbarous treatment. At about five o'clock the next morning, he came to himself, and found his head bleeding profusely from a deep cut he had received.'[12]

These mobile hells were every bit as illegal as their more solid counterparts in the West End, and often operated by the same people, who would come from London and set up these portable facsimiles of their urban operations. Indeed, it was noted that many of the London hells actually closed during such major race meetings as the Derby and relocated to the racecourse. But if the witnesses before the Select Committee were to be believed, those in charge of the daily running of the racecourses were in complete ignorance of the law on this matter. Typical was the evidence of one John Rushbridger who, when asked if he was aware that it was against the law to operate a gambling booth, answered, 'No, I am not; I have understood it is generally done at race-courses.' What made Rushbridger's admission particularly embarrassing was that he was in charge of running Goodwood, the Duke of Richmond's race-course, and the two booths there had been first let some twelve or fourteen years earlier by the duke's brother. The reasoning was very simple, as Rushbridger pointed out: the two booths were let for £125 each, while a similar-sized refreshment booth might rent for 10 or 15 shillings.

The attitude was the same at racecourses elsewhere. As it happened, Goodwood was remarkably restrained in letting just two booths (a third operator had offered £150 to run one but had been turned down by the duke, who had said that he did not want another and rather wished he could get rid of the other two). At Egham some fourteen booths were let for gambling, in addition to some rooms in the grandstand. At Hampton the clerk to the course put the case forcefully for gaming booths as vital to the continuance of racing: 'I am confident, as far as our race is concerned that it would be impossible that our races should exist under any circumstances whatever without the canvass upon the ground.'[13] And the booths were certainly enough of a tradition at Hampton to warrant an appearance in Dickens's *Nicholas Nickleby.* 'Of the gambling-booths there was a plentiful show, flourishing in all the splendour of carpeted ground, striped hangings, crimson cloth, pinnacled roofs, geranium pots, and livery servants. There were the Stranger's club-house, the Athenaeum club-house, the Hampton club-house, the St James's club-house, and half a mile of club-houses to play IN; and there were ROUGE-ET-NOIR, French hazard, and other games to play AT.' (The Stranger's and the Athenaeum were well known hells of the early 1840s.)

Written at the end of the 1830s, this passage is part of a much broader description that is the written companion to Frith's essay in oil and canvas. Dickens, like Frith, is charmed by the scene, which embraces pickpockets and fortune-tellers alike as players in a familiar and much loved pageant. 'The attention so recently strained on one object of interest, was now divided among a hundred; and look where you would, there was a motley assemblage of feasting, laughing, talking, begging, gambling, and mummery.' There is 'a little knot gathered round a pea and thimble table to watch the plucking of some unhappy greenhorn'; elsewhere the eye alights on the 'wide circle of people assembled round some itinerant juggler'. The air is alive with noise, 'ventriloquists holding dialogues with wooden dolls'; 'Drinking-tents were full, glasses began to clink in carriages, hampers to be unpacked, tempting provisions to be set forth, knives and forks to rattle, champagne corks to fly.'[14]

Dickens's narrative picture of 'the little race-course at Hampton ... in the full tide and height of its gaiety' was a snapshot of the England he loved – 'one of those scenes of life and animation, caught in its very brightest and freshest moments, which can scarcely fail to please'.[15] For him the gambling booths, with their gaudy exteriors and stuffy interiors thick with the fumes of sherry and cigars, were an inalienable part of the appurtenances of the early Victorian racecourse. Nowhere was this more true than at Epsom. But the economic ecosystem of the early Victorian race-course was a finely balanced organism. This was not a matter of sentimentality to be exploited by authors and artists, but, so the racecourse operators argued, concerned the financial stability of the sport of racing. An important source of income, the gambling booths enabled those who ran the courses to put up bigger prize money – to attract more entrants of higher quality, bigger crowds, and more customers to the booths, whose holders would pay higher prices when the time came to bid for ground for the following year. The gaming booths were themselves an attraction, bringing in other booth-holders. At Epsom, for instance, gambling was described as 'the main stay of the other booths, such as the publicans' booths'.

Timothy Barnard, who in 1844 had been letting the grounds at Epsom for almost thirty years, told the Select Committee that he had never known of any attempt to suppress the gambling booths. 'The steward [of the racecourse] has always said to me, "Now Barnard, do keep them as much out of sight as you can, so that

I have no complaint." And I have always obeyed his orders.' The question was then put to him: 'Supposing persons were not allowed to bet upon a horse-race, and that gaming-booths were not allowed to be erected upon the course, do you think anybody would come to see the races?'

The answer was unequivocal: 'I think you would not have half-a-dozen people.'[16]

With the Derby now a matter of weeks away, his answer would soon be put to the test.

I I

Raid

═══

'The feeling being so much excited about these gaming houses, we do not find the same difficulty in obtaining the oaths of the inhabitants as heretofore.'

Richard Mayne, Commissioner of the Metropolitan Police Force, before the Select Committee on Gaming (26 April 1844)[1]

═══

Shortly after one o'clock on the morning of 8 May 1844, the bell of 12 Bury Street, St James's, was rung smartly. To the passer-by no. 12 Bury Street presented the façade of a cigar shop, but the real business was conducted in a room at the rear of the property where play at the hazard and roulette tables was now winding down. An hour or so earlier the room had been fairly busy, but now only three men remained. Hoping for a little late business the owner Mr Leadbitter instructed his doorman to open up. Immediately he did so the passage was filled by eighteen policemen, headed by Superintendent Samuel Hughes. Acting on information that had been gathered in the preceding days, Hughes left some men to guard the suspects then opened a side door to another passage to find his way barred by 'a very strong door, cased on the inside with strong iron binders and bolts'.[2] But he had come prepared. Police constables equipped with a sledge hammer and crowbars now went to work, getting the door open in time to apprehend two men and seize three roulette tables, a hazard table, dice, money, counters and other gambling equipment. Hearing some noise from above, Hughes sent men on to the roof, where another gambler was caught.

In a few minutes it was over and the five men, together with the gaming accoutrements, were carted off to the police station.

At exactly the same time, similar scenes were being played out at a further sixteen addresses where the police had reliable information that illegal gaming was being carried on. The night air was rent with the sound of splintering wood and cries of 'Police!' The early hours of 8 May saw more than three hundred police across the West End breaking down doors, scuffling with porters, forcing windows, scaling ladders, wriggling through trapdoors, chasing across rooftops, overturning roulette wheels, smashing up gaming tables and making dozens of arrests.

Each of the fifteen gambling hells that Metropolitan Police Commissioner Mayne had identified in his evidence before the committee, plus a further two that had subsequently come to his notice, were entered by police. It was a spectacular operation conducted with an almost military precision. Its scale and scope were unprecedented. The law required that only a superintendent could lead a raid, so superintendents had to be drafted in from different divisions including Finsbury and Greenwich. The same was true as regarded extra constables: around 350 police took part in these simultaneous raids, many of whom were brought in from other parts of London and none of whom, with the exception of the superintendents, were told in advance what they were to do.

The results of the raids varied: twenty-two men were arrested at a gambling hell masquerading as a coffee shop; at another establishment a partially dressed man was found in bed with two women, his belongings packed up and ready to move, having heard about the intended raids in a nearby public house the day before. At 27 Regent Street premises known as the Stranger's – the presence of which Dickens had noted at Hampton racecourse and with which Charles Russell of the *qui tam* actions was linked – were, so the visiting superintendent noted, 'beautifully furnished, and brilliantly lighted up by numerous chandeliers'. But the place was empty of gamblers – 'it is obvious the parties anticipated a visit from the police' – and the superintendents had to content themselves with taking a few servants into custody and seizing some gaming apparatus. However, patrons of the anti-Semitic Berkeley had not been so well informed, and a number of arrests were made.

As it happened, the amounts of money seized were negligible, under £30 (£3,600) in total. But it was the high-profile action taken that was judged to be important. Plainly, the pressure of public opinion had made itself felt. Since setting up the parliamentary inquiry, of which the Victorian age could boast an immense number, the legislature appears to have been caught by surprise. Until the Select Committee convened at the insistence of members who felt that Bentinck's (or, rather, the Duke of Richmond's) 'Manly Sports Bill' was a case of parliament protecting the interests of a privileged clique, gambling hells had been regarded as little more than a regrettable fact of life. As something that offended the burgeoning moral sense of the bourgeoisie but that unenforced and inadequate laws seemed powerless to control, they could be compared, say, to the issue of child labour. The preceding year had seen the Factory Bill brought in to reduce the working hours of children, and now the besetting social ill of gambling had come under public scrutiny. Until that moment, since Victoria's coronation barely half a dozen gambling houses had been raided. The obstacles to achieving convictions had been enough to discourage even the most zealous and conscientious policemen such as Thomas Baker, who saw them as a scourge.

Now, within a matter of weeks, public sentiment on the matter was running high. The sense that something needed to be done was stronger than ever. As Commissioner Mayne put it, 'The feeling being so much excited about these gaming houses, we do not find the same difficulty in obtaining the oaths of the inhabitants as heretofore.'[3] Already on the morning of 7 May two public-spirited householders had been persuaded to give their oath against some neighbouring premises; they 'had reason to believe, in the words required by the Act, that they were common gaming houses'.[4] Having obtained the necessary affidavits the Commissioners gave the order that the premises should be entered. The criteria for the raids were simple enough. The targets were 'Common gaming-houses where gaming is carried on, and to which all people are admitted, or those called members, after a colourable election, the primary object being play'.

Of the seventeen raided, however, there was one address that was absent: 50 St James's Street. Crockford's had been spared the attentions of the Metropolitan Police. 'I could not consider myself justified, unless authorised by a higher power, in directing an entry to be made into Crockford's, or any club which I believed to be a club of gentlemen for general purposes, as well as for play.' Such was the explanation given by the Commissioner himself, who went on to add, 'I think practically there is an intelligible distinction between Crockford's and mere gaming clubs.'

But not everyone agreed. Some, not least conspiracy theorists, suspected that the attacks on the gambling hells were motivated not so much by a public-spirited zeal on the part of the Metropolitan Police as by the vengefulness of leading turfites: 'The attack is reported to have been for some time in contemplation at the Home Office and as the hellites say, chiefly at the suggestion of certain influential persons of the Turf in revenge for the *qui tam* actions against them by certain broken-down levanters of the play-ring,' observed *The Satirist* on 12 May. 'Why in the name of justice, should the great pandemonium of all [Crockford's] be allowed to escape the attack? Is it because it is the chosen resort of the law-makers themselves that their place of illegal amusement should not be interfered with? This is making fish of one (not to speak irreverently of the great fishmonger himself) and flesh of another with a vengeance.'[5]

I 2

Tension Mounts

'It seemed as though there was here brought before me, in one concentrated and panoramic view, an exhibition of the world's varied allurements of sin.'

Quoted in Stella Margetson, *Leisure and Pleasure in the Nineteenth Century*[1]

Of course, the real surprise was not so much that Crockford's was
not among the common gaming-houses raided, but that Lord
George Bentinck was not called upon to give evidence before the
Select Committee. After all, it was his attempt to get the law
changed for his own benefit that had led to the setting-up of the
committee and the concomitant crackdown on illegal gambling.

However, as far as Bentinck was concerned there were more
important matters facing him in the spring and early summer of
1844. His mother had died, but as Day already indicated, he did
his best to hide his grief. His note to his trainer John Kent,
admittedly on black-edged paper, is eloquent enough about his
feelings. 'My Mother's funeral is fixed for Thursday next in
London which I shall attend & then return here. Under these
circumstances however there will be no objection to my horses
running next week at Gorhambury & I will write to your father
to send up Herens[?] & Haworth for that purpose,' he wrote
peremptorily, having the good grace to add, 'but I shall not be
present at the races myself'.[2]

The big event that occupied Lord George's mind was not his
mother's death, but the Derby, which was to be run on 22 May. By
the mid-nineteenth century the Derby, which had been born and

named under such arbitrary circumstances, was the major event of the sporting world. For the owners and trainers who had horses entered, this race was the culmination of many years of patient work and calculation. Likely horses would be entered as yearlings. The Derby of 1844 attracted 153 entrants, fewer than a fifth of which would start the race, and bets would be made at long odds. Thereafter betting would fluctuate for a couple of years, depending on how the horse and its rivals performed and what money was placed on it. These movements in the betting market were solemnly covered in the nascent sporting press.

By 1844 sweepstakes on the outcome of the Derby were being run up and down the country, and most towns had a sporting tavern or other commercial premises where bets could be made. In York, for instance, there was a famous sporting chemist in Mickle Gate, who took bets as well as dispensing drugs. Attendance at the Derby was now judged to be in the region of two hundred thousand.[3] Months ahead of the big day working-class racegoers in London and other major cities organised themselves into clubs, contributing a regular amount of money to a pool that would pay for a day at the races.

For this year's Derby, Bentinck had two horses entered, Vin Ordinaire and Croton Oil,[4] of which pair only the latter would actually race. But the real favourites were the Ugly Buck and Ratan. The two horses had been the talk of racing circles since the preceding year. Often, in letters dealing with the impending *qui tam* actions correspondents would allude to the performance of one horse or the other and mention the various odds being offered on them. From a letter written by Bentinck to John Kent on 16 December 1843 it is clear that he thought both horses extremely difficult to beat: 'Rattan [sic] & the Ugly Buck are both sure to be in the Newmarket St Leger & they will at once frighten away all others & make it anything but a good engagement.'[5] In another letter he comments, 'Lord Chesterfield says the Ugly Buck is the finest horse he ever saw.'[6] Sir William Gregory, however, was of a different opinion. He wrote in one of his letters that 'as long as

Rattan [sic] flourishes, he certainly is what Wyndham Smith used to call "a hummer", an expression meant to comprise all the aggregate excellencies of the race horse'.[7]

Certainly at the first major engagement of the 1844 flat-racing season, the 2000 Guineas at Newmarket, the Buck had performed impressively. After the Derby and the St Leger, the 'Two Thousand', established in 1809 and the highlight of Newmarket's second Spring Meeting, was considered to be one of the great tests of three-year-olds (the Jockey Club had decided that for the purposes of classification for races the birthday of all horses would be 1 January). A Guineas winner was looked on favourably for the Derby, and given the race's timing, near the beginning of the season, there was an optimistic expectancy about it. As Sylvanus puts it, 'It was the first great muster of the season, and the meeting of all others that might possibly give a clue to the mysteries of the approaching "Derby".' Consequently, Newmarket was filled with all manner of racing men: 'country speculators, London legs, City traders, flash West-enders, itinerant hellites, a stray jock – whip in hand – and every other human ingredient of the turf'.[8] And so the entire sporting world was aware of the Ugly Buck's victory by a neck over Lord George Bentinck's Devil-to-Pay.

However, Bentinck did not seem too put out by the defeat, even though the fact that the Buck was trained by John Day at Danebury must have hurt. The point was that although it was a good race, knowing his own horse as he did, he did not think that the form shown by the Buck was as impressive as that demonstrated by Ratan. It was Ratan that had caught Lord George's eye. Following the horse's performance as a two-year-old in 1843, beating a horse he had backed heavily in the New Stakes at Ascot, Bentinck had taken whatever odds he could get for him on the Derby. Ratan had continued to improve, winning the Criterion Stakes at Newmarket's Houghton meeting. 'This encouraged Lord George during the winter to increase his investments upon Ratan for the Derby,'[9] wrote Kent. On both occasions the jockey was Sam Rogers, who would be riding the horse again in the Derby. And while the Select

Committee on Gaming was interviewing its witnesses in Sir Charles Barry's newly completed Houses of Parliament, Ratan won again at the Craven meeting in Newmarket. Crucially this win came some weeks before the Buck's triumph in the 2000 Guineas, giving Bentinck the opportunity to compare the two horses and to continue to back Ratan heavily.

Although the Ugly Buck was often entered in races as being owned by John Day, *Bailey's Magazine of Sports and Pastimes* describes John Gully as 'half proprietor',[10] and during their long association the two men would share the ownership of many horses. Interestingly, in its form guide to the Derby of 1844 *Bell's Life* of 19 May claims that Day bought the Ugly Buck from Lord George as a yearling. Coincidentally, Gully was also among 'the men of the highest rank and the most respectable character in this country'[11] who had had the misfortune to be threatened with one of Russell's *qui tam* actions. His involvement in the Ugly Buck added extra piquancy to the Derby: it would bring him into competition with his old foe William Crockford who, aged seventy and in failing health, was not expected to get another good opportunity to win British racing's ultimate prize.

However, shortly before the Derby it became clear 'from market operations in Manchester, Liverpool, &c., as well as in London, that there were parties in the ring who were laying immense sums of money against the horse winning. It got rumoured that the horse was certainly made safe as far as regards not winning.' Crockford himself heard from a friend who had previously backed Ratan but was now laying against it that 'the horse was as "safe as if he were boiled," and that Sam Rogers, who was engaged to and did ride the horse for the Derby, was in the plot to prevent Ratan winning'.[12] Futhermore, as Derby Day neared, Bentinck, doubtless through the Argus-eyed Harry Hill, John Gully's old crony, got to hear of some dubious betting by Rogers. In particular he learned of some highly suspicious wagers with Gully.

As well as riding for Crockford, Rogers was one of Bentinck's jockeys. He had ridden Devil-to-Pay in the 2000, and Gaper in the preceding year's Derby; at the time questions had been raised about Rogers's conduct during that race. It was well known how much Bentinck had riding on Ratan and he was not, of course, a man to leave anything to chance. But before he took action on this account he had other business to settle. In a letter dated 18 May, the Saturday before the race, addressed to the stewards of Epsom racecourse and penned in his firm, fluid handwriting, Bentinck opened up a huge controversy, one that would remain unequalled in the annals of racing:

Gentlemen

We the undersigned owners of horses engaged in & intended to run for the approaching Derby, having thorough reasons for believing that the horse meant to be started as Mr Goodman's Running Rein is not the b.c. [bay colt] by the Saddler out of Mab by which pedigree Running Rein is detailed in his earlier nomination but some other horse & one above three years of age which has been substituted for the colt by the Saddler out of Mab, request you as Stewards of Epsom Races to investigate the matter and to oblige the owner or owners of the horse to prove his identity by evidence; – and above all through a proper examination of his mouth by Veterinary Surgeons of character & eminence of your selection to satisfy you before he is permitted to start, that he is not more than three years old.

And we the undersigned hereby engage and undertake to bear you harmless of all expense incurred by any such investigation and further to indemnify you against the consequences of all expense incurred by any such investigation and further to indemnify you against the consequences of any action at law which might be brought against you should you in the discharge of your duty as Stewards think it proper to hinder the colt in question from starting until you shall have been satisfied that the colt intended to be started as Mr Goodman's Running Rein is no more than three years old the identical animal described in the entry for Derby.

We have the honour to be

Gentlemen

> Your obedient humble servants
> G. Bentinck
> John Bowes
> John Scott[13]

Racing was in such a rotten state by the 1840s that substitutions of older horses were far from unexpected. In the Derby of 1840, the first and last that the young Queen Victoria attended, the 50–1 winner Little Wonder, trained by the wily 'Old Forth', was strongly suspected of being a four-year-old. The difference here was that Lord George had been following Running Rein's career. Along with his campaign to rid the turf of defaulters and to have the law changed to save him and his friends from huge penalties in the *qui tam* actions, the management of his own considerable racing establishment, the pursuit of his vendetta against the Days, the making of his betting book, and the gathering of information about the making of other people's betting books and about the form of almost every thoroughbred racehorse in training, Lord George had found time to pursue his suspicions about Running Rein and its owner Levi Goodman.

Abraham Levi Goodman was one of Victorian England's outsiders; as a Jew he would have been a victim to what today would be seen as systemic discrimination, ethnic slurs and racial abuse. To these socio-environmental factors he added his own predilection for dishonesty. Not enough evidence of his character emerges to ascertain whether his criminal activities were motivated by a desire to retaliate against a social system that used him shabbily, but certainly he would have accepted that – to use a term that he would have been familiar with – the dice were loaded against him. Still, he was a man of ambition and intelligence, and these qualities were unfettered by any scruples.

At about the time when Lord George Bentinck embarked on his career as a racehorse owner, Goodman too was making a name for himself on the Turf, as a petty swindler and practiser of short cons. In the summer of 1828 he was one of a gang charged on suspicion of having robbed a woman of £300 at Hampton Races on 26 June. Their victim, a bearer of the splendidly Dickensian name Mrs Dunkin, had arrived at the races in search of her husband. 'On her arrival on the course,' *The Times* reported, 'she met Goodman Levy [sic], and having a slight knowledge of him as a tradesman, she spoke to him and told him for what purpose she had come there.'[14] Goodman told her that he knew her husband and would help her look for him, but suggested that first they take a little refreshment. Together they went into one of the booths where 'they had some sand-wiches, and a glass of brandy and water. While partaking of the refreshment, Levy offered her some indecent familiarities, and not wishing to remain in his company, she got up, and he having paid for what they had taken, they both left the booth.'

Levy walked with her a little while until she fell into company with a William Pitt, who also offered to help her look for her husband. At this point Mrs Dunkin became 'anxious to rest herself, and expressed a wish to Pitt to go to the Coach and Horses', perhaps feeling that another brandy and water was in order. Pitt, however, steered her into a booth where thimble-riggers were practising their art and, Mrs Dunkin feeling like trying her luck, reached into her embonpoint and fished out a roll of notes, selecting one to change and returning the remainder to her bosom. At first she must have thought she was the subject of yet another indecent familiarity as Pitt reached inside her dress, but it was not her breasts but rather her bundle of banknotes that he was after. As he sprinted from the tent, the blowzy brandy-and-water-befuddled Mrs Dunkin tried to give chase, but was held up by various accomplices including Goodman. Pitt was apprehended the following day trying to change the notes at the Bank of England.

When Goodman appeared in court 'a person named Raphael, of the Jewish persuasion',[15] gave him an alibi. It might well have been this same Raphael who was cited in a court case in 1836 in which Goodman was judged to have obtained by fraud a bond of indemnity upon which he brought an action to seize 'the goods and chattels of a person of the name of Hayward'. Although the sum of money involved was not particularly significant, the methods used were certainly a step up from getting a lone woman drunk at a racecourse and acting as an accomplice in robbing her. By the late 1830s Goodman was connected with a hell called the Little Nick in Leicester Square. At the end of the decade he was described as having 'kept the oyster and wine-rooms at the corner of Bow Street, Covent Garden, and been fined for allowing gambling in the house'.[16] But by the 1840s his plans had become more complex and much more grandiose, and he had shifted his attention from oyster-shucking and small-time hell-keeping to the Turf.

In a race for two-year-olds at Newmarket in 1843, Running Rein had won so comfortably that he had aroused Bentinck's suspicions. But only the owner of the second-placed horse could lodge an objection with the stewards of the meeting, asking for the stakes to be withheld pending an investigation. Using the same mixture of cajoling, moral blackmail and sheer willpower that characterised his behaviour in the *qui tam* affair, he succeeded in getting the Duke of Rutland, whose horse Crenoline had finished second to Running Rein, to make the necessary application to the stewards.

The inquiry was not handled expeditiously. Had the horse's mouth been examined on the spot by a competent professional, the matter would have been resolved there and then. Horses, like humans, shed their milk teeth, but unlike humans they lose specific pairs of their incisors between fairly accurately defined times, allowing an extremely reliable estimate of the horse's age to be made.

Instead there was a delay of a fortnight and the outcome hinged on the testimony of a stable lad called Kitchen who had seen the 'real' Running Rein born and had the animal under his care when it was a foal. The lad was brought to Newmarket and confirmed that the horse was indeed the one he had known. It would appear that either he was bribed by Goodman, or the horse was switched.

Unable to substantiate their allegations, Bentinck and Rutland saw their case collapse and Goodman was awarded the stake, but not without some adumbration of his reputation. The stewards considered it wise to recommend that Running Rein should not run again at Newmarket. Although he was the victor in this instance, Goodman's conduct had been brought into question by the stewards. But far more seriously for him, he had courted the opprobrium of Lord George, who was able to nurse a grudge for years. As seen in Bentinck's behaviour with every adversary since Captain Ker during his early days in the Army, he would go to any lengths to avenge himself.

In his letter to the stewards at Epsom Bentinck had made a mistake about the owner of the horse. Since the disputed victory at Newmarket it had passed to a corn-chandler called Alexander Wood, who, it was said, had taken the horse in settlement of a debt on the condition that it would still be entered for the Derby. Clearly, it was not the ownership of a Derby winner that motivated Goodman but rather the betting coup that he would pull off in the event of Running Rein coming first. And perhaps Bentinck's mistake was intentional, drawing the stewards' attention to the man he considered the miscreant.

The Derby is known as being the severest test of a three-year-old's legs. The initial climb, still one of the steepest on any major racecourse in the world, places immense strain on the limbs. The pace is terrific from the start, as jockeys try to get a good position before rounding the corner and descending the hill. On the course on which the Derby was run until 1847 Tattenham Corner was much sharper than today, and after the corner the ground dropped almost as steeply before rising slightly towards the winning post. For most of this punishing course a horse would be running flat out at speeds of around forty miles an hour. Physical stamina apart, according to one trainer of a Derby winner the key difference between a three- and a four-year-old would be the strength of the bones – a four-year-old's legs would be stronger than a three-year-old's. As for mental stamina, a four-year-old would be more mature, less likely to be startled and get upset. A good three-year-old could beat a poor four-year-old, but, like for like, the older animal would enjoy a tremendous advantage over the Derby course. Moreover, in appearance a four-year-old would not look substantially different from a three-year-old – a few pounds heavier, perhaps – whereas the difference between a two- and a three-year-old would be more marked, which is what had probably aroused Bentinck's suspicions the year before.

A couple of days later, Lord Maidstone, who had been prepared to be a martyr in the *qui tam* actions, weighed in with further accusations against Running Rein and another horse:

> Gentlemen
>
> Sinister reports have been prevalent with regard to the identity of Leander [a horse belonging to German owners called Lichtwald] and Running Rein.
>
> I therefore think it highly important to give the respective owners an opportunity of proving their pedigrees, and their ages.
>
> Under these circumstances I think it right to enter an objection to both of them for the Derby – and beg to say that I shall cheerfully bear all or any part of the expenses which may be incurred by the Stewards in prosecuting an enquiry so essential to the very existence of Horse Racing
>
> Gentlemen I have the Honour to be
> Your obt servant
> Maidstone[17]

As Maidstone was an intimate of Bentinck's it is difficult to imagine that Bentinck had not put pressure on him to write.

But if Bentinck had hoped for decisive action from the stewards of the course he was to be disappointed. As had happened in the Gurney affair, the authorities were inclined to take the course that would incur the least disturbance.

It was fully expected that both cases would have been gone into by the stewards previous to the race [commented *Bell's Life and Sporting*

Chronicle on 26 May 1844] but such was not the case. The stewards simply confined themselves to calling upon the parties connected with the two horses to produce their certificates, and, this having been done those gentlemen considered that sufficient evidence had been adduced to warrant them in permitting the animals to start, with an understanding however, that should either of them win the Derby, the stakes would be withheld, and the objection more fully discussed.

Bentinck was unimpressed with what he saw as a pusillanimous decision, and piled on the pressure: Lord Glasgow now wrote to complain, as did another four men including, interestingly enough, Crockford himself.[18] For the old man who had worked his way from an eighteenth-century fish shop, using guile and a head for figures, to an ostensible position of early Victorian respectability living in a grand house on the newly built Carlton House Terrace, this was his last chance to win racing's ultimate prize. Once again it is possible to see the hand of Bentinck at work here. By now it was well known that he had invested heavily in the Derby favourite Ratan and had suspicions about the jockey Sam Rogers. Moreover, he was not squeamish about forging alliances outside his class when the need arose. The hideous Hill was one of his closest associates, and he would even receive him in his bedroom in Harcourt House, the family's impressive London mansion, while others were made to wait in the hall.

While whipping up a campaign against what he plainly believed to be a substituted horse, Lord George was still pursuing inquiries about the betting on Ratan and the Ugly Buck. In particular he had learned, most likely through Hill, that some suspicious bets had been laid by Rogers against Ratan. He summoned Rogers and asked him to produce his betting book. It took a brave man to stand up to Lord George, both as the panjandrum of the Turf and as a spoilt aristocrat used to getting his own way. However wily Sam Rogers might have been, he quailed in front of Bentinck. 'The long and the short of the matter was, the jockey was taxed by Lord G. Bentinck with secretly betting against the horse which he was going to ride to win, and Rogers, it is said, confessed such was the case,' recorded an anonymous history of horseracing published in 1863. As well as making a full confession of his part in the plot, 'it appears he promised to do his best to win the race, and he was allowed to do so, and the knowledge of what had transpired about the secret kept close, in order that the guilty parties should have the tables turned upon themselves, and let in the hole by means of their own roguery'.[19]

Bentinck suspected John Gully and the Days. In his peremptory manner he convened a highly public kangaroo court at the Spread Eagle Inn. The Spread Eagle served as the headquarters of the Turf during Epsom race week, when part of it was transformed into the landlord Lumley's 'subscription betting-room',[20] entry into which cost five shillings. Mounting the steps at the front of the handsome old coaching inn, in his stag-skin breeches, a whip tucked threateningly under his arm, sunlight glinting on 'the gold pencil case in his fingers', Bentinck produced Sam Rogers's betting book with the flourish of a lawyer presenting a key piece of evidence. He cleared his throat and, surveying the curious crowd that had gathered, addressed them in his curiously accented, reedy, grating voice.

'Gentlemen, I'm going to call over my jockey' – even though Rogers was riding for Crockford this was personal business, and seldom had the feudal nature of the relationship between aristocrat and racing groom been so clear – 'I am going to call over my jockey Samuel Rogers's book, and will thank you to answer to your names and bets.'

A susurrus of incredulity circulated amongst the 'besatined, Circassian-creamed plebeian legs', reported Sylvanus.

'Mr Gul-ly?'

'Here!' growled the veteran leg, removing the cigar from his mouth, which creased into a rictus that was half snarl, half sardonic smile.

'You have bet Samuel Rogers 350/35 against Ratan, I perceive,' observed Bentinck, riffling a little further through the pages of the book. 'Ah! But he stands in a pony with you on the Ugly Buck, it seems.' He glanced up, observing that although the amount was written down the terms of the bet were not stated. 'This has an ugly look.'[21] He paused. 'Are those all the bets you have with Rogers, Mr Gully?'

Bentinck was fishing. At the top of one of the pages was a considerable bet of 10,000–1,000 laid by Rogers against Ratan, and it was this wager that Bentinck was keen to have acknowledged.

But Gully, champion prize fighter, colliery owner, professional hard man and former MP, was not one to be bullied by the shrill aristocrat. He fixed Bentinck with a manly gaze and said slowly, 'If you have any more in my name, and will specify them, my lord, I may then be better able to answer you',[22] after which he replaced the cigar in his jaw and returned to silence.

He was not going to be drawn.

Bentinck went through the rest of Rogers's book, pausing for rhetorical effect to emphasise those transactions entered into with the noted heavy betters of the day. He then snapped the book shut, turned round, and went into the Spread Eagle, leaving the crowd outside lost in an excited babble of speculation about what exactly Bentinck had been trying to prove and against whom he was trying to prove it. Sylvanus, normally a Bentinck enthusiast, comments wryly that it was amusing to see him calling over the book on the steps of the inn, 'as if every bet, under such circumstances, need necessarily be entered in that volume; nor was it less gratifying to see him apparently convinced that Sam was acting fairly by him from having placed it in his hands without demur'.[23]

The decades-old rivalry between Crockford and Gully was to be played out between the two favourites. There were suspicious betting transactions involving huge sums, and sensational allegations that not one, but two horses were a year older than the rules allowed. It was already shaping up to be one of the most contentious of Derbys when the Home Secretary, the autocratic and humourless Sir James Graham, decided it was time he got involved.

*

Back in London on Monday 20 May, two days before the Derby, the Select Committee on Gaming published its report. Broadly speaking, the committee found in favour of Lord George Bentinck and his cronies, recommending that 'Wagering in general should be free, and subject to no Penalty', and expressing the 'opinion that Wagers are not matters which ought to be brought for adjudication before Courts of Law'.[24] Ironically, considering the clouds that were gathering over Epsom as the report was being published, the committee admitted that it had 'some Evidence to show that frauds are occasionally committed in Horse-racing and Betting on the Turf', but they had 'difficulty in suggesting any remedies for this evil'.

They had identified four types of law respecting gaming – those dating from the Middle Ages, sumptuary laws, laws against cheating, but it was the fourth category of law that interested them most: 'those which relate to Public Morals, and which prohibit common Gaming-houses and public Gambling as public nuisances, by which the peace of society may be disturbed, and by which simple and unwary men are liable to be led into dissolute and vicious habits, whereby the morals and interests of the community would be injured'. Unsurprisingly, it was the hells that came in for the committee's opprobrium:

> Your Committee have to express their regret that the existing Enactments for the suppressions of common Gaming-houses have not hitherto accomplished the purpose for which they were intended. It appears that many houses of this description have been open nightly in the Metropolis; and that the parties who are concerned in these establishments have been in the habit of frequenting country races and setting up their Gaming-tables either in booths on the race-course during the day, or in hired apartments in some adjoining town during the night. Your committee cannot too strongly recommend that these nuisances should be effectually put down.

As for the argument that the gambling booths helped pay for the prize money on the racecourses, there was no possible room for misinterpreting their recommendation: the committee 'cannot consider the establishment of gambling-booths on race-courses as in any way an essential accompaniment to racing; and they feel that they cannot too strongly express their opinion, that all such practices ought to be entirely and universally discontinued'. Armed with this report, the Home Secretary swung into immediate and decisive action.

In May 1840 a clergyman visiting England from America had managed – by accident, or so he assured his parishioners – to be in Epsom at the time of the Derby. It was an experience that left a deep scar.

> The first thing that particularly struck me was the mixed character of the multitude. Kindred tastes had brought together, upon that great arena, the extremes of society and into the closest contact. Here were the carriages of the nobility, emblazoned with their appropriate coats of arms and attended by liveried footmen; and the cabs and carts in which not a few of the *ignobile vulgus* had been borne to the scene of dissipation. In the same throng, pressing forward to gaze upon the exciting spectacle, were the gentry and the very off-scouring of the earth, clad in rags and squalidness. In the same group, or standing near each other, might have been seen high born ladies, servant girls, gypsies and the most worthless of the sex, all pressing forward in one broad extended ring to witness the races.

Clearly, the intoxicating social cocktail assembled on the Downs was not a mixture that travelled well: where Frith and Dickens saw a gaudy kind of lyricism the American clergyman saw vice and depravity.

He continued, warming to his homiletic theme:

> How true is it that all the unregenerate whatever may be their circumstances in life possess kindred tastes, which frequently bring them together here and will assuredly place them in the same company and assign them to the same doom in the future world! In the interval between the races, the course ground was filled with

rope-dancers, jugglers, necromancers and various kinds of gamesters; and on the outskirts of the course were fixed up long lines of splendid booths and pavilions, which contained the appliances and paraphernalia of gambling and carousing on the most extended scale.

For him it was hell on earth. 'It seemed as though there was here brought before me, in one concentrated and panoramic view, an exhibition of the world's varied allurements of sin.'[25]

Had this clergyman been visiting the Derby four years later he might not have had such a shock. 'Epsom races commenced yesterday, and a duller commencement we never witnessed,' reported *The Times* on 22 May 1844. The reason was not the weather – after three or four days of wind from the north, a mild south-easterly breeze now brushed the Downs. And after a few early showers the sky brightened and the clouds parted to reveal a 'sunny and genial afternoon'. It was something far more fundamental. Epsom was, if not a ghost town, almost funereal in its demeanour. This was supposed to be the great national holiday, the zenith of the sporting year, the *terminus a quo* or *ad quem* and all that and yet 'there was nothing going on at the inns' and the club houses were shut up 'like houses infected with disease during the prevalence of a plague'.[26] The prospect at the course itself, as already noted, was even more drab. Instead of the lively and licentious carnival atmosphere that had so disgusted the transatlantic cleric four years earlier, 'there was a sort of dullness which seemed to pervade the general business; there was perhaps more moral feeling or at all events less display of what is understood to be the antithesis to it, than on former occasions; there was no gambling, no pea or thimbles, no prick in the garter, no roulette, no rouge et noir, no hazard, no club houses, no anything to excite or even interest.'[27]

The Home Secretary had taken the Select Committee's findings to heart and issued an immediate edict:

All persons playing or betting in any booth or public place, at any table or instrument of gaming, or at any game or pretended game of chance, will be taken into custody by the police and may be committed to the House of Correction, and there kept to hard labour for three months. By order of the Commissioners of the Police in the Metropolis. Thomas Bicknell, superintendent of police. Metropolitan police-office, Scotland Yard, May 20 1844.[28]

The news reached Epsom on Monday evening as the hellites and the publicans, who had paid their money to Timothy Barnard this year – as every year for the last thirty – were preparing their temporary accommodations for race week. All efforts were going into making them as inviting as possible, with their flowers and their awnings, their stocks of sherry, port and cigars and their liveried servants. Even *The Times* felt that 'those who have authorised these new regulations have been guilty of a great breach of courtesy towards the Epsom magistrates in not making them aware of their intentions'.[29]

The citizens of Epsom, too, were taken by surprise, but they were not about to see the great cash crop of tens of thousands of day-trippers who habitually poured into town intent on getting drunk, losing their money and generally having a good day out, go unharvested. Reacting with commendable speed, they got up a petition, a 'memorial of the inhabitants of the Parish of Epsom in the county of Surrey'. This document dispensed with the usual expressions of due respect and got straight down to business. Prefacing their letter to the Home Secretary with the reassurance that they had 'no desire to defend gaming of any description', that is exactly what they tried to do, citing 'peculiar circumstances'. The petition claimed that 'the keeping of gaming tables at the various racecourses around the metropolis has been indirectly sanctioned', pointing out that those 'setting up places for the entertainment of the public' had paid considerable sums which had already been 'appropriated in making stakes for the different races'. It raised the spectre that as a result of this surprise decision 'hundreds of persons must be reduced to a state of destitution'. The inhabitants of Epsom graciously advised the Home Secretary that in future, if given fair warning, they would happily abide by the laws regarding gaming-houses, 'but to do so at the present moment would be a flagrant act of injustice, and would be opposed to every principle of justice and fair play, to which the humblest criminal is said to be entitled'.[30]

A deputation of citizens travelled to London to deliver the document in person to the Home Office, but the Home Secretary declined to meet them. Instead, they had to make do with the Under Secretary, Manners Sutton, who did not give them the answer they were hoping for. Telling them that 'the prayer of their memorial could not be listened to', he informed them that 'Sir James Graham's determination to suppress gambling on racecourses was irrevocable'.

The meeting did not go at all well, and many drew the conclusion that the crackdown on gambling booths was a direct consequence of the *qui tam* actions recently brought against Bentinck and his circle. It would appear that there was a heated exchange between the memorialists and the Under Secretary, giving currency to rumours circulating around Epsom on the night before the race that 'the keepers of the gambling booths and their *employés* would have set Sir James Graham at defiance, and have opened their booths in spite of his interposition and menace'.[31]

Sir James sensed that he might expect trouble from the hell keepers, and fearing a serious outbreak of violence along the lines of the great thimble-riggers' revolt at the St Leger of 1829, applied a lesson learned from the recent gambling-house raids in London. Adopting a measure that was to become popular with many generations of Home Secretaries, he authorised an overwhelming police presence at the race. So, shortly before ten o'clock on the morning of Derby Day, five hundred police, both mounted and on foot, led by armed superintendents, marched through Epsom 'with all the parade of regular infantry and cavalry, as if they were going to take the race-course by storm'.[32] Once on the Downs, they drew up in military formation, then marched off to occupy strategic positions around the course. However, the hellites, doubtless still reeling from the raids on their London premises, had decided to quit the course. All that was left were the skeletal forms of their half-completed and hastily abandoned canvas Sodom and Gomorrah.

13

Derby Day

===

For three hundred and sixty-four days in the year a cannon-ball might
be fired from one end of Epsom to the other without endangering human
life. On the three hundred and sixty-fifth, or Derby Day, a population
surges and rolls, and scrambles through the place that may be counted
in millions.

Charles Dickens, *Household Words*, 7 June 1851

===

The sun rose over Epsom just before 4 a.m. on an overcast Wednesday 22 May 1844, and brought with it a few large drops of rain. But they did little to change the condition of the course, which *Bell's Life* described as 'hard as old nails'.[1] *The Times* concurred: a long drought had left the ground 'as hard, without being as even, as a wood pavement'. Some wags said that the race might as well be run on a turnpike road as the Epsom Downs, where the dust had turned the turf rust-coloured. By about nine o'clock the clouds began to clear, 'making room for the appearance of the sun, which shone pleasantly for intervals during the greater part of the day, its heat being every now and then tempered by large masses of clouds, and by a cooling breeze'.[2]

On Derby Day it must have seemed as though the whole of London was on the move. As Sylvanus picturesquely put it, 'On the eve of the Derby, the mighty Estuary of Life is at flood, and ripples far beyond its usual high-water mark.'[3] In the days leading up to the great contest racegoers from all over the country poured into London. The railway boom was at its height in 1844, the growing network of train lines funnelling huge numbers of racing folk from the north into London. They filled the capital's famous sporting hotels, such as Limmer's on Conduit Street where there was heavy play the night before the Derby. Barely had the nocturnal carousing ceased than the main coaching inns on Piccadilly, such as the White Bear, began to fill up. And from an early hour a sea of traffic made its way over the river to the Elephant and Castle: stately phaetons, elegant curricles and barouches, driven four in hand, with the little grooms known as tigers, like Dickens's Bailey, dangling off the back in their coloured silks. As they scraped alongside rumbling stage coaches and overladen carts they elicited oaths and ribaldry – some good-natured and some not – as all classes of Londoners, along with the many who had travelled by train from the racing centres of the north, moved down through south London and out along the road to Epsom.

Those who did not have a carriage of their own or who had not boarded one of the stage coaches in Piccadilly would wait here to haggle with the drivers of the numerous 'cruelty vans'. These were rudimentary passenger carts, pulled by a single horse typically hauling ten people for a fare of five shillings each all the way to Epsom. Often the horses never made it back to London; returning from the Derby in 1843, Dickens was struck by the sight of horses lying dead at the roadside. Early Victorian England was not yet a sentimental country, so it is safe to assume that the many racegoers who set off on foot at dawn to cover the twenty or so miles to Epsom did so to save their shillings rather than the ill-used and decrepit horses.

The sight of the roads from London to Surrey on Derby Day was one of the great spectacles of the time. In his series of letters to America, Dickens compares this motley matutinal cavalcade to the crowds on Broadway and the triumphs of ancient Rome, but ultimately finds such parallels wanting:

> You can form no adequate notion of the procession to Epsom on the Derby-day. Such leagues of carriages, one closely following another as if linked by design to form a curious vehicular chain, and one in its

linked irregularity so long drawn out. Every possible and impossible carriage was there, including numerous spring-wagons, called spring-vans, or, to speak a-la-cockney, wans (they being generally a bright yellow), filled with the lower orders, journeymen-mechanics with their wives or sweethearts dressed in their holiday garb.[4]

By the time the sun had come out, sightseers had gathered along the road to watch the cavalcade pass by. The inns along the well-travelled Derby route became famous as way stations: the Swan at Clapham, the Cock at Sutton – and, of course, the terminus, Epsom's Spread Eagle. Toll-gates were a favourite spot for spectators to gather, as here there would be lengthy delays (and plenty of oaths and imprecations from the carriages behind) offering a good opportunity to scrutinise the racegoers at close quarters. Some started celebrating the day early – it was not uncommon to see carts loaded with barrels of beer to fortify the passengers on their journey. Boys in the schools that lined the route – Morden Hall Boarding School for Gentlemen was one of the noted landmarks – took great glee in discharging their pea-shooters at the passing carriages.

Although largely good-tempered, the journey was not without its dangers, especially on the return when, much refreshment having been taken, the roads became quite hazardous. Every year the newspapers recorded numerous accidents in ghoulish detail, and 1844 was no exception. A party of London publicans was severely injured when their coach and four was run off the road by another carriage; two northerners got lost, and when returning at dusk to London crashed their gig, leaving one of them unconscious and in a critical condition. Most gruesomely, one of the post-boys from the Spread Eagle was thrown from his chaise while driving a group to the railway station – then in trying to catch up with it again, 'missed his hold, and fell with his neck on the spikes, and powerless to extricate himself was dragged a considerable distance, and, on the chaise being stopped, he was dead'.[5]

The crowds that eventually arrived in Epsom were immense.

'For three hundred and sixty-four days in the year a cannon-ball might be fired from one end of Epsom to the other without endangering human life,' wrote Dickens with pardonable hyperbole. 'On the three hundred and sixty-fifth, or Derby Day, a population surges and rolls, and scrambles through the place that may be counted in millions.'[6] This year, if anything, the crowds were bigger, and, moreover, this Derby was noticed as being different from previous years.

The difference went beyond the excitement in Turf circles about the suspect fluctuation in the betting, the sensational and highly public allegations about over-age horses, the disappointment about the absence of the gaming booths, and even the heavy-handed, quasi-military deployment of police. While the crowd was certainly huge – 'the throngs that poured forth exceeded anything which we had witnessed on previous occasions,'[7] noted one reporter – it was a different type of crowd. *The Times* too noticed something changed about the spectators, who began to arrive from early in the morning: 'There has been a generalisation of equipages, and a stunted economy of appearance and expenditure, which has taken a good deal from the elegance and fashion which formerly graced the Downs: there were more people assembled than formerly, but there was less style.'[8] *Bell's Life* agreed: 'We are bound to say,' noted its reporter with regret, 'that the display of fashionable equipages was far inferior to what we have witnessed in former years.' For the spectators who lined the route from London there were fewer coroneted carriages of 'the quality' to gawp at as they swept towards Epsom; instead, they saw many people rather like themselves trundling racewards in inelegant vans.

'On the turnpike roads the outpouring of vehicles of every possible description exceeded all calculations', generating huge clouds of dust. In particular, the overladen wagons of the working-class Derby Clubs, with their members all dressed up and looking forward to the day they had been saving up for over the preceding months, were seen this year in greater numbers than usual. In many ways this was the first people's Derby. 'In truth, the enormous extension of Derby Clubs, which are now to be found established, not only in almost every house of entertainment in the metropolis and its neighbourhood, but throughout the kingdom, has diffused an interest among all classes,' commented *Bell's Life* in May 1844, 'which creates a stronger inducement than ever to be present at the decision of an event in which the hopes and fears of millions may be said to be involved.'[9]

With Derby lotteries operating in almost every pub in the land, the race was more of a national event than ever before. Country wide, these Derby Clubs had become such a feature that they had attracted the attention of the Select Committee, which had become aware of the worrying trend that in 'some parts of the country mechanics join their five shillings together to back a horse'.[10] The committee heard that 'at those clubs, which are held generally late in the evening, young persons have been induced to meet to spend their time and their money; there they form habits of irregular hours, and the betting and conversation in which they engage tends to weaken the moral principle which ought to govern young men employed as clerks, and entrusted with other people's property'. And if there was one thing more calculated to excite the Select Committee than the weakening of the moral principle, it was the weakening of the moral principle amongst flashily dressed clerks. And it was these same clerks, in their tens of thousands, typified by their irregular hours and their coats of a sporting cut, who made the great exodus from London to Epsom on 23 May 1844.

As the Select Committee of the House of Lords heard, 'It is a great mistake to suppose that the betting is confined to those who go to Tattersall's; men all over the country send up their twenties, fifties and hundreds; it extends all over the country to all classes.'[11] Racing was losing its aristocratic gloss.

Racing was indeed starting to be democratised, for many racing *was* the Derby. By mid-century it was estimated that betting on the Derby was five times greater than on the St Leger (as long ago as 1806 betting on the St Leger had passed the £1 million (£120 million) mark). And this year the number and frequency of railway

services to stations near the course had also increased. The South-
ampton Railway Company ran a service to Kingston station, while
from 7.30 a.m. the London and Croydon Railway was running a
train every twenty minutes to the Stoat's Nest station five miles east
of Epsom Downs. It would be some years before Epsom acquired
its own railway station – the modest wooden structure was built in
1859 – and Epsom Downs station did not open until six years later.
So the three hundred or so passengers who made each trip from
the metropolis had the choice of walking the remaining miles to
the course, thereby combining 'healthful exercise with an agreeable
saving in their exchequer', or taking one of the carriages that were
lined up outside the stations awaiting each train and charged 'from
4s to 10s a-head'.

By midday, Epsom had shed the mournful and wraithlike appearance of a town under martial law that it had presented on the first
day after the Home Office's shock announcement, and regained
something of its usual Derby Day tumult. In particular, an
'immense crowd'[12] had gathered outside the Spread Eagle to follow
the final movements in the betting. The threat of a full inquiry
notwithstanding, there had been more betting on Running Rein
as the race neared. Less than a week earlier the horse hadn't featured,
but since then ante-post betting at sporting taverns such as the
Coach and Horses on Dover Street in London had seen odds of
20–1 coming down to 10 or even 9–1 on the day. Word spread that
getting on to Running Rein even at a late stage and at reduced
odds represented a good investment. But the position at the top of
the betting had not changed. Interest in the Buck had continued
strongly: it was widely held that 'if money can operate in his favour,
his party is certainly the most influential in the market'. Ratan had
remained joint favourite until 'within a very few minutes of the
start, when [he] retired to 3 to 1, leaving Ugly Buck unquestionably
the *premier*'.[13]

This sudden change in the betting could be ascribed to the
physical appearance of Ratan on race day. Sylvanus reported: 'We
ourselves *saw* him grinding up his last supper previous to the race,

with a skin like satin, and muscles of iron. We saw the jockey, Sam Rogers, locked up with him, his bed being made up in the adjoining stall: and we saw Ratan hardly more than twelve hours afterwards, unable to make a gallop, with his coat blue and shivery, and standing in fright.'[14] Another source stated, even more melo-dramatically, that 'his coat was standing like quills on the fretful porcupine, his eyes dilated, and he shivered like a man with the ague'.[15] Dramatic licence aside, it was clear that Ratan had been got at, and in later years suspicion would fall on a Manchester man called Hargraves, memorably described as 'the lucky, screaming gentleman, with the large face and pink eyes'.[16]

From noon to 2 p.m. the course filled up rapidly. Although the 'falling off of the aristocracy was but too apparent',[17] *Bell's Life* commented, there was a knot of fashionable carriages arranged on the hill commanding a fine view of the course, directly across from the grandstand where the other fashionable section of the crowd was gathering. As two o'clock approached, the buzz of conversation among the forest of top-hats by the betting post at the middle of the course intensified. Last-minute bets were made, and shortly before two a huge crowd convened at the saddling area in a hollow just below the starting post to see all twenty-nine horses together for the first time. Upon the ringing of the bell to clear the course, the crowd moved – an exercise accomplished surprisingly readily considering that by now almost a quarter of a million people were on the Downs to witness the greatest sporting spectacle of the age.

The excitement grew, and as the horses made their way to the start the various mounted spectators galloped off to points from which they would follow the race. The practice of the more enthu-siastic to follow on horseback had become increasingly challenging because of the large crowds that now attended the event. Tens of thousands were gathered many rows deep behind the ropes that cordoned off the last eight hundred yards of the course – the final sloping straight, from Tattenham Corner to the winning post. The very back rows were standing on trestles and wagons in order to catch a glimpse of the panting horses and a blur of coloured silk as the horses flashed by on their way up to the grandstand and the finish. The impressive scene was 'rendered still more imposing by the almost breathless silence which prevailed, pending the commencement of the great struggle'.[18]

The stewards had hoped there would be no false starts, but with such a large field there was bound to be some difficulty in getting the horses away cleanly. And so it was on the third attempt, at three o'clock precisely, that the flag dropped and the Derby stakes of 1844 got under way.

The pace was blistering from the outset, and particularly taxing on the horses' legs, given the flint-hard, uneven ground. In addition, it was difficult to follow because of the immense cloud of dust that the twenty-nine horses kicked up. Leander immediately took the lead; the Ugly Buck, ridden by John Day Jr in black with an orange cap, was third, closely followed by Nat Flatman on Colonel Peel's Orlando to his right and Sam Rogers in white silks and a red cap on Ratan to his left. Just behind was Running Rein. The pace was soon too much for all but a handful as they pounded up the hill. After half a mile at this punishing rate, Running Rein moved up easily through the field and took up a position just behind Leander. Then, as they headed into the first turn, with a loud crack like a pistol shot one of Running Rein's hooves made contact with Leander's offside hind leg, above the fetlock. Such was the force of the blow that the bone shattered – into more than three dozen fragments – and Leander's jockey pulled his horse up, letting the rest of the field gallop past. The Ugly Buck kept his position but Running Rein was beginning to ease ahead, now leading by two lengths. It was as the dust-shrouded field cleared the brow of the hill and came into the fabled Tattenham Corner that most of the spectators got their first sight of the horses. They could make out the plain white, albeit dust-streaked, silks of Sam Mann, the jockey on Running Rein, in the lead. Behind him were the purple and orange colours of Colonel Peel's jockeys, with the sky-blue silk and white cap of Lord George Bentinck's Croton Oil further back, visibly weakening as the punishing pace took its toll.

It was only when the horses entered the straight that the distance between Running Rein and the rest became apparent. There were shouts of incredulity that both the Buck and Ratan, backed so heavily and talked of for months, were nowhere. Ratan was in the middle of the field, and on the way down the hill the Ugly Buck had been overtaken by Colonel Peel's two horses, Ionian and Orlando, as well as Colonel Anson's Grey Momus. As they neared the finish it was clear that although the plucky Nat Flatman on Orlando was putting up a good challenge, the race would be won by Running Rein. Orlando finished just under a length behind, confounding the correspondent of *Bell's Life*, who before the race had commented, 'I cannot believe Orlando to have a chance.' Third was Peel's other horse, Ionian, and, aware that the stakes would be disputed, the stewards were careful to place a fourth horse, Grey Momus.

For the final portion of the race along the straight, Running Rein was noticed to have been going with 'consummate ease', 'without even making it necessary for Sam Mann to call upon his horse'. By contrast, the pace had been so strong for the others that the two crack horses Ratan and the Buck, which finished seventh and fifth, were judged to have been 'cut up wretchedly'.[19]

So a few minutes after three o'clock, after two years of training, several months of feverish speculation and a drama-filled last few days, the Derby of 1844 had been won by a horse called Running Rein. Ostensibly owned by the Epsom corn-chandler Alexander Wood, it had seen off challenges from, among others, the brother of the prime minister, the infamous William Crockford, the celebrated prize-fighter-turned-plutocrat John Gully and that aristocratic scourge of the defaulter and levanter, Lord George Bentinck. Except, of course, it hadn't.

Clouds of carrier pigeons were released into the air to carry the results of the race back to London. There the news was eagerly awaited by the legs and the sporting press – the sporting newspaper *Bell's Life* kept pigeon lofts in the roof of its offices (the Derby results were not transmitted by telegraph until 1847). As the news reached London, the Epsom stewards added their signatures to a hastily scrawled note to Messrs Weatherby. 'We the Stewards of Epsom desire you will not pay the Derby Stakes to the owner of Running Rein such stakes being claimed by Col Peel as owner of the second horse.'[20]

The race to win the Derby of 1844 was only just beginning.

14

The Stock Exchange of Betting

'I then attempted to take from my friend a cane he held in his hand to apply it to Mr Scott's shoulders; he resisted giving it to me, and when I turned round I saw Mr Scott, who had in the intermediate time taken off a white coat he had on, in a fighting attitude. I knocked him down.'

Quoted in *Bell's Life*, 7 July 1844

'Tattersal's [sic] which may be called the "Stock Exchange"* of betting, is situated on the right-hand side of Hyde Park Corner, as you enter London from Knightsbridge, and is also the principal horse mart of the metropolis'[1] – thus James Christie Whyte characterised this sporting institution in his *History of the British Turf*. Another observer of London described the eponymous establishment of Richard 'Old Dick' Tattersall: 'Tattersall's gives a *tone* to the *sporting* world, in the same way that the transactions on the Royal Exchange influence the mercantile part of society.'[2]

The foundation of Tattersall's, in 1766, by Old Dick's grandfather and namesake, has an air of folklore about it. The founder had been stud groom to the 2nd Duke of Kingston and was popular with the aristocracy, one of whom, Lord Grosvenor, had one day airily asked him where, in the large fields he owned near the Hyde Park toll-gate – fields today occupied by Belgrave Square – he would like to set up his establishment. Tattersall decided on a charming tavern called the Turf which, as its name suggests, already

---

* An alternative, Turf-centric view resulted in the Stock Exchange being known as 'Little Tattersall's'. E. Hyde, Lords Select Committee, p. 107.

had a following amongst the racing fraternity. Another tavern, Pillars of Hercules, so named as it was on the furthest extremities of the West End, stood on the site later occupied by Apsley House. With the exception of the then modest Lanesborough House, this was the extent of the eighteenth-century metropolis's encroachment on what was a piece of rural England. It was still the resort of highwaymen who might have cantered from the pages of Fielding, with names like Galloping Dick, Gentleman Foster and Seven-stringed Jack.

Roughly coeval with the founding of the Jockey Club, Tattersall's evolved rather than developed, gradually accruing a position of emi-nence in the sporting world rather than having set out to achieve one. It grew quickly; by 1785 it had kennels, coach houses and stabling for 120 horses, as well as a house and offices. Auctions were held at Tattersall's on Hyde Park Corner, known to the racing world simply as 'The Corner', every Monday and Thursday. But increasingly the importance of Tattersall's was being asserted in a different arena, as the home of heavy betting. In the early 1770s Richard Tattersall had opened what had been the laundry of his house as a subscription room,[3] a comfortable club room in which, for a fee, the increasing number of his clients who gambled on horse racing could settle their debts. Settling day at Tattersall's was the Monday following a major meeting. Hundreds of thousands would change hands at The Corner after a classic race – the settling after the Derby of 1816, for example, amounted to £300,000[4] (£36,000,000).

Richard Tattersall is often depicted as an opponent of gambling on horses. This depiction is consistent with the evidence he gave before the Select Committee. Nevertheless, his presence as a witness was indication of his importance in the field. Much as Bentinck evinced both the blithe amorality of the Georgian period and the improving zeal of the age of empire, so Richard Tattersall seems to have been perfectly happy accommodating a personal aversion to betting and a tendency to warn young men against it with his presiding role over the single largest betting market in the world. According to the sporting writer the Druid, who as a young law student had been consulted on the *qui tam* affair, the figures and quotations that came from Tattersall's 'are to racing men what those of Mark Lane* are to the farmer, Lloyd's to the insurer, the Stock Exchange to the broker, or Greenwich Time to the horologist'.[5]

The Corner, as it appeared on settling day after the Derby of 1844, would have been unrecognisable as the homely tavern of the preceding century. Entering through iron railings into a pretty garden-like area of neatly mown lawn, shaded by a large tree and surrounded by a gravel path, the habitué would turn right through a gateway that led to the colonnaded yard, its walls hung with harnesses. Here the auctions were held and horses for sale were paraded amongst the assembled purchasers while the auctioneer surveyed the yard from his rostrum, taking bids. In the centre was an elaborate pump decorated with a fox and horses under a cupola bearing a bust of the 'first gentleman', as George IV had been known as a young man – a rather fitting personage to overlook the raffish scene where the spirit of his reign still prevailed. Not far from the stables and offices and the taproom where the grooms refreshed themselves, the towering townhouses of Belgravia could be seen. The highway robbers (at least, the ones armed with flint-locks rather than betting books) were long gone, and the Duke of Wellington lived in state and splendour just across the road.

The sporting world did not stint itself when it came to its surroundings. The betting men of the Turf had outgrown the old laundry room, and in 1842 a new subscription room had been built and equipped in the manner of the smart clubs of St James's. Although Tattersall would have winced at the idea, his subscription rooms were to horses what Crockford's was to hazard; membership of the rooms was at the discretion of Messsrs Tattersall and Son and had to be applied for in writing along with references. Impressive double doors, ten to twelve feet in height, opened into an imposing, high-ceilinged, almost cathedral-like room. Light streamed in through large sash windows and a central skylight; chandeliers

---

* The *Mark Lane Express* was a weekly farming review.

descended from elaborate ceiling roses. Above the fireplace hung a picture of the famous racehorse Eclipse, near to which race lists and sporting announcements would be tacked to the wall. A reporter was often seen scribbling away in a corner, assiduously noting down the odds being given and taken. A few sporting prints decorated the other walls, joined in later years by 'a couple of engravings of Lord George Bentinck'.[6] To the left, large windows opened on to a patch of manicured lawn known as the 'terrace green'.

Terrace green was capable of accommodating four hundred men, but on the settling day of 1844 there would have been many more at The Corner. Tattersall, although an opponent of betting, according to his *New Rules and Regulations* published in 1843, allowed non-subscribers to enter 'on the annual settling day for the Derby'[7] on payment of a guinea. Thus any little shopkeeper or aspirational clerk with a sovereign to spare who had been turned down for annual membership could come along and play the role of turf grandee for a day. For all Richard Tattersall's personal probity, there were those who, to put it plainly, saw The Corner as a racket. 'The subscription-room at Tattersall's is the private property of the firm from which its name is derived; and the management of it rests solely with the partners of that firm. Without mooting the point, it cannot be to the interest of any one under the moon that it should remain in its present condition – or rather out of condition,' thundered the *New Sporting Magazine*'s reporter. 'And outside the room, around and about the door, what a villainous conclave may be seen on any grand occasion! I never go down the yard, and thread my way through the throng that crowds it at such times without calling to mind Sidney Smith's sketch of the social re-unions at Botany Bay.'[8]

To liken the 'alphabet of faces who congregate in and around the Rooms',[9] to the convicts in Botany Bay is perhaps harsh; nevertheless, Sporting Britain was present in all its roguishness and splendour. The Corner at its zenith was

the most complete place in the Metropolis if you have any desire to witness 'real life' – to observe *character* – and to view the favourite *hobbies* of mankind, it is the resort of the *pinks* of the swells, – the *tulips* of the Goes, – the dashing heroes of the military, – the fox-hunting clericals, – sprigs of nobility, – stylish coachmen, – smart guards, – saucy butchers, – natty grooms, – tidy helpers, – knowing horse-dealers, – *betting* publicans, – neat jockeys, – sporting men of all descriptions, – and the picture is finished by numbers of real gentlemen. It is the tip-top sporting feature.[10]

And on Monday 27 May the excitement was intense. The sporting world was in uproar over the disputed Derby result: nothing like this had happened before. Various rumours about frauds and deception had been bruited about but the story as it was told at The Corner on that eventful Monday was remarkable, even by the standards of the time.

Moreover, the man claiming the stakes was the prime minister's brother. Colonel, later General, Peel was an amiable and, for a soldier, unusually harmless man. Gazetted a few days before Waterloo and judged to be too old to go to war when the Crimean conflict arose, not once did this distinguished soldier see action. Instead, he rose peacefully through the ranks while simultaneously pursuing the parallel careers of Member of Parliament and successful racehorse owner. In possession of a 'princely fortune' and 'a subscriber to all the great stakes', by the 1840s he was one of the most influential men on the Turf. Tall, 'very distinguished in his deportment and scrupulously plain in his costume', his august appearance was further enhanced by the nimbus of smoke from the cigar that was his constant companion.

His prominence in this sordid wrangle must have been an embarrassment for the austere proto-Victorian Sir Robert Peel. However, as racehorse owners went, Colonel Peel was lauded as a model of probity. 'All is based upon the original purpose, the legitimate design of Racing as really a national sport. He is a very extensive breeder of bloodstock, has his private trainer at Newmarket, William Cooper, one of the most respectable men there,'[11] commented the sporting writer Craven approvingly. And as such he looked somewhat out of place among the sporting crowd. On a visit to Tattersall's in 1843 a reporter from the *Illustrated London News* had noted the incongruity of the sight – 'on one side, the gallant brother of the Premier; on the other a group of gentlemen with faces that would compliment an execution'.[12] Whereas others cheerfully called out their bets and flaunted their gambling as a fashion accessory, Peel was discreet in his wagering, seldom betting in public and only then in small amounts. Amidst the brisk and lively atmosphere of The Corner he appeared 'but as a spectator, as carefully aloof from its actual operations as one might be supposed to keep whom chance had associated with a party busied with no savoury office'.[13]

Perhaps the most telling piece of trivia about this popular sporting man concerns the nickname 'Sandwich' that he gave to his horse Orlando upon it winning the Ham Stakes – a sobriquet he thought heartily amusing. No one really considered this man of limited wit capable of uncovering a serious plot to defraud the racing world. Already it was being muttered that the man 'really moving in this matter' was Lord George Bentinck. Peel had not been among the objectors to Running Rein before the race and yet events had moved on briskly after it had been run, suggesting an altogether more focused mind was at work. Already the proposal had been made to refer the matter for arbitration via a barrister appointed by the Lord Chief Justice. This suggestion was put before the horse's apparent owner Wood by the stewards of the Jockey Club, and flatly refused. Upon this, the Club felt they could do no more. 'Colonel Peel immediately placed the matter in the hands of his solicitor, and on Saturday process was served on the stake-holder,'[14] reported *The Times*.

However, for the many gathering at The Corner that day there was much more pressing business to be resolved – namely, the settling of gambling debts. In the early afternoon prominent members of Tattersall's subscription room met to consider what action was to be taken under these extraordinary circumstances. And later that day the following notice was posted: 'At a meeting of the most influential subscribers to Tattersall's interested in the Derby and Oaks settlement, it was unanimously agreed that no possible impediment could exist to the settlement of all accounts on the Derby in which the names of Running Rein and Orlando do not occur, and that therefore the settling will take place this day as usual, with the above exceptions.'[15] Then, with the evening sunlight slanting in through the graciously proportioned windows, the room filled up and bets began to be paid and received.

But that was not all. During the afternoon there had been another surprise – those Derby members were really getting value for their guinea – this one concerning Carlton House Terrace where the famous William Crockford, deprived of his Derby victory, had died. He had been killed, as Sylvanus put it, 'by nothing more or less than sheer anxiety – corroding, gnawing, incurable anxiety'.[16]

His widow promptly wrote to Tattersall concerning her late husband's betting book:

Sir, – I trust that the circumstances which cause me to address you will be a sufficient apology for doing so.

Being ignorant of the custom in use at Tattersall's in situations parallel to the one I now find myself placed in, I consider it best for me at once to place in your hands the betting book of my deceased husband.

You will perceive that in case Running Rein shall receive the stakes there will be a loss of £604, and in case Orlando shall receive them, of £724.

I enclose you, therefore, a draught for the larger sum, and would wish you to apply this sum, together with the receipts from the several losers, to pay, as far as may be, the claims of the several winners.

It is possible that in a case of this sort it is not customary to settle the book; should it be so, I am anxious not to establish a precedent.

With a deep sense of the trouble I am about to impose upon you, I have the honour to be, Sir,

Yours most respectfully

S.F. Crockford[17]

George Byng and Lord Stradbroke, two stewards of the Jockey Club, handed down the opinion that 'every person indebted to the late Mr Crockford on his Epsom account is bound to pay the amount due to the person deputed to settle the same'.[18]

From across the centuries these slips of paper, their pages now brittle and yellowed, may seem straightforward enough, but given the decidedly unstraightforward nature of the world they concerned – the system as imperfect as it was, no single person or body in control, huge sums of money at stake – the result was chaos. It was quickly realised that the decision to a partial settling was flawed. Deferring payment of a portion of the debts would enable unscrupulous betters to take their winnings on settling day and then, if the court case went against their betting books, simply to levant. Furthermore, it was widely held that this partial settling was agreed upon to serve the interests of a few of the 'influential subscribers' who would benefit immediately from the decision.

Soon, angry correspondence on the subject began to fly. 'Sir – the "settling" on Tuesday last is described as a very unsatisfactory affair. How could it be otherwise, when, by the arbitrary dictum of about half a dozen leviathan "bookmakers," the backers of horses who constitute a majority of the subscribers at Tattersall's, were called upon to pay without receiving?' trumpeted one who signed himself Rhadamanthus, annoyed that this compromise favoured professional bookmakers rather than gentlemen speculators. His letter bristled with stentorian rhetoric: 'Now, sir, I ask you, as a man of the world, and one tolerably well acquainted with the present system of Turf speculation, whether this arrangement be either just, or reasonable, or practicable?'[19] 'Fairplay' the sobriquet employed by another indignant turfite, was equally exercised. 'Sir – the decision at Tattersall's of the betters-round [precursors of modern bookmakers] is most favourable to themselves, and most unfair to the backers of horses. The former (by their own rule) get all their gains, save upon one horse, whereas the latter have to pay on all save on two horses. Why should the betters-round (perhaps heavy losers on Running Rein and Orlando) receive nearly all their profits, and retain in their pockets all their losses?' He would have preferred to see 'no settling till the winner of the race was officially announced' or to have all monies deposited in escrow 'in a banker's hands'. Although reasonable, this latter solution was hardly practicable given the rogues who infested the Turf.

A further dimension of uncertainty was added when the settlement of the other major race at the Epsom meeting was called into question, as *Bell's Life* commented: 'In the settlement of the Oaks account, further bickerings also arose, inasmuch as the accounts between the Oaks and Derby races had become so intermixed as to render the adjustments of many books impossible.'[20]

Tempers shortened and, on occasion, snapped. Two members of Tattersall's subscription rooms, a Mr Scott and Mr O'Brien, came to blows in a highly public fracas over the sum of £575 (£69,000). The matter came to its ugly head when, out walking with two friends, Scott encountered O'Brien, who asked of the two men, 'Why do you walk with that wretch?' To which Scott riposted, 'You must not take notice of a thief.' As O'Brien was to put it later, 'I then attempted to take from my friend a cane he held in his hand to apply it to Mr Scott's shoulders; he resisted giving it to me, and when I turned round I saw Mr Scott, who had in the intermediate time taken off a white coat he had on, in a fighting attitude. I knocked him down.' And although O'Brien was to deny it, bystanders said they had to pull him off the unfortunate Scott as he 'kept on striking him on the ground', leaving Scott bleeding 'and in an almost senseless state'.[21]

If the 'sport of kings' maintained any vestigial sense of dignity, it vanished as the circumstances surrounding Leander, the horse whose hind leg was shattered by Running Rein, came to light. Leander had been trained by the less than scrupulous John Forth and was owned by a German father and son called Lichtwald, who were both at the race. Hearing that his horse had been injured, the younger Lichtwald rushed over to Old Forth's deputy, John Norman, and said that he wished 'to have him destroyed on the Course'.[22] Forth himself calmed the nervous Germans sufficiently to advise them against such a precipitous course of action. Instead, the injured horse was loaded on to a van with a couple of other horses and taken back to Forth's stables in Sussex, where it was shot some time between seven and seven-thirty on the evening of Derby Day, and buried soon afterwards.

However, shortly after the remains of the horse were interred, the driver of the Worthing to London stagecoach was spotted walking through Forth's yard carrying a grisly memento: Leander's jawbone. In evidence given later, Norman defended his employer of forty-two years, saying that he would have had no knowledge of this post-mortem amputation. He mentioned that there had been talk of taking a piece of ear or mane by way of a souvenir, clearly inferring that this was little more than tuft-hunting by a racing-obsessed coach driver.

This account is not convincing – cutting off an ear or some hair from the mane is of an entirely different order of butchery from hacking off the lower half of a dead horse's head. Moreover, Forth's son would later contradict Norman's account, saying that the jaw was removed with Old Forth's consent. There can have been only two reasons for this: either he wanted to have the jaw examined to support his contention that the horse was three years old, or it was removed as a precaution against an inquiry into the race calling for Leander's exhumation, whereupon professional examination of the lower jaw would reveal the teeth at a stage of development in advance of a supposed three-year-old. What a vet or horse expert would have been looking for was the loss of what were known as a 'colt's temporary incisor teeth – his sucking teeth', which are present in a two-year-old. 'At two years and a half old, and from that to three, we expect them to lose two teeth above and below – the incisor teeth; and from three and half to four years we expect them to shed four more . . . from four and a half to five we consider that they have their permanent set.'[23]

Of course, all of this might never have come to light had it not been for a group of grave-robbing roisterers. Incredibly, it was not an official inquiry that would discover the half-headless horse. A gang of men had gathered to celebrate the success of John Scott, who had trained Princess, the horse that won the Oaks on the Friday after the Derby. The carousing continued late into the night. As they got deeper in their cups, Julia, the horse Princess had beaten – also trained by Forth, owned by the Lichtwalds and objected to on the grounds of being a four-year-old – became firmly linked in their drunken minds with the well-aired suspicions about the age of Leander. All this, plus Forth's questionable reputation, was enough to have them take action. Fortified by far too much brandy and water, they gathered shovels and lanterns and headed off into the night to the field near Forth's stables where the recently buried Leander lay. Here, having uncovered the body, the guttering lantern light illuminated the gory discovery of the horse's mutilation.

This drunken escapade quickly entered racing folklore, and the events of the evening were turned into a piece of satirical doggerel called 'The Lay of the Lichtwalds'.

> For at Leatherhead, Scott's friends were having a spree,
> And they swore that Leander was four years, not three;
> And the oaths of John Scott, they waxed loud o'er his cup,
> And he seized on a spade, and cried, 'Let's have him up.'
>
> And there lay Leander, all stark on his side,
> With the lower jaw gone that he had when he died;
> And the blood from the cutting lay red on the ground,
> And a four-year-old jaw was the jaw that they found.
>
> And now lies the trainer in sorrow and shame,
> With the cross on his lot, and the cloud on his name.[24]

Keen to avoid the disappearance of the whole head, the grave-robbers decapitated the horse's body, then boiled the head, minus the lower jaw, and took it to a vet, who declared it to be the head of a four-year-old.

The secret was out and Old Forth, seeking to limit the damage and head off (excuse the pun) any accusations, took his part of the jaw to a vet in London, who confirmed what his detractors had been saying: namely, that Leander was a year too old to have been entered for the Derby. It is not clear whether Forth genuinely believed that Leander was a three-year-old or whether he was putting on an elaborate pantomime of his innocence. Be that as it may, he broadcast his injured feelings about the racing world with vigour and warmth. Stopping at Weatherby's office in Burlington Street, he favoured the unfortunate Earl of Stradbroke with his low opinion of veterinary surgeons and with vigorous assertions about Leander's age. But Leander and Julia were not Old Forth's only problems: suspicion was circulating about the age of another horse that he had trained, Foigh A Ballah (sometimes referred to as Faugh-a-Ballah), which had been withdrawn from the Derby at a very late stage, and under mysterious circumstances.

Old Forth brazened it out, firing off lengthy letters to the newspapers refuting their less than flattering reports about him. But his protestations of virtue rang hollow, in particular when answering accusations that, as a trainer who had been working with horses since the previous century, he might have taken it upon himself to look inside the horse's mouth when concerns about age arose. 'I contend that it is not the duty of a trainer to examine the mouth of any horse that is sent to his stables,' he intoned pompously in a long letter to the editor of the *Morning Post*, 'but merely to manage him and to train him to the best of his abilities.'[25]

Clearly, all this gallivanting about town protesting his innocence took its toll on Old Forth. He was too ill to go before the Select Committee of the House of Lords, leaving Forth Jr to explain how his father had sought the opinion of a local vet, John Wood, earlier in the year, who had been categorical in stating that Leander was a three-year-old. But conflicting dates were given for Wood's visits to Forth's stables, and people were more inclined to believe that he had merely been shown another horse that actually was three years old. In addition, by the time young Forth appeared before the House of Lords Select Committee admitting that both Leander and Julia had been four-year-olds, it was clear that if they had ever been in league to defraud the racing world the alliance between the Lichtwalds and the Forths had come to an end. The former had cleared off to Germany, leaving unpaid training bills of £1,000, and were refusing to reply to increasingly irate letters sent by the latter.

Eventually, the Jockey Club swung into action. On Saturday 15 June it met at Charles Weatherby's house on Old Burlington Street in order to close the stable door after the four-year-old had bolted, been buried and boiled, and resolved to tighten up the rules of entry for horses belonging to owners outside the United Kingdom.

Among the staggeringly obvious conclusions they reached were that the fraudulent entries of over-age horses 'not only tend to defraud the owners of those horses that would otherwise have been winners, but are calculated to inflict an injury on the Turf by bringing racing into disrepute, and by deterring honourable men from entering into a competition in which they run the risk of being encountered by such dishonest Rivals'.[26] It recommended tighter controls on the ages of horses entered in races, including, in the case of those from outside the United Kingdom, certification from a relevant racing club. The Jockey Club also staged an inquiry into the Leander affair and banned the Lichtwalds from entering horses in races run under Jockey Club rules.

However, the travails of the Forths, the exhumation and dismemberment of a thoroughbred racehorse and the sundry allegations of skulduggery by dastardly German owners were just an *amuse-bouche* for the banquet of scandal that was about to be served.

15

A Game of Musical Stables

'I have a machine for the purpose and it is easily done.'

Jockey Club Inquiry, evidence from Thomas Ferguson[1]

The scandal concerning the great Derby of 1844 began on 16 September 1841 at Tattersall's Doncaster sales. Abraham Levi Goodman was in a buying mood that early autumn day. He picked up four young horses, including two colts, one black and one chesnut, and a brown filly. But it was a bay colt with black legs belonging to Sir Charles Ibbotson and engaged to run in the Derby of 1843, knocked down to Goodman for £52 10 shillings, that would inspire his audacious plan to steal the Derby of 1844.

As a Jew and a commoner, Goodman did not share Lord George Bentinck's advantages of birth, advantages that counted for so much in the early years of Victoria's reign. However, while he would for ever be an outsider in the patriarchal Britain of the time, he shared Lord George's dream of owning a Derby winner.

Goodman had been accompanied to the Doncaster sales by a friend called Henry Higgins, a Northampton coachmaster. At the same race meeting was another Northamptonshire man, George Worley, a farmer who owed a few pounds to Higgins and agreed to look after the bay colt in one of his paddocks in settlement of his debt. The colt was a fine-looking thoroughbred. Running around Worley's paddock, it stood out from the hacks and hunters and attracted plenty of attention from visitors. It remained with Worley until the end of January 1842, and at some point during its stay with him injured a foreleg. Worley would later recall that 'something frightened [the colt] and he jumped at a wall and hedge and cut himself severely on the arm just beside of the near knee'.[2] But by the time the horse was returned to Northampton at the beginning of 1842 the injury had healed, leaving a three- or four-inch scar.

All this time Higgins is described as having behaved as if he were the owner of the colt, and after George Worley's the animal spent time in the stables at Vigo Cottage, where Higgins lived. By May it had moved again to a paddock owned by a Mr Markham, a Northampton attorney, where it remained during July and August and where it met with another accident, again on the foreleg close to the knee. After that, the horse disappeared to London, so Higgins said, adding that it was owned jointly with Goodman and was to be entered for the Derby of 1843. Nor was this bay colt with its much injured knee always known by the same name; sired by Gladiator, it was originally intended to be called Spartacus, but the name was later changed to Maccabeus. And it was by this name that Higgins and Goodman talked him up throughout the winter of 1842–3, suggesting to friends that they should 'stand in about Maccabeus'[3] for a few pounds.

Meanwhile, Goodman was busy adding to his stud. Using an intermediary called Henry Stebbings, he paid £28 for a foal sired by the Saddler and born on 11 May 1841 to a mare owned by a surgeon in York called Cobb. And so, at the time the bay colt by Gladiator was running in Mr Worley's paddock in January 1842, another bay horse with black feet arrived in London by train from York and was taken to Goodman's stables in Chapel Mews. It stayed there for two nights and a day before being moved, on 20 January, to livery stables kept by James Wilson Pearl near Dorset Square. There it remained until the end of the month, when it was taken to William Bean and put in the paddocks around his house in the then semi-rural village of Finchley, staying there until 24 September.

It could be a coincidence that the foal under Mr Bean's care in Finchley was almost identical in colouring to the colt sired by Gladiator that Goodman had bought in Doncaster the preceding autumn. Accidentally or not, this other bay foal soon acquired a scar near the knee on the near foreleg that was uncannily similar to the one carried by the Gladiator-sired colt. Mr Bean would later claim that it was in 'getting over some low palings to get to some horses in the adjoining field of mine'[4] that horse sustained a slight injury, breaking the skin and taking off some hair. And it could also have been that Goodman had no particular plan in mind for the Gladiator colt beyond entering him for the Derby of 1843. However, some time during the spring of 1842 Goodman's undeniably agile and dishonest mind began to conceive an elaborate deception.

In July that year, when Goodman was at the Liverpool races, he met the characterful Irish owner and jockey Thomas Ferguson. Ferguson was another of the fascinating individuals inhabiting the murky world of British racing during the early years of Victoria's reign. Described as possessing natural gifts of horsemanship and a similarly innate ability to judge a horse, he had originally been apprenticed at a linen factory but had soon made the switch to racing, prompting the witticism that he was 'exchanging calico for silk'. By the 1830s he was a winning rider and owner: in 1838 he was the owner who won the greatest number of races in Ireland. But he felt that Ireland was not a large enough canvas to accommodate his designs: 'There is not a butcher in Liverpool who would make more in one throw over a match for a pony than the greatest robber of all would make in Ireland if he began with the Kirwans in June and ended with the Rossmore Handicap in October.' The following year he entered three horses in the Grand National, riding one himself. Ferguson was a strong character who liked to get his own way, and 'it was not only your money that was in danger if you interfered with his plans'.[5]

Hot-tempered and prone to gout, which did not improve his mood, his nickname was Choleric Tom. He was certainly not above the sharp practices of the day when it came to manipulating horses and races; he once rode the favourite in an Irish race into the sea because it suited his betting arrangements. His ambitions and his abundant natural ability, alloyed as they were with a minimum of scruples, inevitably brought him into the orbit of Lord George Bentinck. And he employed many of Bentinck's signature tactics, such as threatening to scratch a horse from a race unless he got the odds he wanted. The two men were similar in many ways and their relationship seems to have swung between friendship and enmity. In a letter written to William Gregory in 1841, Bentinck recalls what sounds like a very pleasant day spent at Ferguson's home, Rossmore Lodge, looking over racehorses and seeing Ferguson's famous Harkaway in training. But then, unable to get decent odds on this superb horse at a particular race because Bentinck had taken the best odds and effectively closed the market, Ferguson is supposed to have ranted about his lordship: 'By God, the public must understand that Harkaway is my horse, to win money for me, and not for any damned fellow, either a lord or a lord by courtesy and a thief by the curse of God.'[6]

Here, thought Goodman, was a man with whom he could do business. He made particular inquiries about one of Ferguson's horses, Goneaway, asking detailed questions about his colouring and establishing that he was a bay like Maccabeus, albeit with a white heel and white star. He arranged to hire Goneaway from 20 September 1842 to 20 September 1843, for £500 and half of any prize money that the horse might win. Goodman in fact had no interest in running Goneaway to win anything – at least not as Goneaway. As it happened the horse was not handed over to him until 6 January 1843, by which time he had written to Ferguson requesting that he 'send him some of the black hair from the horse's leg'.[7] Goodman went to Liverpool to collect Goneaway. The two men met at the quay and repaired to the Mersey Coffee House to complete their transaction, Goodman handing over £400 and an IOU for the remainder. Ferguson then returned to Dublin and Goneaway joined the merry-go-round of horses that comprised Goodman's highly mobile stud, circulating as it did between his house in Sutton and sundry farms, trainers, horse breakers and London stables.

The next time Ferguson saw Goneaway was at Goodman's house in May of 1843, not long before the Derby, by which time he had become sufficiently friendly with Goodman to be his houseguest. Goodman thought it was time to take Ferguson into his confidence and into the stables, where he asked if he could identify the horse standing in front of them: Ferguson recognised it as Goneaway, but with some difficulty. His appearance had altered dramatically. The 'very long bushy square heavy tail which reached nearly to his hocks'[8] was gone; 'his tail had been cut and his foot and near hind pastern had been dyed black'. The colouring had been so well done that it was impossible to tell it apart from the others. Ferguson was furious and rounded on Goodman: 'To be sure I would know him anywhere, but damn you, you have cut his tail off and what do you mean by that? You might as well cut his head off or his leg off and say that would not hurt him.'

Goodman, clearly hoping to recruit him into his plan, informed Ferguson he was going to run Goneaway in place of Maccabeus in the Derby. According to evidence he was later to give at a Jockey Club Inquiry, Ferguson was outraged at the suggestion – although perhaps his indignation was retrospective. He insisted that Goneaway was sure to be recognised and that if questioned he would not collude in the cover-up, apparently saying, 'I will not tell an untruth for any man living.' But Goodman knew men as well as he knew horses. He assured Ferguson that 'Lord George Bentinck saw the horse at William Sadler's' – Sadler was Goodman's trainer – 'and he knew Goneaway and he did not recognize him.'

The way Ferguson recounted it later, nothing, not even the tantalising prospect of deceiving his upper-class rival, would shake him from his determination to foil Goodman's plan. If he is to be believed, it was at this point that Goodman cancelled his plan to enter Goneaway as Maccabeus for the Derby. Disappointed on finding that Ferguson was not the man he thought he was, Goodman told him that he might as well take the horse away, which he agreed to do. However, when Ferguson suggested that he might run Goneaway for the Goodwood Cup, Goodman became anxious and 'urgently remonstrated against him entering him to run in England in his proper name as he would be sure to be recognised as the horse he had run as Maccabeus at the Epsom Spring Meeting'[9] where the horse had finished second. Ferguson was to claim later that he would have carried out this threat and entered the horse – had events not overtaken him.

That Ferguson continued to visit Goodman and felt it necessary to move his horse at about two o'clock in the morning of 7 June to the Foley Place livery stables, then immediately to Euston Station, ensuring that he and the horse were aboard the *Britannia* by the time it steamed out of Liverpool harbour at six o'clock that evening, indicates that his conscience was not entirely clear. The passage, which lasted twenty-four hours, was so rough that the ship lost its foremast and Goneaway its life. By the time the horse was unloaded in Dublin, again at 'night between 12 and 1', it was very sick and by nine o'clock the same morning it was dead. The carcass sold for five shillings to the carrion butcher, carrion butchers being 'the people who go about buying sick and dead horses for dog's meat',[10] as one Dominick Holland put it at the Jockey Club Inquiry.

So a little over a week after the 1843 Derby had been run, the horse that had been second favourite had been spirited out of England and made into Irish dog food.

Goneaway's death and tidy transmutation into a comestible was undoubtedly convenient for Goodman, as, when he had entered it for the Derby under the name of Maccabeus, it had attracted considerable attention as a likely winner. One press report had noted that 'Maccabeus has become decidedly second favourite, the party have backed him to win an immense stake, and do not *hedge*'.[11] In the event neither Maccabeus nor any horse bearing that name started in that particular Derby, to the disappointment of George Worley, the farmer who had looked after the real Maccabeus and had gone to Epsom to watch the race. Bumping into Higgins, he had asked where Maccabeus was, and was told curtly that the horse 'was ill and could not run'.[12] Shortly afterwards Higgins put the word out that Maccabeus was dead, only a slight distortion in that the casualty was the horse pretending to be Maccabeus.

This was far from being the end of Goodman's plans to steal horse racing's greatest prize. Like a megalomaniac villain in a melodrama, he thought big: he may have been foiled in his bid to rob the racing world at the Derby of 1843, but he would be back. He had built up a complex machinery of disguise and deception with which he hoped to win the Derby not once, but year after year.

While at Goodman's in Sutton in May that year Ferguson had been shown another horse, an inch or two over fifteen hands, 'a stout bay'. As the horse placidly munched grass nearby, with a flourish Goodman announced to the astonished Ferguson, 'That is Maccabeus and I mean to run him next year for the Derby.' He asked if Ferguson did not think him uncannily like the made-over Goneaway, and was about to enlarge on his plans when he heard a carriage pull up. He left Ferguson in the stable with the horse for about fifteen or twenty minutes, during which time the Irishman looked into its mouth three times and came to the opinion that he was a three-year-old. While still at close quarters with the animal he also noticed 'a mark on one of his forelegs'.

Later on, once his visitor had left, Goodman showed Ferguson another horse, at grass on the lawn outside the house. He was 'a little darker than Maccabeus', but presumably it was nothing that a little expertly applied dye could not sort out. This, announced Goodman with pride, was a horse sired by the Saddler, a prize racehorse owned by the diminutive sportsman Squire Osbaldeston whose own feud with Bentinck had ended in a farcical duel. Goodman declared that he would enter it in another's name for the Derby of 1845. By now even the fiery Ferguson was taken aback and unnerved by the audacity and scope of the operation. When he thought Goodman was out of sight he decided to look inside the mouth of his own horse, Goneaway. Goodman surprised him in the middle of his extempore dental examination and asked what he was doing.

'I thought you might be playing tricks with his teeth as well as his tail,' answered the nettled Irishman.

'I knocked the tusks out of him but they are springing up again,' said Goodman blithely, adding in an offhand tone, 'I have a machine for the purpose and it is easily done.'[13]

For some years it was a puzzle to racing historians how Maccabeus, a much fancied second favourite for the Derby of 1843, died and then came back to life to win on 9 October of the same year at Newmarket as a two-year-old called Running Rein, claiming the Saddler pedigree of the horse that Ferguson had seen on Goodman's lawn during the summer. 'It seems incredible that, with such an obvious clue, no one should have challenged him as the quondam second favourite for the Derby whom Goodman had run at Epsom the previous April and can scarcely have been so soon forgotten by everyone,'[14] wrote the author of *The History of the Racing Calendar and Stud-Book* in 1926.

Given that the horse that was second favourite for the Derby of '43 was in fact the dyed, docked and shortly thereafter dead Goneaway, and the real Maccabeus now appeared as Running Rein, Goodman's success is more explicable – though it did not go entirely unremarked. 'There were some grounds for supposing that Mr Goodman's Running Rein was a year older than he ought to be to qualify him for a two-year-old race; and, to speak plainly, the colt is as well-furnished as many of our bona fide three-year-olds,' ran one report. While commenting on the betting coup, James Rice in his *History of the British Turf* (1879) remarked, 'Mr Goodman made a good speculation of this, but, as we have before observed, the paying was done under protest. Running Rein, if he be only two years old, is one of the forwardest that ever caught our eye.'[15]

This was the race at which Goodman was nearly caught out by Bentinck, who prompted the Duke of Rutland, whose horse had finished second, to lodge his objection. For a while it was touch and go for Goodman as to whether he would pull it off. A meeting of the stewards of the Jockey Club was called, where the duke demanded 'that the horse's mouth should be examined by competent persons'. Goodman flatly refused, and instead called upon some witnesses including Mr Bean of Finchley to support his case. At the Jockey Club Inquiry Lord Stradbroke stated, 'The stewards repeatedly urged Goodman to allow the horse's mouth to be examined for the sake of his character' – perhaps not the most compelling and persuasive argument to use on a man like Goodman – 'and to prevent future objections.'[16] But Goodman was implacable and in the face of his obduracy the duke did not press his objection.

Privately, Goodman was seething with rage at the behaviour of his confederate, Higgins. When, on the day of the race, Higgins had encountered the Northamptonshire farmer George Worley at Newmarket, he had said that he recognised 'Running Rein' as the horse he had looked after during the winter of 1841–2. Goodman's problem was that Higgins was a loudmouth who had not been particular or careful about whom he had talked to concerning the plan. With Higgins at the Newmarket meeting that day was a trainer called Drage who also recognised 'Running Rein' as the Gladiator colt he had examined for an injury to the near leg just above the knee. Higgins admitted to Drage that the 'colt bought from Cobb was bought for the purpose of being personated by the colt by the Gladiator which was a year older'.[17] During July Higgins had visited Worley with a horse dealer called Odell and boasted, 'I can tell you who will win the Derby next year' – then, running his finger down the list of entries in his copy of the *Guide to the Turf,* pointed to the line reading, 'Mr Goodman's Running Rein by the Saddler out of Mab'.

Irritated by Higgins's gloating, knowing air, Worley had said, 'Damn it Henry I think that was my horse', meaning the bay colt he had looked after.

Higgins hesitated, then spoke confidentially: 'There are only us three present – it is the colt you had but that is to go no further.'[18]

Some time later Higgins had tried to bluff Worley into believing that he had lied and, angry at being taken for a fool, Worley had started talking about the plot to anyone who would listen. Doubtless word got back to Goodman, who sent Higgins round to apologise and patch things up, even going as far as inviting Worley to the Derby.

In light of his close shave at Newmarket, Goodman took care not to race the impostor Running Rein again until the Derby, notwithstanding the horse's engagements which included an entry in the prestigious 2000 Guineas. In January 1844 the horse was sent to William Smith, a trainer at Epsom, where one of Smith's employees heard that the horse was more than three years old and examined the mouth. He found, in spite of Goodman's machine for removing them, the telltale 'tusks'. He was later to aver that he 'never saw a three year old colt with tusks nor a four year old without'; moreover, he noted that 'he had the ways of an old horse, turned around with docility and appeared to know what was required of him'.[19] Clearly, the concerns about Running Rein's age were not going to go away. So Goodman took steps to distance himself from the controversial horse, hoping to obscure the situation by ostensibly relinquishing ownership of it to the Epsom corn-chandler Alexander Wood.

The accepted version of events is that Wood was the unwitting dupe of Goodman, receiving the horse in lieu of money owed to him and honouring its engagement at the Derby. However, from the testimony given at a subsequent inquiry set up by the Jockey Club to look into the scandal, it would appear that Wood was more closely involved in the fraud than has hitherto been thought. Goodman was seen frequently at Smith's yard, sometimes visiting the horse with Wood even though he was no longer supposed to own it. Moreover on 24 April 1844, while at Newmarket, he paid the forfeit for the entry he had made for the 2000 Guineas, when by that time the horse was supposed to be owned by Wood.

Nor was Wood's behaviour that of an unwitting honest man. Lumley, the landlord of Epsom's premier sporting tavern the Spread Eagle, had also heard the rumours about Running Rein's age. He engaged John Bartlett, a vet from Dorking, to examine the horse at Smith's stables, which he did on 9 or 10 January. Bartlett's initial verdict was that it was the mouth of a three-year-old, but added that he was not certain and that he would welcome a second opinion, recommending a vet on Bond Street. Wood did little to allay Bartlett's suspicions when he told him that he 'should stand £100 to nothing', to which he made no reply. Calling back at Smith's stables a few days later, Bartlett asked whether the other vet had been to see 'Running Rein', and was told that 'Mr Wood had made up his mind that no more veterinary surgeons should see the horse'. At that moment Bartlett noticed the horse walking in the paddock, so went and examined his mouth on the spot. This time, his eye sharpened by suspicion, he saw marks indicating that the last four incisors had had their sharp edges 'filed down nearly close to the mouth' and, upon looking closely at all the other teeth, he saw evidence to indicate that they had all been filed or cut so as to give the impression that the horse was at a less advanced stage of development than was the fact. He was now in no doubt that the horse was four years old and informed the trainer, Smith. He then went on to Lumley at the Spread Eagle, who told him to go and tell Alexander Wood. He was on his way to Wood's house when he met him in the yard and told him the news, whereupon Wood 'begged that [Bartlett] would not say a word about it'.

After that, the whole business seems to have taken on the character of a personal crusade for Bartlett. He went back to the trainer the following day to give him a lesson in equine anatomy, comparing the mouth of 'Running Rein' with that of an actual three-year-old. Smith appreciated the difference but, like Wood, begged him to say no more about it. However, to keep silent was clearly not in Bartlett's nature. On 24 January he presented himself at the Spread Eagle and informed Lumley – presumably, the nearest that out-of-season Epsom had to a racing official – that unless Wood made Bartlett's views known, he would write to the Jockey Club. Lumley called for Wood, who said he was busy and could not come, so the two men then went to Wood's house. They found him walking in his yard. When Bartlett told him he would be writing to the Jockey Club, Wood turned on him. There was no more begging – rather, plenty of abuse and sinister accusations that he was 'mixed up with some party'. The fire of righteousness burning in his breast, Bartlett told Wood that he would find him at the Spread Eagle in a quarter of an hour, should he want to suggest any alterations to the letter that he was going to write to the Jockey Club. Wood, of course, declined the invitation and Bartlett wrote to the 'parliament'* of racing:

> Dorking 24th January 1844
> To The Hon'ble the Stewards of the Jockey Club
> My Lords and Gentlemen
>   Having lately been called up by Mr Alexander Wood to examine a horse of his now standing at Mr Smith's stables at Epsom and which is entered in the name of Running Rein for the next Derby, particularly with reference to the age of the horse I think it my duty to apprise you that my decided opinion is that the horse is four years old and that such was my opinion I forwarded in writing to Mr Wood. I inform you of this in order that you may take any steps you deem necessary to make the fact known to the public.
>   I am yrs
>   John Bartlett junior.

He was still waiting for a reply on 4 February when an item in *Bell's Life* caught his eye, prompting him to write again. This time he sent a letter not to the parliament of racing itself, but to its civil service arm, Weatherby's, repeating his conviction that Running Rein was a four-year-old. He then went on to add,

> In today's Bell's Life in London there is a letter from Mr Alexander Wood on the subject in which after giving a most incorrect version of the circumstances attending my giving the opinion in question he concludes by saying that he has applied to the breeder from whom he has received sufficient evidence to prove that the horse is not yet quite three years old. I still retain the same decided opinion as before and as the correctness of it is thus unfeigned it would be satisfactory to all

---

* 'Horse-racing . . . has also its code of laws – a club called a Jockey Club being its parliament.' Charles Dickens, Letter XXXI, *American Notes for General Circulation* (1842), p. 70.

parties if my opinion was refuted or confirmed and I shall esteem it a favour if you will inform me whether supposing Mr Wood too assents the Jockey Club would appoint a competent person to examine the horse of what steps would be taken by them in the matter. I trust you will excuse my troubling you with this and will favour me with a line by Monday or Tuesday's post.

The following day Charles Weatherby, Clerk to the Jockey Club, did favour Bartlett with more, though not much more, than a line on the subject, but it was hardly what he hoped for.

Sir

I am directed by the stewards of the Jockey Club to acknowledge the receipt of your letters of the 24th January and the 4th inst, and to inform you in reply that the question of the age of the horse called Running Rein is not at present in such a shape as to give them any power to interfere in the matter.[20]

Displaying a complete absence of interest that would have impressed Pontius Pilate, the Jockey Club declined to act on the concerns now being widely voiced; leaving Wood and Levi Goodman able to proceed with their plan to use Maccabeus, alias Running Rein, to steal the Derby stakes.

16

The Full Majesty of the Law

─────

I knew the individuals composing the Running Rein party, and their solicitor; I immediately put myself in communication with them and they advised me not to hedge a shilling because every pound I hedged was money lost. The solicitor's name was Gill, and he being in possession of all the evidence, and a lawyer, too, I was guided entirely by his advice and opinion. He also assured me that theirs was a 'plain unvarnished tale' and it was impossible to upset it.

Squire Osbaldeston, *Autobiography*[1]

─────

If the Jockey Club had been reluctant to get involved in the case, the same was not true of Lord George Bentinck. He had been thwarted the previous autumn when the Duke of Rutland's objection had not been upheld and, as has been shown, he was not a man to take such a defeat well. He approached this new challenge with redoubled energy. He was most fortunate to have on his side the good-natured and tractable Colonel Peel, who as the owner of the second-placed horse was entitled to lodge an objection. As well as being a man of Bentinck's own social circle with a relatively clean reputation – the only shadow over his good name was a libel action he had fought and won against the *Sunday Times* when it printed a story suggesting he had scratched a horse from a race to suit his betting book – he was an easy-going individual who was easily managed.

How different it would have been if, instead of colliding with Running Rein, Leander, as the other four-year-old in the race, had gone on to take second place. Given that the Lichtwalds and Old Forth were as blackguardly as Goodman, Higgins, Wood, Stebbings et al., any protest against the result would have been highly unlikely. This would have left Goodman clear to claim the stakes, plus the tens of thousands in bets owing to him, and to start planning his assault on the Derby of 1845. Indeed, there were those who believed that the Goodman and Lichtwald camps had forged an alliance in order to pull off just such a coup. There was a precedent for this type of scam: in 1840 suspicions had been voiced about the circumstances in which Goodman's Mungo Parke had won against Lichtwald's horse Shark in a match at Newmarket during the Houghton meeting.

Bentinck doubtless appreciated his good fortune that the Leander fraud had already been uncovered and the danger neutralised. Nevertheless, he was anything but complacent. Even though he, or rather Peel, would have his day in court, the outcome was far from sure.

Life, as Bentinck saw it, was a series of battles. For his existence to mean anything he needed to have a fight on his hands and a focus against which to direct his anger and his energy – whether the rascally Days or, in later life, the free-traders. For the moment, however, the Running Rein case was the fourth act in the ongoing drama of his class-inspired struggle against the disreputable elements in British racing. First he had pursued individual defaulters; then those defaulters had fought back by launching their *qui tam* actions. He had countered this with his skilful manipulation of parliament, which had resulted in the Select Committee and the crackdown on gambling hells; and now the battle was moving into a new phase in which he would have to play a new role, that of detective. The idea of a detective was an alien one in the Britain of 1844; the police force itself was a relative innovation, and it would be over forty years before the first of Arthur Conan Doyle's Sherlock Holmes stories would appear. But Lord George Bentinck's work on this case would have impressed Dr Watson.

With millions at stake, he was far from being the only one looking for, or hoping to conceal, vital clues that would swing the case one way or the other. His adversary was his equal in terms of the single-mindedness and ruthlessness with which he would pursue his goal. 'Where money is in the way, Goodman Levy does not stand upon trifles,'[2] noted C.M. Prior in his *History of the Racing Calendar*. But then nor was Bentinck above turning the relationships of others to his advantage. He lost no time in starting his investigations, mobilising his informers in the racing world.

'At the time when the Derby of 1844 was run, I was on terms of the warmest friendship with "Tom Ferguson," of Rossmore Lodge, Curragh, who had no secrets from me,' one racing man was to recall later. He continued:

> This fact was well known to one of Lord George Bentinck's most trusted commissioners, who upon the evening of the day on which Running Rein ran first for the Derby, came post-haste from Epsom to my house in London and induced me to write to Ferguson, so as to obtain from him information with which he was acquainted as to the substitution for the Maccabeus colt of an Irish horse who, under the name of Running Rein won the Derby in 1844. The commissioner in question stood to win a very large stake on Colonel Peel's Orlando, and promised me faithfully that he would put me on a large sum to nothing if I assisted in unveiling the fraud. In addition, he pledged me his most solemn word that Tom Ferguson's reply to my letter should be kept secret, and shown to no one.
>
> When Ferguson's letter reached me three or four days later, Lord George's commissioner was at my house expecting it. I, little knowing what sort of man I was dealing with, was persuaded by him to let him have the letter, which he solemnly pledged himself to return to me the same evening. From that day forward I never again was in the same room with him, and never spoke to him again. His promises proved to be as faithless as he was himself.[3]

This piece of work has Harry Hill's dirty fingerprints all over it.

It would appear that the frank and candid letter sent by Ferguson to a trusted friend and purloined by Bentinck was sufficiently damning to send Bentinck to Ireland. With his usual pre-cipitousness, he set off the instant he read the letter, the weekend

The betting post at a racecourse was a scene of frenzied pre-race speculation as last-minute bets were made. The throng clamouring to make their wagers in the tense minutes before a major race such as the Derby could be immense.

Overleaf The journey to Epsom was almost as much of a spectacle as the race itself, with spectators lining the road from an early hour. The taverns en route became much cherished landmarks on the annual exodus from London.

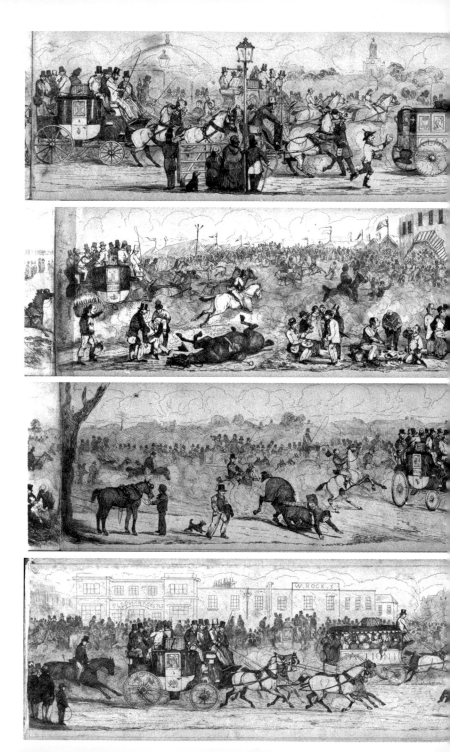

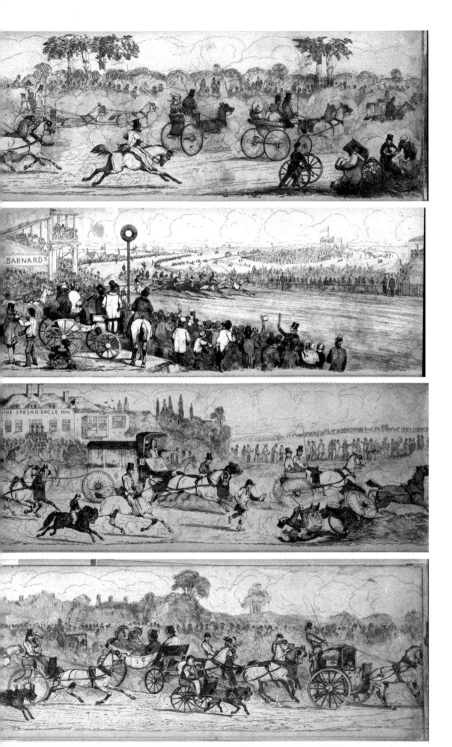

The Derby of 1844 was the most crooked ever run, and also the longest: it started at 3 p.m. on 22 May, but the final result only became clear in early July after a sensational court case that, for a few days, obsessed the country.

Although this early photograph was taken in the following decade to aid Frith in the composition of his canvas, it gives a flavour of Epsom racecourse on Derby Day in the mid-nineteenth century.

The journey back to London could be lethal. Returning from the Derby in 1843, Dickens was struck by the large number of horses lying dead by the side of the road, these worn-out nags were simply unequal to the task of hauling their human cargo back to the metropolis. Congestion was terrible: race-goers in an advanced state of refreshment frequently lost control of their carriages adding to the mayhem, while criminals lurked on the country roads ready to waylay those who had had a profitable day at the races.

TATTERSALS. *Tom and Bob, looking out for a good one, among the deep ones.*

Tattersall's was the metropolis's premier equine auctioneer and the epicentre of the heavy betting on horse races. Given the financial significance of the transactions carried out there it was known as the Stock Exchange of Betting, though there were Turfites who considered it more appropriate to call the real Stock Exchange 'Little Tattersall's'.

Settling Day at Tattersall's, when the racing world gathered to settle its debts, was a solemnly observed ritual – or it was before the Levanters and confidence tricksters moved in.

An excerpt from a letter from Lord George Bentinck to his brother William after the sale of his stud in September 1846.

Alexander Cockburn represented Wood in court and his performance is chiefly remembered for his scathing attacks on Lord George Bentinck. He expressed his repugnance for the sordid world of racing in splendid terms, saying that 'the spotless purity of the judicial ermine is sullied and soiled when it is brought into contact with impurities so gross as those which connect themselves with the Turf'.

Baron Alderson: the sporting judge who presided over the legal proceedings seemed to enjoy being the centre of national attention and always had a quip to hand, yet his wise-cracking exterior masked the mind of a brilliant classical scholar and supremely talented lawyer.

The Court of Exchequer was one of the picturesque anachronisms that characterised the British legal system in the early Victorian era. For sheer pageantry, eccentricity and obfuscatory mumbo jumbo the Court of Exchequer is right up there with the Court of Chancery that casts its long shadow over *Bleak House*, and Doctors' Commons, affectionately satirised in *David Copperfield*.

The Solicitor General, Frederick Thesiger, represented Peel and, by extension, the interests of the aristocratic Turfites. The outcome of the case hinged on pieces of evidence such as a bottle of hair dye, which Thesiger produced with a flourish, holding the offending colourant aloft and peering at it as if the truth were dissolved in the inky liquid.

following the Derby. On arrival at Rossmore Lodge, Bentinck found Ferguson ill in bed with gout and not disposed to see him. Not to be put off, Bentinck sent word that he had his letter, whereupon Ferguson agreed to see him in his bedroom and tell him everything he knew about Goodman's use of Goneaway.

Armed with Ferguson's information, Bentinck returned to England to pursue his inquiries with customary vigour, turning his time and his seemingly inexhaustible energy to what had become a full-blown detective investigation. He had been lucky to get hold of Ferguson's letter and, convinced as ever of his own rectitude, had absolutely no scruples about the methods used to acquire it. One of the most promising leads to come out of his sickbed interview with Ferguson in Ireland was the dyeing of Goneaway. He was determined to uncover the source of 'the "Tyrian dye," celebrated for the mutation of whiskers, for application to the leg of Goneaway'.[4]

The problem was that in 1844 London was a teeming metropolis, and male vanity, while perhaps not at its Regency zenith, was still considerable. In *Martin Chuzzlewit*, published the same year, one of the features frequently remarked upon is the lustrous dyed black hair of mountebank financier Montague Tigg. Public figures including Lord Palmerston, who sat on the Select Committee investigating gambling, wore rouge. So a middle-aged man purchasing hair dye some months earlier was not the sort of event to stick in a barber's or a chemist's mind. But Bentinck would not be dissuaded from looking for the needle in the haystack. With deductive analysis that would have reflected well on any fictional sleuth, he reasoned that Goodman, a notorious hellite, would probably have bought the colouring from a shop that he passed on the way from his house in Foley Place to Piccadilly or Leicester Square.

Bentinck visited every chemist the length of bustling Regent Street. Nothing. Undeterred, he started on the hairdressers, and this time he got lucky. Talking to a woman behind the counter of the hairdresser Rossi's, he ascertained that a large quantity of hair dye had been sold to one customer who answered Goodman's description. It is strange to think of this tall, earnest, slightly awkward aristocrat, fixing this hairdresser's assistant with his intense gaze as he cross-examined her, asking her repeatedly if she was sure about the details. 'Yes,' answered the woman at Rossi's till, she was entirely sure 'because he ordered a second jar, and forgot to pay for it'.[5] It was as much Goodman's compulsive dishonesty, 'forgetting' to pay for the materials for his criminal masterwork, that gave him away, as it was Bentinck's equally characteristic doggedness. Bentinck probed further and discovered that the customer had requested specially prepared dye, a fact that tied in perfectly with Goodman's request to Ferguson for some hairs from Goneaway, enabling him to effect a perfect colour match.

Bentinck wanted to be absolutely sure that it was indeed Goodman who was bulk-buying bespoke dye from Rossi's. It would appear that he spent the rest of the day having Goodman followed, ascertaining his movements. Bentinck appeared again the following morning at the hair salon and asked if Rossi himself would accompany him in a cab he had waiting. The slightly bemused hairdresser complied and in a short time he found himself outside the Regent Street shop of baker and biscuit-maker Adam Glen, watching customers come and go. Among them he identified Goodman. Bentinck was satisfied, and took a written statement from the hairdresser.

The story of Rossi the Regent Street hairdresser was just one of many truffles that Bentinck unearthed in the course of his detective work. He also found and questioned a horse breaker called George Hitchcock who had broken horses for the Epsom trainer William Smith, and elicited from him suspicions that one of the horses had been broken before. Hitchcock claimed that Smith had horse-whipped him for saying that the colt he was breaking was a four- rather than a three-year-old. A woman called Fanny Humphries, née Page, was found who knew about dubious transactions undertaken by Mr Bean of Finchley that would, if necessary, cast a shadow over any testimony he might make.

As has been seen, Lord George's zeal in assembling evidence to support the case was not always ethical. In today's terms it does seem that some of his methods bordered on harassment, intimidation and witness-tampering. It would emerge that when he had investigated the result of the race in which the Duke of Rutland's horse Crenoline had been beaten by 'Running Rein', he himself had tracked down the lad Kitchen and kept him under the supervision of his valet and his trainer until he could be cross-examined by the stewards. Bentinck had been unsuccessful in the Crenoline inquiry and did not take the failure philosophically. For two weeks before the trial William Smith complained of being watched and followed, at one point counting seven men surrounding his house. But Bentinck, of course, did not care. He was riveting together links in a chain of evidence that, he hoped, would shackle his – or rather, Peel's – courtroom adversaries.

Just as Bentinck was using Peel's name to further his own crusade against what he saw as villainy on the Turf, so Alexander Wood's name was similarly employed by the rival coterie. 'Mr Wood's beneficial interest in the stake being but small, he endeavoured to avoid a lawsuit, and to have the dispute settled by the Stewards,' wrote his lawyer, doing his best to present Wood as the reasonable and magnanimous party in the case. He added that when Peel began his action Wood had been reluctant to litigate, 'but being positively assured, and believing that the horse was Running Rein, he, upon receiving a bond of indemnity, permitted those who had greater interest than himself in the stakes, to use his name for the purpose of trying the question, and to employ their own Attorney, the use of Mr Wood's name being necessary for the purpose'.[6]

Throughout the month of June the 'subject was mooted daily among the aristocracy and nobility'.[7] As soon as the case had been announced, bets were offered and taken on the outcome, and fluctuated constantly as any information, however insignificant it may have seemed, was seized upon. Of course, nobody was under the misapprehension that it was just a matter of settling a difference of opinion between two men. It was, instead, a clash of two value systems, dividing neatly along class lines. Like rival teams, their supporters united behind one or the other with an almost tribal loyalty.

As Monday 1 July, the date of the trial, neared, excitement mounted and many could think and talk of nothing else. Charles Greville's diary pages are blank for the days leading up to the trial. 'I have been for the last 10 days too much occupied with the trial of Wood v Peel to find time to write anything here,' he noted afterwards. Even though he had no direct interest in the case, aside from any bets he might have placed on the outcome of the race, the sense of identity he felt with the defendant, Peel, is palpable throughout his account. He writes of '*our* [my italics] great case of Orlando and Running Rein'; that 'never was there a case so got up as *ours*'; that '*we* have all worked hard in different ways', and so on. In spite of their personal feud, he even acknowledged 'the indefatigable activity and the intelligence and penetration of George Bentinck, who played the part both of Attorney and Police-man in hunting out and getting up the evidence'.[8]

Meanwhile, typical of those who backed the Wood party was another victualler – a sporting cheesemonger, sometime defaulter, small-time racehorse owner, occasional *qui tam*-action bringer, and on the whole rather endearing opportunist who had been mixed up in the Gurney affair, called John George Dixon. He had gone before the Select Committee on Gaming and been remarkably free and frank about the methods in which a racehorse could be 'made safe'. Moreover, when asked whether he valued his reputation on the Turf, he had answered cheerfully, 'Not at all', adding by way of clarification a little later, 'I do not think that there is much honour on the turf.'[9] Dixon embodied the new breed of Turf men. Cheese was his business and horses were his recreation; he had little time for quasi-chivalric notions of honour and was just out to enjoy himself. He was said to have been among those who guaranteed Wood's costs in the case.[10] Another of Wood's backers was Adam Glen, the same Regent Street baker in whose shop Goodman had been spotted by Rossi. The sporting biscuit-maker 'had a very large pecuniary interest in the result'.[11] He was known on the Turf as a commission agent, having even done some dirty work for Bentinck on one occasion, laying against a horse that he subsequently withdrew from the Derby.

For its part the Wood contingent, or at least its legal advisers, felt just as confident as Lord George Bentinck that it had an unbeatable case. Of course, the outcome was an event of immense financial significance and information was eagerly sought by all who had an interest in the outcome. For instance Squire Osbaldeston, who had duelled with Bentinck and whose horse Saddler had sired the real Running Rein, had thousands of pounds on Running Rein. 'I knew the individuals composing the Running Rein party, and their solicitor; I immediately put myself in communication with them and they advised me not to hedge a shilling because every pound I hedged was money lost. The solicitor's name was Gill, and he being in possession of all the evidence, and a lawyer, too, I was guided entirely by his advice and opinion. He also assured me that theirs was a "plain unvarnished tale" and it was impossible to upset it.'[12]

The court in which this extraordinary case was to be heard was the Court of Exchequer, itself a suitably esoteric setting for a strange affair. The Court of Exchequer was one of the picturesque anachronisms that characterised the British legal system in the early Victorian era. It was exactly the sort of institution that Dickens adored to lampoon in his novels. For sheer pageantry, eccentricity and obfuscatory mumbo-jumbo the Court of Exchequer is right up there along with the Court of Chancery, which casts its long shadow over *Bleak House*, and the Doctors' Commons affectionately satirised in *David Copperfield*.

Sadly, the Court of Exchequer is no more; it was absorbed into the High Court in 1873, six years short of its eight-hundreth birthday. It was founded by William I in part out of homesickness for his Duchy of Normandy, where a similar court existed. Overhauled in the reign of Edward I, it was thereafter not much altered; indeed, litigants from that time would have found much that was familiar in the summer of 1844 when the court prepared to hear the case of Wood versus Peel. The name was derived from the chequerboard-like cloth, a large carpet lying before the judges, except that this being the Court of Exchequer they were not called judges, but barons, alluding to a time when only barons were eligible to serve as judges in this court. In Westminster Hall, a coloured engraving of the early nineteenth century shows the court in all its majesty. Even the light falling in shafts through the windows seems respectful of the armorial tapestries and the bewigged figures on the tiered seating. At the centre of the scene is the giant checked carpet, a sort of early medieval spreadsheet, or woven abacus, on which the accounts used to be tallied using counters and which nobody had had the heart to do away with for over 750 years.

Parliament may have been reformed, the industrial revolution may have been transforming Britain from an agrarian to a manu-facturing economy, the railways may have been criss-crossing the nation, fortunes may have been forged in the white heat of the iron masters' furnaces, the new police force may have been raiding the illegal gaming hells, the Home Secretary may have been fretting about the peril to the nation's morals posed by the racecourse thimble-riggers – but the Court of Exchequer carried on as majestic as ever. The nineteenth century had nibbled away at it slightly, with some reforms during the reign of William IV, but it maintained its dignity. Slumbering in its treasury was the 'Great Roll of the Exchequer' or the 'pipe roll', which contained the Crown's revenue from the time of King Stephen to Queen Victoria. 'To this docu-ment nearly every ancient pedigree is indebted; it has a perfect list of the Sheriffs of the different counties, and almost every name in English history,' noted John Timbs, the awestruck author of the *The Curiosities of London*, in 1855. On occasion the Privy Council would meet in the Court of Exchequer to regulate the election of sheriffs; at this time the Chancellor of the Exchequer himself would preside on the bench 'in his figured silk gown, trimmed with gold'.[13] On even rarer occasions, when the barons could not decide on a judgement, the Chancellor would be called upon to adjudicate in solemn, Solomon-like manner. By the time the case of Running Rein was heard, though, that had not happened for a century: 'The last case in which the chancellor was required to sit, owing to the barons being equally divided in opinion, was that of Naish against the East India Company, Michaelmas Term, 1735, when Sir Robert Walpole was Chancellor, and his decision in a question of very considerable difficulty was said to have given great satisfaction.'[14]

The Chancellor of the Exchequer would not be sitting in judgement on the case of Wood vs Peel. Instead, it was to come before Mr Baron Alderson, a famous racing judge. He was hardly an impartial figure but, as senior judges went, an expert on racing and possessor of a brilliant mind, as Greville found out when he met him at a dinner given by the Chief Justice.

> I sat next to Alderson, and found him a very agreeable man, Senior Wrangler, Senior Medallist, a Judge (and really a Lawyer), a wit; a life all of law and letters, such as I might have led if I had chosen the good instead of the bad path. I always think of this when I meet such men who have 'scorned delights, and lived laborious days,' and now enjoy the benefit thereof. He told me he had been writing an exercise in the morning for one of his sons at Oxford, a dialogue between Erasmus and More, on the preference of the Latin to the Greek as an universal language.[15]

In Mr Baron Alderson the Court of Exchequer had a judge worthy of its antique and eccentric dignity. A painting of him in his robes shows a vulpine face with intelligent features, quick eyes peering mischievously out from beneath a wig that carpets his shoulders and spills halfway down his chest. He was not a man to be trifled with. Already in the preliminary hearing when the lawyers representing the two parties had 'state[d] their respective claims, in order that the case might be dealt with by the court',[16] he had raised the issue of whether it was not Goodman who was the 'real party'. Moreover, the possibility was raised that Peel might try to prove 'at the trial of this issue that there are more parties than one to whom Running Rein belongs'. Which, while probably true, would have been hypocritical, given that it was also noted in this pre-trial session that the protest at the result of the Derby of 1844 'was delivered by Lord George Bentinck on behalf of Colonel Peel'.

And the preliminary hearing set the jocose tone that was to continue throughout this high-profile case. At times transcripts of the trial read like a libretto by Gilbert and Sullivan. The normally arid legal language was larded with racing references – how the case had been referred from Tattersall's and how Peel had sought to 'jockey' Wood out of the stakes – plus jokes about the plaintiff not being allowed to 'ride off on a bye point' and much more in this vein. And given that this was 1844, when racial stereotyping cast Jews as grotesque moneylenders or Fagin-like corrupters of the gentile gentleman, there was the occasional low anti-Semitic comment at Goodman's expense. As *Bell's Life* reported on 9 June:

> Mr Baron Alderson: ... the issue will be, whether Running Rein was a colt foaled in 1841, whose Sire was The Saddler, and dam Mab? That involves two propositions in one issue – namely the identity and age of the horse, and to it should be appended permission to the plaintiff, Colonel Peel, to give in evidence the acts and declarations done or made by Mr Goodman. What's his Christian name?
>
> Mr Martin [counsel for the defendant]: Oh no. Abraham Levi-Goodman [laughter].

And so the cast was assembled: from the haughty and disdainful aristocrat to the pantomime villain, the affable younger brother of the prime minister, the wisecracking scholarly racing judge, two teams of highly qualified (and highly paid) lawyers; and a supporting cast of dozens including trainers, stable keepers, farmers and vets. The sporting world waited expectantly for the drama to commence in one of the most majestic and ancient courts in the land. Who would win? Would it be the racing and social establishment represented by the arrogant and publicly virtuous Bentinck? Or would the audacity of the new men, the social outsiders, triumph – the sporting tradesmen and the audacious criminal mastermind?

Wood v Peel was a snapshot of a country trammelled in change. And if the social drama was not sufficiently compelling, the court-room duel in prospect was given added piquancy by the fact that thousands of men up and down the country, from the mechanic in his Derby Club to the sporting squire Osbaldeston with his thousands wagered, had a financial interest in the outcome.

17

Their Day in Court

———

'I cannot help, somehow or other, feeling that the transcendent dignity
of the judicial office – the spotless purity of the judicial ermine – is sullied
and soiled when it is brought into contact with impurities so gross as
those which connect themselves with the Turf!'

Alexander Cockburn at Wood v. Peel, quoted in *Bell's Life*, 7 July 1844

———

And so it was on Monday 1 July that the two opposing sides drew
up their batteries and faced each other across the chequered field
upon which they would do battle. The heavy legal guns that were
wheeled into position were scarcely less impressive than the brilliant
and quixotic Baron Alderson. For Wood, his lawyer Gill had
engaged the services of Alexander Cockburn, a fearless and brilliant
advocate who would later become Sir Alexander Cockburn and
Lord Chief Justice. Cockburn was an impressive figure, often pictured looking witheringly down his long nose. He was assisted
by Messrs James and Lush. Ranged against them was no less an
individual than Sir Frederick Thesiger the Solicitor General, later
first Baron Chelmsford (whose son would acquit himself so dis-
astrously in the Zulu war of 1879), at the head of a crack team of a
further six lawyers – three barristers and three solicitors.

From an early hour that Monday morning, a vast crowd assembled in Westminster comprising 'persons of all grades, and we may
also say from all parts of the country, whose interests were deeply
involved in the inquiry'. Mr Baron Alderson was not to take his
place until ten o'clock, but spectators keen to get a ringside seat
had arrived early and when the doors were opened at 9.30 there

was a stampede for seats, with much jostling and elbowing. Such was the crush that the Bench and other places normally reserved for officials were rapidly occupied by the numerous witnesses and hundreds of sporting men determined to see the sporting trial of the age. As expected, the nobility and gentry were well represented. Among those fortunate enough to get seats were Osbaldeston, who sat near the judge, Greville, Lord Stradbroke, Sir Gilbert Heathcote, Baron de Tessier (one of the Epsom stewards), Poodle Byng, Sir Charles Ibbotson and Colonel Anson. Indeed, the dignity of the proceedings was sometimes imperilled by the propinquity of the spectators. At one point, when Greville was handed a letter, Baron Alderson, clearly feeling it was not on for spectators to be receiving correspondence in court, was moved to comment: 'I wish you would not bring things upon the bench. I do not like to be sitting with persons who are taking a part. I do not like it at all. I feel myself in a very difficult position.'[1]

Lord George was of course there and, typical of his arrogance, was seated directly behind counsel for the defence. He spent the day whispering instructions to the Solicitor General; it seemed that the fiction of Peel being the prime mover in the case had been dropped entirely. Recalling this rich scene in his autobiography, Squire Osbaldeston makes the pardonable error of saying that 'Lord George sat close to *his* [my italics] counsel'.[2] Already a physically imposing presence, Bentinck's overly apparent sense of entitlement can be imagined. Having assembled the evidence like an investigating officer, having harassed those witnesses he could not buy or otherwise inveigle into appearing to support his case, he was now forgetting himself entirely and appearing as the defendant. It was simply too much for Wood's counsel, and as soon as the special jury had been sworn, Cockburn was on his feet.

'My lord, before the case proceeds, your lordship will, perhaps, be good enough to order the witnesses on both sides out of the court.'

A murmur of surprise and perplexity echoed around Westminster Hall.

Mr Baron Alderson raised a quizzical eyebrow. 'You particularly want, to have all the witnesses out of court?' he asked, as if he had not heard correctly and was inviting clarification.

'Yes my Lord,' came the brusque, unvarnished reply.

But before Alderson could reframe his question, Sir Frederick Thesiger rose, perhaps prompted by a hurried whisper in his ear from Bentinck, to object. He saw exactly where this was going, even if Alderson pretended he didn't.

'My lord, I must appeal to your lordship in this case whether it is necessary that Lord George Bentinck should leave the court: he has been subpoenaed by the plaintiff as a witness and I have not the slightest expectation that the plaintiff intends to call him. I believe the object is that his lordship should not remain in court.'

There then followed some legal fencing between the two men, with the result that some of the less significant witnesses did leave the court, but the main racing witnesses, including Bentinck, were permitted to remain.

Battle had been joined.

Just in case anyone was in doubt as to why they had all crammed themselves into Westminster Hall that summer morning, the jury was acquainted with the case. 'Alexander Wood is the plaintiff and Jonathan Peel Esq is the defendant,' said one of Wood's barristers explaining that the issue to be tried was 'whether a certain colt called Running Rein which came in first at a certain race at Epsom this year, was or was not a colt foaled in the year 1841, whose sire was The Saddler, and dam Mab' – adding for good measure, 'The plaintiff alleges that it was; the defendant that it was not.'

The barrister then sat down and allowed Cockburn to begin. As Cockburn's exploratory skirmish about clearing witnesses from the court had indicated, he was in a fighting mood. He lost no time in sketching out that the jury was being asked to decide no normal case but an issue of national importance. As he saw it, this was not just about bets and money won or lost, but nothing less than a question of Britain's very identity:

In a country like this, where horse racing in its various forms has so formed a feature in our national habits, it is not to be wondered at that a question like this should excite a very great degree of interest, not only in what are commonly called sporting circles, but indeed I may say among all circles and classes of society. When we recollect what this Derby race is – that from the peer to the peasant all classes congregate and crowd to witness it – that the gravest senators, ministers of state, members of the learned professions, all flock to the scene – business is forgotten on that day, and all classes hasten to see that scene of excitement – one can't at all wonder that very great interest is attached to this race.

His emotionally charged peroration continued in much the same way, moving seamlessly from the word picture he had painted of the pageant of British sporting life on to the subject of the huge sums of money at stake, 'which really would quite astonish those who were not acquainted with the manner in which all these things become matter of speculation'. From this, all it took was a suggestive nudge and he had arrived at the nub of his argument: 'The plaintiff in this issue has to contend with individuals connected with the Turf of very great influence, of very great activity and energy, who have got enormous sums depending on the issue in this contest.' It is safe to assume that, pausing for emphasis between the three key words 'influence', 'activity' and 'energy', Cockburn allowed his gaze to travel beyond the end of his nose and rest upon the auburn-haired and languid figure of Lord George Bentinck.

A great many of Cockburn's opening remarks were flimsily veiled attacks on Bentinck – in fact, most were not equipped with even the scantiest of veils but mentioned him by name again and again. He accused him of having 'got the witnesses together – kept them together – fed them – entertained them – clothed them and paid them'. He mentioned that he would be unable to call a particular witness 'because he is in the service of Lord George Bentinck, *that* is quite enough for me'. Nevertheless, he undertook to show that the horse *was* the horse Wood said it was, and that his client was a perfect innocent who had taken Running Rein merely because Goodman was unable to pay him for the corn he had bought.

Cockburn also decided to play the class card, in a cunning way, when commenting on the judgement of the Jockey Club on Running Rein's victory over Crenoline, making much of the probity of the proceedings:

> It was known that a public investigation had taken place before the stewards of the Jockey Club, competent authorities on this subject, submitted to ordinarily by all persons connected with the Turf, *this* was perfectly well known, and it was known that the decision of the stewards, of that competent authority, had been in favour of the colt, that they had decided him to be a *two year old*, and not a three, and that they had awarded the stakes to his owner, rejecting the claim of no less a person than his Grace the Duke of Rutland. The whole thing was perfectly fair and impartial; there had been that impartiality which I trust there always will be between British noblemen and gentlemen of high birth, rank, and station, when they are called upon to adjudicate between one of their own class and one of an inferior class; that impartiality which I know, whatever may be hoped or expected in other quarters, will be exercised here today by you whom I have now the honour to address.

Once again the accusation was clearly directed at Bentinck and his role as self-appointed paladin of the Turf. It would be intriguing to know exactly what Bentinck thought of this attempt to shame him by implying he was wanting in what he would have called, in his old-fashioned way, the 'aristocratick principle'. He probably allowed himself a mirthless chuckle at Cockburn's highly coloured version of the inquiry the previous year at Newmarket, at which Stradbroke had pleaded fruitlessly for Goodman to allow the horse's mouth to be examined for the sake of his good name.

But Bentinck can barely have had time to ponder this when Cockburn followed up his attack with the allegation that certain noblemen and gentlemen interested in this matter [had] bet against this horse to an enormous amount, with this comfortable conviction on their minds, that they had a double chance, that if the horse was beaten according to ordinary running they were safe in their bets; and if by accident he should win, they had another hook on which they might hold themselves harmless. That is what you call the honour of the Turf – that is the honour of British noblemen and gentlemen, who, with this knowledge, bet thousands and thousands of pounds, with the intention of lodging a protest against the horse the day before he runs.

Again, just so there was no doubt as to whom this explosive broadside was aimed at, Cockburn was careful to add, in honeyed tones, 'Do not let me for a moment be supposed to mean that Colonel Peel has anything to do with this dirty transaction', while warning darkly that 'there are those who, if they venture to put themselves in to that box, I will venture to say I will turn inside out'.

He might have ended there, but instead went on to ever higher planes of rhetoric, expressing the 'deep, heartfelt, unbounded veneration' that he entertained for the 'sacred callings and functions of a British judge'. His personal view was that the shocking Turf transactions that would come out during the trial betokened 'a lamentable demoralisation among all classes of society'. In moving terms he spoke of 'the transcendent dignity of the judicial office' and 'the spotless purity of the judicial ermine' that 'is sullied and soiled when it is brought into contact with impurities so gross as those which connect themselves with the Turf'. But the subject of the soiling of the judicial ermine would not be allowed to keep him long from the main thrust of his opening address: the denigration of Lord George Bentinck's character.

Before calling his witnesses, he permitted himself one final sally against the man even now whispering instructions in the Solicitor General's ear. Referring again to the Crenoline inquiry and freighting his voice with all the irony and sarcasm at his disposal, he admitted Bentinck as an honorary member of the legal profession, accusing the Duke of Rutland of 'acting under the advice and led by the direction of that excellent advocate, my Lord George Bentinck, who in this case will be found to have played the part of attorney – of a party interested – I believe I may almost say of a policeman; for you will find him watching with all the vigilance of one of those quick sighted and quick witted functionaries'. The allusion to the police force was hardly a flattering one: drawn from the working class, the so-called new police were viewed with little enthusiasm. One of the names given to the embryonic force was 'crushers', as in crushers of liberty. It was widely held that a police force, especially one founded on solving crime on a scientific basis, was in some way unEnglish and contrary to the prevailing notions of liberty enjoyed by Her Majesty's subjects. And having called him a 'crusher', Cockburn again alluded ominously to what would come out in the trial, with the words, 'My Lord George Bentinck may think it might have been as well if he had taken my hint and gone out of court.'[3]

After such coruscating opening remarks, the supporters of Running Rein could have entertained high hopes for the way the case would go. Certainly Osbaldeston, one of the interested spectators crammed up near Mr Baron Alderson, thought so, commenting that the 'Running Rein party seemed to be winning in a canter'.[4]

However, any euphoria occasioned by Cockburn's blistering beginning started to evaporate when the cross-examination of the witnesses took place. As before, Cockburn set out to prove that it was Bentink rather than Peel who was behind the case and that he was manipulating the proceedings much as he might manipulate a horse race. But when he was questioning the lad Kitchen on how Bentinck had kept him effectively locked up during the Crenoline inquiry, Mr Baron Alderson interjected, saying, 'The question solely is as to the identity of the colt. A good deal of examination as to Lord George Bentinck is utterly immaterial.' Moreover, as the proceedings wore on, the sheer weight of Bentinck's preparation began to tell: Kitchen, for instance, was made to look unreliable when questioned in detail about any promises of emoluments made to him by Wood's team in the event of the case being decided in their favour.

As the procession of shifty and evasive individuals was paraded in front of the court with a view to building up a compelling chronology that would prove the real Running Rein had won the Derby, Baron Alderson's irritation became more apparent. In the midst of the painstaking examination of a servant to Henry Stebbings about the events of 1841 and the colour of the foal's legs, which he had not seen for three years, Alderson, as if musing aloud, said, 'I suppose it is close by, and if the jury wish to see it, it is to be seen. We can have it brought into court I daresay.' Bringing a horse into the Court of Exchequer was just the sort of thing that would have appealed to Alderson, and it also gave Peel's counsel the opening they were looking for.

'Under an order of your lordship we have been desirous of seeing this horse, and we have been refused,' came the quick-fire response from the Solicitor General.

'Refused!' Baron Alderson had shaken off his dreamy hypothetical manner and was instantly outraged. First the soiling of the judicial ermine and now no horse.

Cockburn did his best to deflect the attention from the horse and back to Stebbings's manservant and the colouring of the foal's feet three years earlier: 'Your lordship will hear under what circumstance when the time arrives.'

But for Baron Alderson there was no time like the present; he was getting bored with the rather drab witnesses filing before him and, as a student of the Turf himself, he decided he would much rather be looking at a thoroughbred racehorse. 'We shall see it tomorrow morning; I am quite sure both the jury and myself would like to see him; don't you think you should like to see him gentlemen? Would it not be reasonable for us to see it?'

'I should think so,' came the smart response from the jury.

'I think I should like to see its mouth,' announced Baron

Alderson with the satisfaction of a cat looking forward to a bowl of cream.

Examination of the manservant, who admitted that he had seen the horse for a full three or four minutes in 1841, served only to harden Alderson's resolve. 'You had much better send for the horse; nobody will be satisfied without it. I am sure, whatever the verdict may be, it will be set aside if the horse is not seen, therefore be prepared,' he said. He then invoked the full majesty and spirit of the law that gave Cockburn ample return for soiling the judicial ermine. 'This is an issue directed to satisfy the conscience of the court, and we act not in an ordinary way, as in a common cause, but with a power to make such orders as requisite for the purposes of the justice of the case. I think it requisite that the horse should be seen.'

Cockburn was only able to splutter, 'If your lordship's order has been used in a proper way—' before he was cut off.

'I do not care whether it has been used properly or not. It must be brought up now.'

It transpired during the bickering immediately afterwards that a deputation from Peel's team including vets and the omnipresent Lord George – 'half London', as Cockburn sourly put it – had been down to the stables but had had no luck.

As the day wore on, a pattern in the proceedings began to make itself apparent. Inconclusive testimony was given by a variety of people tasked with keeping Goodman's constant merry-go-round of a stud in perpetual motion. Stables in Chapel Mews, Foley Place, and Langham Place as well as various paddocks outside London were employed much as a thimble-rigger used his cups to conceal the elusive pea. The general unreliability of the witnesses appearing for Wood was suggested by telling questions, such as those directed to Mr Bean about his prior bankruptcies and insolvencies (two of each), formed on the basis of information acquired by Bentinck's detective work. Baron Alderson became increasingly exasperated, asking of one witness, 'Are you so much in the habit of committing frauds that when it is put to your memory you can't remember

anything of the kind?' Upon hearing evidence from William Mar-
shall, a Finchley cow-keeper who used to deliver milk to Mr Bean,
Alderson asked imploringly, 'You do not mean to call many more
of this sort of people?' Towards the end of the afternoon he got so
bored that he started cracking puns on the names of various horses
mentioned in evidence, one of which was called Dr Phillimore,
prompting the groaningly awful exchange:

Cockburn: 'Two Fillies.'

Baron Alderson: 'And one Phillimore! [laughter]'

But Baron Alderson was certainly not laughing when the Epsom
trainer William Smith was called into the witness box. Smith gave
an account of Goodman's unpaid bills and described how Goodman
had asked Wood to take the racehorse to meet the balance of money
owed to him. The next, crucial, part of his testimony concerned
the horse that Baron Alderson and the jury were so keen to see.

It had disappeared.

The court was asked to believe that Smith had 'begged Mr Wood
to get the horse out of my hand' because 'I was in fear. There had
been from one man to six or seven around my house for the last
fortnight. I was in fear they would take the horse away.' And in
this helpless state he had handed the horse over to a tall, red-faced
mystery man called Ignatius Coyle, who, he believed, was going to
take the animal to Wood. What made this revelation even more
piquant was that Coyle had been spotted in court that morning.

Baron Alderson was apoplectic. 'It was the day before I ordered
the horse to be shown *Sir! That* was what you were afraid of. You
had better be a little more cautious; or we shall have you up in the
court next term if you do not mind. Do not be contemptuous of
the orders of the court; take good care what you are about. I can
assure you I shall not be satisfied again with any such story.'

Enraged that Smith would hand over a valuable piece of evidence
without even a written order from Wood, Alderson branded Smith's
conduct a 'gross fraud' and called again for the horse. Cockburn,
doing his desperate best to keep his case from being derailed,
announced that he was 'perfectly ready to produce the horse'. This

calmed Alderson sufficiently to allow the proceedings to continue. But for the rest of the day the trial was prone to eruptions from Alderson along the lines of 'You wish me to suppose that at Epsom the police cannot keep people from stealing a horse?' When Cockburn dared to suggest that even bringing the horse would not prove anything, as he thought the Bentinck–Peel party quite capable of producing witnesses to swear to whatever was most expedient, Wood supporters in the court burst into rapturous applause. But Alderson was withering, calling with 'much warmth', as *Bell's Life* put it in its issue of 7 July, for the ushers to clear the court. He eventually calmed down enough to let the case continue.

But by now there was no disguising the fact that Wood's case was in serious trouble, giving the Solicitor General the opportunity to gloat as he opened the case for the defendant.

> I confess that I have rather been taken by surprise that the case on the part of the plaintiff, should have so suddenly, and it appears to me so abruptly terminated, because, considering what was the nature of the issue which the plaintiff took upon himself to establish, and who were the persons who were acquainted with the important facts which ought to be communicated to you to guide your judgment, it does appear rather astonishing that my learned friend should have been satisfied with establishing, by means of the witnesses he has called before you, what I shall show you presently to be a very imperfect case indeed; and I can only account for the very great boldness with which my learned friend opened his case for you, from his having been kept in ignorance most improperly and most unfairly to my learned friend, of some very important particulars which it was absolutely essential he should know; because I cannot for one moment believe that those who have instructed my learned friend on the present occasion are not perfectly aware of what is the nature of the dispute between the parties – what is to be alleged in answer to this attempt on the part of the plaintiff, and in what manner the defendant will establish that there has been a gross and scandalous fraud com-

mitted by the plaintiff, or by those to whom the plaintiff entrusted his interest.

Having thus expressed concern that his learned friend had been so shockingly misled, Sir Frederick continued his lengthy opening remarks, moving on to address the attack Cockburn had made against Lord George Bentinck.

My learned friend has thought proper in the course of his address to you to make some very strong remarks indeed with respect to my noble friend Lord George Bentinck. I think that he has hardly treated him with common courtesy. My learned friend's observations were pointed and strong. I trust that before this case comes to its close that he will be satisfied that they are not justified. Lord George Bentinck has most unquestionably taken a very active and a very prominent part in this investigation. Lord George is desirous, as many other distinguished persons connected with the Turf are, that frauds of this description should be detected and defeated; and acting under that impulse, Lord George Bentinck is ready to avow that he has taken a part in this investigation – that he has been particularly anxious that the witnesses who could furnish on the subject might be forthcoming on the day of the trial, and that there might be nothing wanting to a full and searching inquiry as to the merits of the case. But my learned friend insinuates that there has been something unfair in the conduct of my Lord George with regard to this proceeding. I defy my learned friend to prove anything of the kind; I defy him, if the whole of Lord George Bentinck's conduct was laid before you at the present moment, to find anything which would indicate more than that strong and earnest disposition which all of us must have, that frauds of this kind should not be permitted to pass with impunity.

Thesiger also wondered aloud why Goodman had made himself scarce, thinking 'it more prudent not to appear at all in public before you'. He pointed out to the jury how dextrously his learned friend had piled opprobrium on to the absent Goodman as the villain, portraying Wood as hapless dupe rather than co-conspirator.

The Solicitor General threw everything he had into his opening remarks. He too had come well prepared, right down to bringing with him a bottle of dye from Rossi, the Regent Street hairdresser, to reinforce his assertion that Goodman had dyed Goneaway's white pastern black. 'This is handed to me as the mixture which was used,' he said gravely, holding a bottle of the offending colourant aloft, peering at it as if the truth were dissolved in the inky liquid, 'which was bought of a person of the name of *Rossi*.' Lord George must have been delighted that his detective work was being put to such dramatic use.

However, Mr Baron Alderson was not at all keen on involving Goodman. As he saw it, the case before him was Wood versus Peel and he wanted it to stay that way. 'I want to keep it clear of Mr Goodman; we have nothing to do with him, this is the case of Mr Wood' – a sentiment with which Goodman, had he been in court, would have heartily agreed.

And talking of agreement, there was one aspect of the case about which both the Solicitor General and his learned friend Cockburn, although on different sides in the matter, concurred: the national significance of the case. Thesiger continued:

> I do consider it, for the reasons which I have mentioned, to be a most important case in its result. I am most anxious for your patient and earnest attention, in order to discover, if we can, the fraud which has been practised, and, by the verdict which you will pronounce, to read a statutory lesson to persons in the station of Mr Goodman, which may have the effect of clearing the Turf from intruders of this kind – persons of a character who disgrace the amusements, and who are likely completely to destroy all the interest which the public take in it as a national sport.

It was at this moment that Bentinck stepped into his public role as the spotless champion of sporting honour and integrity, selfless servant of the public desire to purge a wholesome and manly amusement of cheats, crooks, swindlers, and other sundry practitioners of any and every branch of the 'science of chicanery and fraud'.[5] No matter that in his time he had been guilty of pulling strokes that were as underhand as anything that was being tried in court that July day, or that just a few months earlier he had used his privileged position as nobleman and MP to force a cynical change in the law to protect his betting interests and those of his cronies. Here in the ancient and revered Court of Exchequer, with the eyes of the nation on the proceedings, the Solicitor General himself, bottle of Rossi's hair dye in hand, was protecting him against the accusations of the opposing side's lawyers, praising his efforts and his 'strong and earnest disposition . . . that frauds of this kind should not be permitted to pass with impunity'.

The Solicitor General then called his first witness, Lord Stradbroke, one of the stewards of the Jockey Club who had presided at the inquiry into Crenoline's defeat by Goodman's 'Running Rein'. The sporting nobleman was something of a contrast to the preceding parade of shifty characters. Even though Mr Baron Alderson had warned the Solicitor General to keep Goodman out of his argument, Stradbroke pulled him back to centre stage, recounting how Goodman strenuously objected to anyone looking, even for an instant, into the horse's mouth:

> He positively objected to it . . . I replied, 'If the horse was really a two year old, there could be no possible objection to having his mouth examined; that it could not in any way prejudice the case, and that it was a straight forward case, it was to his interest the horse's mouth should be examined.' His reply to that was, that he had been advised by, I think he said, his legal adviser, not to permit the horse's mouth to be examined, to which I said, 'Whoever that man may be, I consider him a dishonest man for giving you such advice.'

His continued attempts to persuade Goodman to allow examination were fruitless. 'I walked with Mr Goodman from the stables back to the New Rooms, conversing with him on the folly of not allowing the horse's mouth to be examined.'[6] The other racing heavyweight asked to give evidence was Charles Weatherby, publisher of the *Racing Calendar*, clerk to the Jockey Club and author of the stewards' letter to the whistle-blowing vet Bartlett, earlier in the year, stating that 'the question of the age of the horse called Running Rein is not at present in such a shape as to give them any power to interfere in the matter'.[7]

And then, after a long and eventful day, the court adjourned.

18

An Eventful Evening

That night, as if in sympathy with the drama unfolding in the venerable Court of Exchequer, the heavens opened. As the rain fell, Lord George Bentinck, awake in splendid Harcourt House and finding it hard to sleep after the excitement of the day in court, replayed the day's events in his mind. It seemed that he had finally learned the lesson that his father had exhorted him to heed after the disagreement with Squire Osbaldeston – he had kept his temper under control. However tempting it might have been, he had not reacted to Cockburn's goading. Nevertheless, the words used against him rankled, and taking pen and paper he sat down to write to the Queen's Counsel who had savaged his character in court.

Harcourt House, July 1 1844
Monday Night
Sir

I am too fully cognizant of your duty as well as privilege as a counsel, and much too highly appreciate the value, and usefulness of such a privilege, for a moment to question the propriety of the remarks which you felt it right, I doubt not, in obedience to your instructions, to pass upon my conduct this morning.

I am quite aware that an honest counsel is professionally bound to assume as true all that is stated in his brief, and would betray his trust if he were to spare the feelings of anyone against whose integrity and uprightness he either had, or might be misled by his instructions to believe he had, any facts, proofs, or evidence to adduce.

Conceiving the latter to be your position this morning, I admired the manliness and honesty with which you made your attack, though I myself was the victim of it, perfectly content on my own account patiently to abide my time, when I confidently anticipated you would put me into the witness-box, and thereby at once prove your words to be true, or convince yourself and all the world besides, that grave charges were never made with less foundation against mortal man, than those you hurled at me.

As in duty bound, I was in court under your client's subpoena, and had brought with me all the documents in my power to bring, in faithful and honest obedience to the wide scope of your *duces tecum* subpoena: bound by my oath, I should have had no chance but to answer freely every question you had thought proper to put to me; but more than that I pledge you my word as a man of honour and as a gentleman, that if you had put me in the witness-box, or will still do so, where your instructions or your own acuteness had fallen, or may fall, short in directing your examination, I would have freely and frankly supplied, and will still as freely and frankly supply, the want, and fully disclose every act of mine, connected with the transaction.

Having said thus much, I appeal to you, not in the way of threat (for I have none to make, and have none in thought or reservation), but I, as a suppliant, appeal to you as a man of honour, honesty, and truth, to afford me that redress to which I have pointed, without which your opening speech cannot be justified. I appeal to you either to make good your charges, or in open court as publicly and as loudly as they were made, to acknowledge and proclaim that they have no foundation save in your false instructions.

Lastly, I appeal to you for the sake of the English bar, which scarcely prides itself more for its unrivalled ability and talent, than for its exalted sense of honour and integrity, not in your person, who ought to be one of its brightest ornaments, to dim its lustre degrading it into the base instrument of the wanton, wilful, wicked, and revengeful calumnies of detected and defeated fraud.

I have the honour to be Sir

Your obedient and humble servant

G. BENTINCK[2]

Here the new Bentinck can be seen emerging from his chrysalis in all his *soi-disant* humility, his spotless character positively glowing with honour, integrity, honesty and truth. The chivalric vocabulary might have come from a Walter Scott novel and would have appealed to the Young England conservatives, nostalgic for a return to a merrie medieval Neverland in which selfless oath-bound noblemen like Lord George championed manliness and purity. Gone was the unscrupulous fixer of horse races, the hypocritical cheat, the callous liar and the tyrannical bully; in his place, bending over his writing desk that wet Monday night in his family's London palace, was a man imbued with the moral certainty of the new convert, a man who revelled in his rectitude. The histrionic assertion that 'grave charges were never made with less foundation against mortal man, than those you hurled at me' must have pleased him inordinately.

And thus, having unburdened his mind and dispatched the letter, it is agreeable to think of him extinguishing the light and retiring to bed to sleep the untroubled sleep of the self-righteous.

Wood, however, was suffering a different order of wakefulness following a wearing day in court. Understandably, Baron Alderson's constant refrain that the horse should be produced weighed heavily on him.

After the Crenoline inquiry and the subsequent fortnight's delay between the complaint being lodged and the Jockey Club hearing, it would have occurred to Bentinck, himself experienced in racing deception, that Goodman might well have substituted the real horse for the four-year-old. As it happened, Stradbroke's evidence, testifying to Goodman's adamantine refusal to allow the horse's mouth to be examined on that occasion, suggests that the horse was the four-year-old; and also that Goodman had suborned the lad Kitchen, whose testimony in the Court of Exchequer was shown to be at best suspect, in light of the pecuniary promises made to him Nevertheless, it is doubtless with this fear in mind that Bentinck kept the Epsom trainer Smith under close watch, and it was this watch that had prompted Smith to explain to an unimpressed Alderson that he had handed the horse over to Coyle, assuming that the man was acting on Wood's verbal instruction. Coyle was, as befits the whole story, a scoundrel and jack of many criminal trades, having been variously identified as a defaulter, forger, pickpocket and, inevitably, small-time hell keeper. At the time he denied having anything to do with the disappearance of Running Rein, but even though his is a cameo role in this racing melodrama it is of pivotal importance.

It was only twenty years later that he finally admitted the story of his role in the most infamous racehorse kidnapping until that of Shergar in the late twentieth century.

It was the morning after the St Leger of 1864 and John Corlett, proprietor of the *Sporting Times*, went down to breakfast in his hotel where he encountered Dr Shorthouse, the founder of that paper, and Jackson, 'the great bookmaker of the day',[3] in the company of the red-faced mystery man of 1844, Ignatius Coyle. By this time Coyle plainly felt that enough years had passed for him to enjoy some of the notoriety of the celebrated Running Rein affair. 'Coyle was unfeignedly proud of the picaresque audacity he had shown in getting Running Rein away from the stables, and at the breakfast table told the whole story as an excellent joke.' The account was relayed by a correspondent to *The Times* who had heard it from Corlett, although the chronology does not tally with Smith's account in court, which states the Wednesday preceding the trial as the date of Running Rein's disappearance. Coyle, probably for dramatic effect in the retelling, states that it was the very morning of the trial when, 'having business with the trainer, [he] rode his hack into the stable-yard. Having finished his business, his hack was brought to him, he remounted and rode away. The "hack" he rode away on was Running Rein, which from that moment disappeared for ever.'[4]

If this horse *was* the three-year-old Running Rein, then the chief suspect in the orchestration of its unauthorised removal from Smith's yard would have been Bentinck. 'Whether or not Bentinck was responsible for the secret disappearance of the three-year-old Running Rein must be open to conjecture and doubt,' writes Bentinck's biographer Michael Seth-Smith in 1971.

But it was not the last time that Running Rein was seen alive.

The exact circumstances of the horse's disappearance, rather like those surrounding Shergar's, are difficult to ascertain. However, if an account of the strange events that took place on the Sunday before the trial in the yard of the Lord Nelson inn at Cheam in Surrey is to be believed, Lord George was not guilty of spiriting the horse away. And while apparently clearing him of involvement, it adds another tantalising layer of intrigue to the affair that was gripping the nation.

A matter of yards away from Westminster Hall where the Court of Exchequer was in session, the Select Committee of the House of Lords was still meeting to inquire into the canker of gambling that was gnawing at the very soul of Britain. The committee had stopped hearing evidence in May, but the Lords continued their examination well into July, long enough for them to digest the important news from the Court of Exchequer. On 8 July they heard from William Coleman, who was both a veterinary surgeon and keeper of the Lord Nelson inn at Cheam, a well-known watering hole for those en route to the Derby.

Coleman was already linked peripherally to the Derby, through knowing Old Forth and having treated Leander. He made a series of astonishing revelations about the horse that Baron Alderson had been so keen to see: he admitted that Running Rein had been in his stable only 'last Sunday week', placing the elusive racehorse, for which a good portion of the racing, veterinary and judicial worlds were scouring Epsom, in the stable of his Cheam pub.

It was around seven o'clock in the morning and Coleman was

leaving for Leatherhead on a veterinary call just as some men arrived in a carriage. 'All I know about it is, a young man came to me, and said, "Could you allow me to shift a little entire* horse out of the Box?" They wanted room for this other horse to come in, and I gave consent.'⁵ Presumably keen to get on with his journey and used to seeing a great many horses pass through the stables of his inn during the space of a day, Coleman thought little of it and went on his way. Only later, on his return, asking who these gentlemen were was he told that they were a pair of lawyers, 'Attorney and Counsel'. He gave the Select Committee the attorney's name as Gill, the preparer of Wood's case, but could not recall the name of the counsel. He did not know where the horse had been or where it was going although, in addition to the two lawyers in the carriage, he did recall seeing another two men arrive in a light two-wheeled, one-horse carriage. And when asked, 'Did you see a man there with a great deal of eruption about his face?' he answered, 'I think it was one of the Gentlemen who came in the Gig' – the term 'gentleman' being used loosely as it was here, in likelihood, the red-featured Coyle. Moreover, he thought that he saw Goodman in the yard as well, while the ostler confirmed that one man had the key to the box in which the horse was kept, and at various times of the day opened it to let other men in and out. It did not take gossip long to circulate around the yard and the pub that this was the famous Running Rein.

If Coleman was correct, Running Rein, Wood's legal team, Coyle and Goodman were all at the Cheam pub early on the Sunday morning. It was no coincidence. The sadness is that this dynamite information was not brought before the petulant Baron Alderson, but instead lay undisturbed amongst the hundreds of frequently tedious pages of evidence given to the Select Committees appointed to look into 'the laws respecting gaming'.⁶

It would perhaps have been some scant consolation for the sporting judge to learn that he was not the only one being kept in

---

* [not castrated]

the dark about the horse's whereabouts. Although Wood's lawyers, his friend Goodman and the acne-blighted Coyle who apparently removed the horse from Smith on his instructions were all at the Lord Nelson to see the horse and to dine together, Wood was uninvited. It seems that for some reason Goodman had decided to betray his accomplice. Coleman did not recall seeing Wood at the inn, adding, 'Neither do I believe he knew the horse was there.' The Epsom corn-chandler only got to hear of it on the Monday night, after the court had adjourned. An agitated Wood turned up at the Lord Nelson and sought out Coleman to ask if Running Rein was in his stables.

Perhaps not yet appreciating the significance of the comings and goings of the preceding day, which he had only incompletely witnessed and set little store by, Coleman was surprised.

'Good God, not that I know of, if he is—'

'If he is, then,' said Wood, cutting in hysterically, 'lock him up, and take care of him for me; don't let no one have him.'

But, double negatives or not, Wood was too late. Eighteen pence having been paid to the ostler for two feeds of corn and hay, Running Rein had been ridden out of the Lord Nelson's busy yard at five or six o'clock on the Sunday afternoon and was last seen heading 'towards Sutton',[7] where, it will be recalled, Goodman had a house and stables.

And so after a worrying night during which he failed to locate the horse, Wood resolved to make contact with the Epsom steward Baron de Tessier.

19

The Verdict

'If gentlemen would only race with gentlemen there would not be any difficulty in the matter; but if they condescend to race with blackguards they must condescend to expect to be cheated.'

Baron Alderson, quoted in *Bell's Life*, 7 July 1844

The diluvia did nothing to quench the fierce and burning interest now surrounding the case, and the 'court was again thronged at an early hour'. As the *Times* reporter put it punningly, 'The disclosures of yesterday [have] rather served to whet than damp the anxiety of those concerned in this exciting proceeding, and the curiosity of those who merely looked upon it as an interesting trial.'

As the crowd waited expectantly for Baron Alderson to take his seat and raise the curtain on the day's proceedings there was a lively ripple of interest around the door of the court, where Baron de Tessier appeared and beckoned both Colonel Peel and Lord George Bentinck to join him outside. Speculation increased when Wood, his face doubtless etched with the concerns of his sleepless night and his fruitless inquiries at the Lord Nelson, was spotted among this little knot of men. 'Some proposition would seem to have been made to the Colonel,' observed the *Times* reporter, 'for he decidedly shook his head, and retraced his steps to his seat near his counsel.' But the agitated Wood was soon on his feet once more. 'The plaintiff descended to the floor of the court, and approaching Colonel Peel, again entered into conversation with him, and showed him a letter which he held open in his hand.'[1] Meanwhile, Cockburn was seen in conversation with the Solicitor General.

Finally, the arrival of Mr Baron Alderson in his wig and robes heralded the resumption of proceedings. He asked the Solicitor General to continue with his evidence. The farmer George Worley from Northamptonshire had just been called when Cockburn interrupted: 'I feel that after what fell yesterday from your lordship on the subject of the production of the horse, that I am bound, my lord, to place myself at once in your lordship's hands.'

It was only just ten o'clock and the court had already enjoyed plenty of unusual activity. Now this.

'I am quite sure you wish to produce it,' remarked Alderson, who appeared to be calmer than he had been the day before. Perhaps he even waved away, with a flick of his bony white hand, what he thought was an apology from Wood's legal team, and turned to concentrate on the evidence of the farmer.

'If your lordship will be good enough to hear me for a moment, your lordship will hear the circumstances in which I am placed. It appeared, of course, to myself and my learned friends, whose assistance I have, that it was our bounden duty, after the view your lordship had taken of the case, to have the horse produced. In that view I am bound to say that the plaintiff, whom I represent, Mr Wood, most fully concurred.'

'I have no doubt he would if he was a respectable person,' said Alderson, a note of impatience creeping into his voice.

'He fully concurred in it,' continued Cockburn. 'I am now to say, in addition to that, I have Mr Wood's assurance – which I have reason to believe – that the horse was taken away without his sanction, approbation or knowledge – that as to the man having come to him, it was a mere *feint*, if it ever took place – that he never gave his approbation for the horse being taken away, and did not know where it was gone to.'

'It has gone away without his knowledge,' said the irritated Alderson, concisely paraphrasing counsel's orotund rhetoric.

'That he has since, my lord, been to get the horse at a place' – the Lord Nelson inn at Cheam – 'where he, in consequence of an inquiry that he made yesterday, was informed that it was gone to, and that the horse has been again removed, and that Mr Wood does not know where it is.'

By now Baron Alderson was losing it. 'Why does he not apply to the police to take up the people for horse-stealing? That is obvious – they are guilty of horse-stealing. I can only say if I try them I will transport them for life, for a dead certainty.'

'That,' intoned Cockburn gravely, 'is a matter for ulterior consideration. The only question, with which I have any concern at present, is the position in which Mr Wood is placed.'

'If Mr Goodman, or any of that sort of people, have taken away that horse, for the purpose of concealing it, against Mr Wood's will (which I suppose), I have no doubt it is a case of horse-stealing, and a case for the Central Criminal Court. Of course you can't produce a horse that is stolen away from you.'

'I feel, after what fell from your lordship yesterday, that it would be in vain to struggle against the effect that must necessarily be produced in the case by the non-production of the horse,' said Cockburn, none too subtly alluding to the prejudicial nature of Alderson's comments the preceding day. 'I can only say, on the part of Mr Wood, that he perfectly concurred in the view that his counsel took of the necessity of its production, and I have his assurance that he has done his utmost to ascertain where the horse is, and to produce it – that the horse has been twice removed without his knowledge – that he is in perfect ignorance where the horse is, and in consequence we are not in a situation to produce the horse.'

'Then what,' asked Alderson icily, 'is the result to be?'

The Solicitor General could hardly contain his glee: 'All I can say is, my friend must pursue whatever course he pleases; we are quite prepared to go on with the case, and to prove our case distinctly. My friend in his discretion will adopt whatever course he pleases.'

And go on with the case is precisely what Sir Frederick Thesiger did. Worley proved to be a staunch and credible witness, who appeared in no doubt that the horse he had had in his paddock as a yearling and then as a two-year-old during the winter of 1841 and 1842 was exactly the same horse he had seen at the Derby of 1844. He was absolutely unshakeable in his testimony, swearing that he had got off his horse in order to take a closer look. 'I thought I should like to see him again,' he said perhaps a trifle disingenuously. When asked how far he had been from Running Rein at the Derby, he cast about for something nearby in the court and said, with an outstretched arm, 'As close as I am to that bar', a distance of 'about a yard'. Worse was to follow for Wood, as the horse dealer Odell, who had been a co-conspirator with Higgins, was called to give evidence. He corroborated what Worley had said, and what by now everyone in the courtroom knew: that the horse that had come first in the Derby was a four- rather than a three-year-old. As Worley and Odell hammered the nails into the coffin of his case, Wood conferred frantically with his legal advisers.

Cockburn was on his feet again:

My lord, although I saw my client, Mr Wood, before we came into court, and received instructions from him with respect to the impossibility of getting at the horse, I did not see him at the moment just before I was addressing your lordship. I now find he had intimated to the gentleman connected with this very affair – to Colonel Peel – before the case was coming on, that he was convinced that he himself had been deceived, and that he did not intend to go on with the case. He has been conversing with me while this conversation is going on, and Mr Wood begs me emphatically to repeat – and I trust he will be believed by Colonel Peel and the other gentlemen who have known him, and have known his character, which has hitherto stood unimpeached.

Wood, realising that he had been abandoned by Goodman and fearing that he was to be used as scapegoat, clearly understood that unless he capitulated right away further evidence might come out that would implicate him as part of the scheme rather than as the unknowing dupe that he hoped to be taken for. And as most subsequent accounts cast him in this light, it appears that

Cockburn's silver-tongued oratory achieved exactly that end.

There was, however, another matter to clear up before Wood's team submitted to a verdict in favour of Peel. Craving the indulgence of the slightly mollified Alderson, Cockburn asked:

Will your lordship allow me to avert for a moment to another matter which is immediately connected with this case and in what I am about to say, I trust I shall give offence to no one, and possibly may remove it. My lord, I have received a communication from my Lord George Bentinck, couched, I must say, in terms of perfect courtesy to myself, and perfectly unexceptionable in every point of view, in which his lordship complains of my having made a charge against him yesterday, with respect to his conduct in the matters connected with the case, and that I have not put him into the witness box, or called witnesses to prove that charge. My lord, I will just explain in a moment the position in which I stand; my instructions were clear, specific, positive and unqualified as to _this_ – that my Lord George Bentinck had (for I can use no milder term) tampered with the plaintiff's witnesses; that he had held out threats to them, and where threats had failed, had held out promises to them to induce them to withhold their evidence. That he had procured by the greatest exertions, and by the use of his personal influence, witnesses to appear for the defendant; that he had to a certain degree associated with those witnesses; that he had them at Harcourt House, his new place of residence, that he had fed them, that he had clothed them, that his valet had been seen to take one of them to a tailor's to fit him out with clothes, and that his lordship had helped out to another a pecuniary promise – had actually given money, and had held out a pecuniary promise. I was instructed, my lord, that from his lordship, if he was called as a witness for the defendant, I should be enabled to extract these matters. I was instructed, that from the defendant's witnesses, when called, I should be enabled to elicit these facts; and I was instructed, that with regard to one of them, especially one to whom it was alleged a promise had been made, that I should be enabled if he denied the fact, or denied his admission of the fact ... to call a body of witnesses to whom he had made such admission. Under these circumstances, my lord, it being a fact in the cause, if Lord George Bentinck was not a party in the cause, still he had been the great mover in it, which is not denied by my learned friend the Solicitor-General. I thought it better at once to open these matters, in order that my learned friend, the Solicitor-General, might know the course I should adopt when the witnesses for the defence were to be put into the box; that the observations that I might think myself called upon afterwards to make on my Lord George Bentinck, might not be made by me when there should be no opportunity of replying on me.[2]

So much for the removal of offence! With the consummate skill and artistry of a truly great advocate, Cockburn thus managed to give voice to all his accusations about Bentinck's conduct, enumerating them in considerable detail (although it was a shame that he did not get round to disclosing which tailor had been used), while simultaneously 'apologising' for having attacked Bentinck's reputation. His 'withering and sarcastic',[3] as *The Era* described it, tone was not lost on those who listened to his 'apology'.

For his part, Alderson, having acted the despot on the preceding day, fell over himself to reassure Cockburn that 'there is nothing in this case in the slightest degree that has been done improperly by you'. He added for the sake of even-handedness, 'Nor (and so far I am bound to say) has any impropriety been in the slightest degree shown to have existed on the part of Lord George Bentinck. Undoubtedly he did that which was perfectly right – he has traced out the truth, and the truth has come out.' One of Peel's team then stood up to make the point that Bentinck would have relished nothing more than the chance to give evidence in court, and that only the abrupt cessation of the proceedings had denied him this opportunity.

The mood of excitement flickered through the courtroom and like electricity sped things on to their natural conclusion, with Baron Alderson cast in the role of Greek chorus or as the authorial voice in one of the young Mr Dickens's novels. He addressed the jury.

Gentlemen the only remaining matter, it being now admitted that the verdict must be for the defendant, will be for you to proceed to give your verdict. Give me leave to say that this case has produced a very great degree of sorrow and disgust in my mind. I have seen the opening out of a most atrocious fraud which has been practised, and I have seen with great regret gentlemen associating with persons of infinitely lower rank than themselves, which is the cause of it all. If gentlemen would only race with gentlemen there would not be any difficulty in the matter; but if they condescend to race with black-guards they must condescend to expect to be cheated.[4]

20

Gentlemen Triumphant

Those followers of the Turf who had not been able to squeeze into the Court of Exchequer had done the next-best thing and headed to Tattersall's, where they had watched that sure barometer of the respective cases, the fluctuations in betting. On the Sunday before the trial, odds of '5 and 6 to 1 could have been obtained' on Colonel Peel's Orlando, reported the *Sporting Life*. But on Monday the odds were shorter, dropping to 3–1 at the start of the trial but rising to 4–1 'after the evidence of Wood's trainer'. Thereafter the odds continued to move in a direction that indicated a victory by Orlando.

But the ramifications of the Running Rein case extended well beyond Tattersall's subscription room. The disputed Derby had absorbed the country's attention; for weeks the outcome had been a topic of intense debate. It had illuminated the hitherto closed world of the early Victorian Turf, and the general impression was of a shadowy realm riddled with dishonesty, in which anything and everything was done in pursuit of financial gain. This picture was doubtless compounded by the near-simultaneous crackdown on illegal gambling that had struck at both the London hells and their satellites, the booths on the Derby course at Epsom.

At first there was relief in the racing world that a result had been reached and that it was in the favour of the sporting Establishment. 'On the news reaching Newmarket,' recorded *Bell's Life* on Sunday 7 July 1844, 'the exultation was extraordinary, all the bells were set ringing, bands of music paraded about the streets, the place was in a perfect uproar of delight'. Settling day at Tattersall's was declared to be the next day, the 8th, 'and this example will be followed throughout the kingdom' while 'the funds which have been locked up in Derby clubs will be distributed'.[1]

The obvious scoundrels emerged as Goodman, Higgins, Bean and Smith, and press reports suggested that they would be made the subject of further proceedings. It was rumoured, for instance, that Thomas Ferguson, who in the event had not needed to give evidence, was offered, and refused, £2,000 (£240,000) 'to absent himself'.[2] There were still questions about Wood's part in the matter, with a suspicious *Bell's Life* calling for him to make 'the fullest and most candid explanation of his connection with the whole of this nefarious transaction' in order to save himself from 'public condemnation'. Nevertheless, his abrupt capitulation had at least distanced him from the malefactors, and in the days following the trial he played to the full his part of the injured and innocent party. He had his solicitor write an 'exculpatory statement' to *Bell's Life* in London, presenting him as a decent tradesman of Epsom, 'where his real character as an honest and upright man is well-known'.

The letter also raised concerns about the fallibility of examining a horse's mouth to determine its age. It even suggested that the vet who had examined the horse in question had changed his mind because of public opinion – neatly forgetting that the same vet had raised the matter with an entirely uninterested Jockey Club at the beginning of the year. Wood let it be known that he had tracked Goodman down and 'demanded restitution of the horse', and that Goodman had 'said he should never see the horse again, but might have a quarter of him if he chose'. It was apparent that 'the poor horse has been made the sacrifice of this abominable conspiracy, and has been actually destroyed'.[3] Clearly, lessons had been learned from the Leander case regarding the leaving of evidence; it was said that the animal's mouth had been tampered with, one of the teeth knocked out, the carcass boiled and the head removed and burnt.

And Wood found that after the trial his costs were almost as difficult to find as the missing horse. He paid £1,555 4s 10d in costs to Colonel Peel, but then the following year he had to take Glen, the sporting baker of Regent Street, to court in an effort to have him honour the bond of indemnity that was supposed to cover him. By this time it was noted that Levi Goodman was living in Boulogne.

The Jockey Club, meanwhile, emerged as a largely self-interested and ineffectual body, at best foolish and negligent.

There were, in short, plenty of villains to populate this sordid tale, but where there are villains there is a need for a hero, and the sporting press and public accorded that role to Lord George Bentinck. There was an almost unseemly rush to support him. The trial had been over for merely hours when a meeting 'of gentlemen of the highest respectability connected with the Turf decided to present Lord George with a piece of plate to congratulate him. Even though individual contributions were capped at £25, the figure pledged had risen to £300 within just 'a few minutes'. What happened just as quickly was the linking of Bentinck's detective work during the Running Rein case with his wider campaigns to regularise racing, and in particular his merciless pursuit of Turf defaulters. *Bell's Life* believed that this piece of plate, contributions for which were pouring into Weatherby's, was in token 'of the high sense entertained of his indefatigable and successful exertions not only in this case, but we believe for the services which he has rendered by promoting the stability and prosperity of racing in general'[4] – even though those indefatigable exertions had, among other things, precipitated the whole *qui tam* farrago and prompted him to fall out with the Jockey Club, calling for its abolition.

The contributions kept on coming and rather than a single piece there was soon enough to purchase an entire service. But in line with his new selfless persona, following the principle that virtue is its own reward, Bentinck 'refused to accept any tribute, either in the form of a service of plate, or otherwise, and at his express wish the "Bentinck Benevolent Fund", for the benefit of the widows and the children of deserving trainers and jockeys, who had been left in necessitous circumstances, was established with the sum of money which had been subscribed'.[5]

Even those who had disagreed with him in the past succumbed to Bentinck mania. 'It has been our lot to differ more than once with his Lordship in our record of Turf matters, and most probably it will happen again,' commented the *The Era* of Sunday 7 July, before embarking on an orgy of praise for his 'stupendous efforts to regenerate the Turf' and contrasting his 'glorious activity' with the Jockey Club's 'effeminate supineness'. Manliness was clearly high on everyone's list of essential virtues – *The Era* described him as the 'Hercules of the Turf, cleanser of the Augean stable', and cast his opponents as 'fraudulent Jews, and horse-dealers, and hell-keepers and men in the back ground'. It was eagerly hoped that the 'perfect and consummated re-union of his Lordship and the Club' would 'insure us a clear and purified atmosphere after the tremendous moral storm with which we have been visited'; and in this reunion the newspaper saw the 'prelude to the revival of the one, original Court of Honor, where all disputes can be arranged without the interference of a Court of Law'.[6]

The Jockey Club too, which had hitherto regarded Bentinck as an irritant, decided that thanks were 'eminently due' to him for his 'energy, perseverance, and skill'. The near-hysterical adulation of Lord George in the sporting world continued in the following years with, amongst other things, the inauguration of the Bentinck Testimonial Stakes in Liverpool in 1845, accompanied by a piece of plate carrying the following admirably fawning inscription:

Honourably to commemorate the public spirited exertions of Lord George Bentinck, by whose zeal and perseverance a fatal blow was struck at the late irregularities and growing malpractices of the Turf;

a wholesome but unflinching lesson was read to the owners, trainers and riders of horses; punctuality, order, obedience and fair play were re-established at the Starting Post, and thus, to the frequenters of the racecourse, whether attracted to the National Sport by pleasure or by speculation, confidence and satisfaction were secured.[7]

The author of these words was being rather optimistic. The Running Rein scandal marked only the nadir of the reputation of the Turf, not its recovery. A mere fortnight after this most corrupt Derby, the winner of the New Stakes at Ascot, a race for two-year-olds, was found to be a three-year-old called Bloodstone. In August, a further scandal was uncovered when it was found that 'letter carriers' of the General Post Office had been intercepting 'letters directed to noblemen, gentlemen, and others connected with the sporting world', among them Lord George Bentinck and Richard Tattersall. These men had been in the habit of opening letters to and from sporting celebrities and then selling the information on to betters – or, indeed, 'betting themselves to a large amount'.[8] The following year the Derby was overshadowed by allegations that John Gully's horse Old England was to be 'made safe'. Gully brought the matter out into the open at Tattersall's much in the way that Bentinck had attempted to expose the plot to fix Ratan on the steps of the Spread Eagle. The Days, who trained Old England, were found guilty, and associated parties included veterans of the Derby scandals of 1844 including Henry Stebbings and the pink-eyed Hargraves.

Nor had the Derby of 1844 finished inscribing names on its roll of dishonour. The conduct of the jockey Sam Rogers, whose betting book had been the subject of highly public investigation at the Spread Eagle in Epsom, was looked into more fully by Lord George Bentinck, who did not like what he found. It turned out that Rogers had indeed been mired in extremely murky betting transactions and had lied to him in the run-up to the Derby. Bentinck gave what was euphemistically termed a 'sharp lecture' to Sam Rogers, after which, *The Satirist* noted on 29 September, the jockey 'went home to his wife with something of the sensation of a whipped child to its mother'. Mrs Rogers was made of sterner stuff than her husband, though, and wrote to Bentinck asking for an interview with him to plead on her husband's behalf. Bentinck appeared at Rogers's house in person and, *The Satirist* continued,

> had no sooner set foot in Sam's domicile, than Mrs Sam and her sister-in-law, Mrs Boyce, were down on their knees in a moment, and begging his lordship's merciful consideration of Sam's conduct. Had they contented themselves with this, things might have gone off smoothly; but when in addition they declared very fervently Sam's entire innocence – that he never dreamt, poor fellow, of doing wrong in laying against Ratan, and that his only object was to protect the horse – his lordship began to wax impatient, and plainly told the ladies that their tale was rather *too* good to be quite true, and notwithstanding the eloquence of tearful eyes and streaming locks, he speedily took his leave with a polite good morning.

The Jockey Club was similarly unimpressed with Rogers. At a hearing held in secret in the autumn of 1844 it emerged that he and an accomplice called Braham had plotted to influence the betting and had employed commission agents to bet for them against the horse. They also admitted that they had no intention of paying out if the horse Ratan won (although with Rogers on its back that seemed unlikely). Rogers was warned off the Heath and banned from riding or training horses 'at Newmarket, or at any place where the rules of the Jockey Club are in force'. And in an arch act of humbug the Jockey Club issued a statement that 'the committee cannot express too strongly their opinion of the impropriety of gentlemen betting large sums of money for jockeys or for parties intrusted with the charge of racehorses'.[9] Still, at least Crockford received posthumous vindication of his deathbed assertion that the horse 'had been "served" for that was not his running'.[10]*

---

* However, the club relented after a few years. But riding the Derby in 1859 Rogers was once again involved in controversy surrounding a plot to pull a horse up.

*

Meanwhile, fired up with virtuous zeal, Bentinck set about exposing what he saw as malfeasance elsewhere. He was on the attack in the House of Commons, where the issue of the *qui tam* actions and the legislation to protect those made subject of them was still being debated. The Manchester MP Milner Gibson continued to champion the Turf defaulter Charles Russell and his dubious solicitor brother James, requesting that their lawyer be allowed to address the House of Commons. On 10 July the Russells' counsel appeared at Westminster only to find that the Chancellor of the Exchequer was not going to allow him to speak because 'he had received information that the petitioner was not himself the party interested', but 'a person put forward by others, who were the real plaintiffs, in order to conceal their own names'. But even if Russell *were* directly interested, 'there were sufficient reasons why, in the present stage of the proceedings, he should not be heard', reported *Hansard*. Two days earlier Charles Russell had appeared before the House of Lords Select Committee inquiring into gambling, chaired by the Duke of Richmond, who it seemed had leaked details of Russell's evidence to Lord George Bentinck, who was about to use this evidence to embarrass Gibson.

The sound of the Establishment closing ranks was clearly heard by Gibson, who could now vent his impotent fury 'that Government had allowed his hon. and learned Friend (Mr Christie) to believe on one day that it would not oppose the hearing of counsel at the Bar, and on the next had resisted a Motion to that effect'. He accused ministers of pursuing 'a timid and shilly-shally course unworthy of a strong Government', of acting 'as if they wished the [Actions for Gaming Discontinuance, or 'Manly Sports'] Bill to pass, and yet were ashamed of standing forward until they saw some indication of public opinion in its favour'.

The accusation of shilly-shallying prompted another member to pitch in to support Gibson, observing that 'he agreed with the hon. Member for Manchester, that the recent Indemnity Bill would never have been introduced at all, if it had not affected persons in high and conspicuous situations, connected with Members of the Legislature'. Furthermore, he found it remarkable 'that the Select Committee on Gambling had not said one word on the subject of horse-racing, and yet only a few days after they had made their Report, one of the grossest cases of fraud in horse-racing had been brought to light, so gross that the Judge who presided in his charge had expressed his astonishment that Gentlemen consented to associate with the characters concerned in it'.[11]

Thereafter the debate warmed up, and a verbal brawl ensued as accusations were batted back and forth. Somewhat foolishly Colonel Peel took exception to Alderson's rather outspoken closing remarks, calling them 'an unfortunate expression'. Peel claimed that he had never seen the blackguards in question until they entered the court; and 'as to their meeting in a public place', he was as powerless to 'prevent that, as their walking over Westminster Bridge'.

In drawing such a narrow and literal interpretation of Baron Alderson's salty opinions, the gallant colonel put his foot in it again, amply demonstrating a lack of judgement that showed why his brother rather than he was prime minister. As *The Times* humiliatingly pointed out,

> Colonel Peel says he cannot prevent certain individuals coming into the same room that he goes into. Certainly, but Colonel Peel need not go into the room at all. Colonel Peel knows that such persons go there. He connects himself with a system in which he knows all sorts of swindling and cheating go on, and attends the same meetings that swindlers and sharpers come to; and when he and his friends find themselves bit and stung, they fly to their kind nurse's apron strings, and take refuge behind the honourable House.[12]

It was over to Bentinck, who thought that Milner Gibson 'had sought to make the Committee for which he had moved, an instrument for the person who had brought these qui tam actions'.[13] This turned the comment about gentlemen and blackguards on to Gibson. His voice creaking in the heat of the exchange, Bentinck flung out the shrill accusation: 'If we associate with blackguards, what have you been doing? Whatever the honourable member for Manchester may say of other men's associates, his associates he could not deny were self-convicted felons.' It is a wonder that Lord George could get the words out in his excitement.

Certainly Gibson was taken by surprise. All he could manage in response was a feeble 'I don't know that'.

'Yes, plaintiff and solicitor alike. For if not convicted by law, at least they were by their own acts, in compromising felony,' continued Lord George, most likely unable to keep the note of exultation out of his piping voice. He accused the honourable Member for Manchester of 'associating with persons who had robbed their own uncle's hell'.

'No,' came Milner Gibson's less than convincing denial.

'The honourable gentleman said no. But before long,' countered Bentinck, members 'would see it in print that those persons went frequently to the house of the honourable gentleman'.

'I deny it.'

'Why,' drawled Bentinck with sarcasm, 'the honourable member himself has said that he would see persons who came on business without caring what their characters might be.'[14] As to his own reputation, Bentinck declared himself 'quite content to leave his character before the public with respect to anything he had done himself, or had been said or done in the Court of Exchequer'.[15]

This game of pots and kettles was called by *The Times* 'unquestionably a perfect piece of nonsense and absurdity. On the one hand what has Parliament to do with a squabble between the gentlemanly and blackguardly sections of that very ambiguous department the turf?' asked the Thunderer. 'What use the betters and gamblers of the turf are to the country it is difficult to see. The country, and even the turf itself, could do very well, and much better without them.' However, the paper also castigated Milner Gibson, saying that he might have objected quite effectively to this measure 'without holding private meetings with scamps and swindlers', adding that he might have been 'opposed to the gentlemen of the turf without patronising its blackguards'.[16]

Bentinck's virtue proved impervious to the barbs of *The Times*, and the *qui tam* debate did eventually play itself out in court. In a gesture that added lustre to his reputation, Bentinck was actually prepared to face the Russells in court. The hearing that took place in Guildford on 8 August in front of Mr Baron Parke brought together some of the most colourful Turf characters, including John Day, John Gully and Harry Hill, who all gave evidence. In just the sort of muscular behaviour that Bentinck's supporters applauded, although he had voted on the passing of the Act to protect his fellow betters from prosecution, 'he declared that it was not his intention to take advantage of the statute, nor to plead the statute'.[17] This further evidence, if it were needed, of Lord George's manliness, honour and so forth, moved one Victorian Turf historian to write:

> It was like the thoroughly plucky spirit of such a sportsman as Lord George, who had at different times more than his share of vexatious actions, to wish to see the question settled on its merits, once and for ever, if possible; as he had been advised no jury would ever find a verdict for the plaintiffs in actions of this description. It was also characteristic of the learned Baron Parke, who had a strong regard for all good English sports, to second the desire of the defendant to take the verdict of his country rather than move the Court above on the point of law.[18]

A clue to the outcome of the trial can be gleaned from the court's reaction to Hill's admission that he was unable to produce his betting book, because he had burnt it. Asked when he had destroyed it he answered, 'Oh as soon as I heard tell of these qui tam actions.' As he said this there was 'great laughter, in which the learned baron joined most heartily'. The *qui tam* actions had become, literally, a laughing stock.

Doubtless sensing the way the trial was heading, the Russells' counsel chose to use his opening remarks to broaden the scope of the particular case being tried. 'You will agree with me, that while the humble gamester, who is said to infest the race course is put down by the police constable, we ought to take care that there is no class in the community, the members of which shall consider themselves privileged to do those acts, for the doing of which their humbler companions are regularly punished.' He went on to enumerate in some detail the complex and tangled betting transactions that had taken place. These had been further obscured by the use of a commission agent in the shape of Hill and the passing of bets between various participants, namely Gully and John Day. The lawyer admitted that he had met the greatest opposition when trying to assemble the case. He then returned to his general theme. Gambling, he said, was a mischief and anyone with any sense of morality would applaud a statute that penalised it.

Why should there be a distinction of classes? Why are men who have booths and tables to be swept from race courses, while other men who pursue the same occupation of gaming, in perhaps a different manner, are to be allowed to go unnoticed? For what reason is this difference to be made? Why are immoral practices to be condemned in one class and allowed in another? Wherever they exist they lead to dissoluteness, extravagance, ruin and roguery and therefore ought to be put down. I ask again gentlemen why should a man in a higher station of life be allowed to do anything, when those of a lower rank are thus to be punished for doing the very same thing? Can that difference be reasonable, can it be honest, can it be just? I say, therefore that whatever may be the topics urged on the other side with respect to application of this law, there is not one of you gentlemen who will not go along with me in saying, that the law of England equally and justly applies to all sorts of gaming, by whomsoever practised, and that in this respect, as in all others, there is no difference whatever in the eye of the law, whether the offences against the law are committed by the poor or rich.[19]

But this was England in 1844. Despite hearing evidence that bets of many thousands had indeed been offered and taken, the jury found for the gentlemen rather than the blackguards, and 'at once returned a verdict for the defendant'.

Epilogue

———

It was the evening of the third day of the Goodwood meeting of 1846, and the Duke of Richmond's dinner guests were discussing the day's racing and how Mr O'Brien's Grimston had won the Cup. But gradually the talk turned to racing's grandee, Lord George Bentinck. Two years on from the summer of 1844, Bentinck was at the height of his powers, respected and revered as the Hercules of the Turf. The preceding year had been his most successful as an owner of racehorses. Of course, he was one of the duke's guests that evening, and it seemed that the dinner now coming to an end had had a soporific effect on him – he 'appeared to be more than half asleep', commented John Kent in his *Racing Life of Lord George Cavendish Bentinck*.

However, while his eyelids might have been closed his mind and his ears were open. 'As the guests assembled around the Duke of Richmond's table fell to discussing the magnitude of Lord George's racing establishments, and the large number of horses that he had in training', the subject of their conversation, his eyes still closed, joined the conversation in a most unexpected way: 'Will any of you give me £10,000 (£1,200,000) for all my lot, beginning with old Bay Middleton and ending with little Kitchener, and take them with all their engagements and responsibilities off my hands?'

It was a typically Bentinck moment: headstrong, unexpected and apparently arbitrary. But earlier that year Bentinck had begun to talk to his trainer of his 'deep regret that, by reason of the severe pressure of his parliamentary duties, he found himself unable to devote as much time as he could wish to managing, engaging, and watching his race horses in training'.[1] Horse racing, which had been his ruling passion for over twenty years, no longer interested him. It is rather fitting that as a young man in his early twenties he had had his first taste of racing riding at Goodwood, and now as a public man in his forties he chose Goodwood to announce his abandonment of the sport.

It is almost as if the virtuous glow accruing to him from his efforts over the Derby of 1844 had put him in search of new worlds to conquer. 'The pastimes and fortunes of the turf, in which his whole being seemed engrossed,'[2] wrote Disraeli, suddenly lost their power to captivate him. He had done with the Turf: he had won its prizes (except, of course, the one he most craved, the Derby), and he had risen to be, depending on one's view, its dictator or its saviour. Now he was channelling his energies towards what he saw as righting another wrong, cleaning another Augean stable – except this time he would be undertaking a labour on the national stage and his opponent was not a horse faker or a disgruntled hellite but Sir Robert Peel the prime minister, the man whom Bentinck, unable to determine shades of grey, saw as the betrayer of the landed interest.

'If you will give me till to-morrow at noon, Bentinck, to consider the matter, I will either accept your offer or will pay you £300 if I decline it.' George Payne was the first to speak and so secured the option on what was the sporting sale of the century.

'Agreed!' muttered Bentinck. The two men sat down together and 'entered into a long *sotto voce* conversation with each other'.[3]

As it happened, Payne paid his £300 to Bentinck the following day and the stud was eventually purchased by a young nobleman called Mostyn. The first thing he did was to reduce the vast number of horses that Bentinck had kept.

Lord George seemed almost dispassionate about the dismantling of the epic racing establishment that had been his life's work. He wrote to his brother that September:

My dear Jock, My stud will have proved a wonderful bargain to the Purchasers. I have no doubt but that they would have realised £15,000 clear if they had sold everything; but I always estimated that they would sell for £5,000 more in anybody else's hands than in mine.

They [Mostyn] have refused 7,000gs for Planet & Slander* & I was told 3,000gs for three bar those two; & they have already sold 33 lots for 3,700gs (there were 205 lots in all). I fancy they mean to sell nothing worth keeping except at extortionate prices; they sold Comrade for 200gs. He has been a begging for 3 months at 50gs. He is a crib biter, a roarer, & frequently breaks a blood vessel in the head & falls consequently without notice in his gallop!!! Old Plantation, now past breeding sold for 17gs last year when heavy in foal to Emilius so one at the hammer bid 5gs for her.

I see Crozier was put up at 4,000gs & I believe they might have got 600 or 700gs for him with his engagements; last year I put him up at the hammer at Tattersall's to be sold for a guinea if it was bid, it would have been happy for me had someone bought him for a guinea, but no one would bid half a guinea for him!!!

I regret Planet more even than Crucifix; Planet is a better horse than ever Crucifix has yet bred. However I should like to have kept them both, but I knew if I kept anything back the Stud would not sell at all. I was dying to be out of it – they were costing me £40 a day & when I gave away the 2,000gs stake to Gully & John Day through mismanagement in running Crozier instead of Planet for it, I was so disgusted & so satisfied I must be ruined if I went on with a racing establishment without having time to look after it & attend to it myself that I felt quite a load off my mind as soon as they were sold for 10,000gs – though I had valued them in my own mind in consultation with Kent at 23,000gs with their engagements.

Bentinck was winding up his racing life and tidying up the loose ends. His letter continues:

I owed Drummonds [bank] £17,000. I have paid them off £7,000 & mean to pay them off the remaining £10,000 at Christmas when

* Slander was the last horse to run in Bentinck's colours, winning the Prince of Wales stakes at York in August 1846.

Mostyn is to pay me for the Stud, unless you will let me pay off the £7,000 I owe you (exclusive of the interest I ought to have but never have paid you for God knows how many years). You need have no scruple in the matter because I shall now have more income than I shall know well how to spend & you will bear in mind the Duke of Richmond owes me £10,000 on bond. In that I think the money is more wanted by you & would be turned to better account by you now than by me.[4]

Bentinck was to die only a couple of years later, at the age of forty-six, of a heart attack, which many thought had been brought on by overwork and his insistence on starving himself during the day so as not to dull his wits; this habit also had the result of rendering him extremely bad tempered. But by that time his apotheosis was complete. His Turf career, which had dominated most of his adult life and which had seen him stoop to some unscrupulous tricks, was forgotten, outshone by the lustre of his chivalric stand against the repeal of the Corn Laws. To many Bentinck was a hero, in particular to the youthful romantics of the Young England movement.

'It is impossible to write on any other subject than that awful catastrophe which has deprived us of the most true, warm-hearted of friends, and the country of the purest, most self-denying, least selfish of patriots. How great a loss in private and in public life! It was only a day or two before the session closed that I was complimenting him on his unusual good looks after such severe and continuous fatigues,' wrote Lord John Manners to his father, virtually inconsolable, on 27 September, six days after Bentinck's death.

The poor Duke of Portland! What can comfort him, humanly speaking, in this terrible bereavement? Truly, like the Patriarch of old, his grey hairs will be brought with sorrow to the grave. If universal demonstrations of sorrow may alleviate his grief, those certainly he does not lack. Mr Chapman writes me word that all the shipping in the Liverpool Docks hoisted colours half mast high, on the fatal news being made known – and everywhere and from all people expressions of the sincerest sorrow are heard. I think many now perceive and appreciate his great and irregular qualities, who before were blind to them.[5]

It took a more mature and informed observer to see the true picture. Charles Greville confided to his diary:

I have not the least doubt that, for his own reputation and celebrity, he died at the most opportune period. His fame had probably reached its zenith, and credit was given him for greater abilities than he possessed, and for a futurity of fame, influence and power which it is not probable he ever would have realised. As it is, the world will never know anything of those serious blemishes which could not fail to dim the lustre of his character; he will long be remembered and regretted as a very remarkable man, and will occupy a conspicuous place in the history of his own time.[6]

It was these last sentiments that were shared by Lieutenant F. Nugent Macnamara, the poetaster who cobbled together a 'MONODY Written on the Death of the late ever to be lamented LORD GEORGE BENTINCK', dedicated 'to the noble House of Portland':

'His saltem accumulem donis, et fungarinani munere.'
'Munere.' – VIRGIL.
Gloom o'er proud Welbeck [Bentinck's family seat]
    waves her sable hand.
Behold a train of real mourners stand,
Affection's tribute render'd to his bier,
Worth – Talent – Title, pay the ready tear.
Bentinck! thy loss our country must deplore,
And who convince us now to grieve no more.
Say, shall the Senate not confess thy loss,
Who tested honesty, – detested dross,
'Faithful among the faithless,' truly known
True to the people – loyal to the Throne;

Poor Erin weeps thy noble plans undone,
And India lost a true untiring Son,
Whose Soul of Chivalry, and patriot fire,
Would even apathy itself inspire;
Religious freedom with thy name's enshrined,
Pure was the purpose of thy manly mind;
What fond emotion with thy name we blend,
True to those duties taught in early dawn,
Bright was the promise of thy rising morn;
Alas before thy bright meridian ray,
Lost is the story of the promised day,
Departed hopes, – appears the cypress wreath;
The blank – the terror of thy fatal death,
Who will not miss thee from the courtly sphere?
Beloved by all, – the peasant and the peer:
The Farmer's friend and patron of the Soil,
Where native Industry expends its toil,
Foremost to serve, or by exertion prove,
The rural interest of the peaceful grove,
To nerve the souls and sinews of that band,
The British yeomen – honour of our land.
Friend of the Turf, its ever trusty guide,
With love of sport fair principle allied,
Eager to punish or detect a flaw
Of petty Tricksters, and their men of law,
Until thy name became the Turf's defence,
'Gainst needy jobbers and their foul pretence.
Where'er I turn, where manly actions prove
A love of country, and a patriot's love,
Thy name I find: identified with thee,
The frank and noble hope of liberty.
'Mild charity, the maid divine,' appears,
Bedews thy tomb with ever grateful tears,
Religion's calm alone can render peace
And Heaven's mercy bid our sorrows cease.

> Ours the keen pang of fitful memory's pain,
> 'Who ne'er shall look upon thy like again.'[7]

It is easy to see how a string of racehorses and a reputation for sharp practice might have seemed out of place in 'the purest, most self-denying, least selfish of patriots'.

The sale of Bentinck's stud and Mostyn's subsequent disposal of many of the horses through Tattersall's was one of the sporting sensations of the decade, and the break-up of this vast racing establishment was not the only sign that the world was changing. The previous year the *Sportsman's Magazine* had run a lengthy obituary on the passing of another monument of an earlier age, taking its readers on a tour of what it called a 'deserted shrine of avarice and ruin, which still rears its head though its guests have departed and its owner has gone to his last reckoning'. Crockford's still limped on, but it was rudderless; its creator had already retired before his death and the culture that supported and tolerated it was dying too, casualty of 'the war which has of late been carried out by the police and the parish of St James's against the various hells of the vicinity'.[8] The end for Crockford's came soon enough. Writing to the gambling radical MP Thomas Slingsby Duncombe on Christmas Eve 1845, one R.W. Graham informed him: 'It is all over with Crocky's, and the place is to be closed on the 1st January; and it appears there is no intention to form another club out of it. In fact, it is such a motley set that there would be great difficulty to do so.'[9]

The same year, 1845, saw the first of three Acts to curb gambling, though horse racing was of course protected. Members of the Jockey Club gathered in Newmarket during the second October meeting of 1845 were accordingly grateful to the legislators who had protected their sport. The minutes of that meeting record:

> That the unanimous thanks of the Jockey Club be rendered to his Grace the Duke of Richmond, K.G., for his Grace's indefatigable exertions, and eminent services in the House of Lords, whereby many obsolete statutes which threatened destruction to the best interests of

the Turf, have been repealed, and the remaining laws in regard to horse-racing put upon a safe and satisfactory footing.
Resolved.

That the Standing Rules and Orders of the Jockey Club be suspended, in order to the election, by open voting, of Viscount Palmerston, as a free member of the Jockey Club.
Resolved.

That Viscount Palmerston be, and his lordship is hereby elected, an honorary member of the Jockey Club.
Resolved.

That the unanimous thanks of the Jockey Club be offered to the Right Hon. Viscount Palmerston, for the invaluable services which his lordship rendered to the interests of the Turf in regard to a revision of the laws affecting the same, and that his lordship be requested to become an honorary member of the Jockey Club, having been elected unanimously by a suspension of their rules.
Resolved.[10]

Nevertheless, the moral tide had turned and rouged roués like Lord Palmerston were members of a fading generation whose cheerful amorality would give way to the earnest and conspicuous high-mindedness of the high Victorian era. Successive Acts in 1853 and 1874 indicated the concern with which gambling was viewed, although on-course betting at horse races was still countenanced. The moral fervour reached its zenith in 1897, when the National Anti-Gambling League tried to ban betting at racecourses. It used a provision of the 1853 Act that stated it was illegal to resort to a 'place' to gamble, arguing that a racecourse was just such a 'place'. The League won its case against the Kempton Park Racecourse Company, but lost on appeal.

From time to time, however, echoes of the old world of hells and hazard could be heard. Every so often the police would raid an old-style hell. At half past one on the morning of 15 July 1857, a policeman knocked sharply on the door of a tobacconist at no. 28

Coventry Street in central London. The shop had been under surveillance for two months, during which time 'little tobacco or none had been sold', the *Morning Chronicle* reported. A young man looked through the window and, seeing the police, ran into a room behind the shop. The police forced the door and apprehended fifteen people; the man caught with the dice box in his hand was Abraham Levi Goodman.

It is rather poignant to read in the newspaper report that Goodman, the man who had once come so close to success in his daring plot to steal racing's most famous race, was running a shabby second-, even third-rate hell that the court considered barely worthy of attention. It was frequented by a crowd that consisted 'not of minors, apprentices, or servants, who are too frequently tempted by the facilities of such a house to make free with their employers' property, but was composed of veteran idlers who, perhaps, might be left to compass each other's ruin without much loss to society'.[11] The previous year Goodman's fourteen-year-old daughter had been abducted to the continent by a married military man called Captain Erlam, and at the subsequent trial Goodman was criticised for his 'disgraceful conduct'.[12] Still, at least he could derive some paternal satisfaction from the fact that his son, the young man who had spotted the police and raised the alarm, seemed keen to continue in the family business. Goodman died of dropsy in the early 1860s, having spent the last two years of his life 'in a most impoverished state, being supported by a subscription'.[13]

By contrast, the horse with which he had hoped to carry off his scheme went on to enjoy a pleasant life. After the excitement of 1844, remarkably enough Maccabeus was not destroyed but reappeared in the ownership of a Mr Parry. After some under-standable resistance, the Jockey Club concluded that it was the horse 'bred by Sir Charles Ibbotson in 1840 ... and that he is the same horse that ran for the Derby in 1844 under the name of Running Rein'.[14] 'But instead of reverting to his original name of Maccabeus, ran at Ascot and York the following season under the name of Zanoni, before being exported as a stallion to Russia, where he stood at Moscow for some seaons. He became the property of Count Bronitskey, and died in 1854.'[15]

As the century wore on and respectability triumphed over rakishness, there was something almost nostalgic about the way some late Victorian writers, commenting from the safe distance of half a century, romanticised the era that ended in the summer of 1844. It was seen as a vanished age that had flourished before 'a paternal government, after much painstaking inquiry, decided to interfere with the development of what was originally an amusement of the leisured classes ... and decreed that facilities for high play in this country should be extinguished'.[16] There is even something heroic, in the vein of Tennyson's 'Charge of the Light Brigade', in the same writer's recollection of how 'the gentlemen of England marched in a compact band through the fishmonger's establishment in St James's Street, and left the greater part of their substance behind'.[17]

The last word ought to go to *Bell's Life*, which in 1886 was rather less sentimental about the age of hellites, turfites and *qui tam* actions, of Bentinck, Gully and Crockford. 'Probably in those days racing was more afflicted with rogues and vagabonds than either before or since'[18] was its unvarnished verdict on the time when gentlemen condescended to race with, and be cheated by, blackguards.

Notes

Prologue

1 Benjamin Disraeli, *Lord George Bentinck: A Political Biography*, pp. 24, 25, 26, 350, 226
2 John Kent, *The Racing Life of Lord George Cavendish Bentinck MP, and Other Reminiscences*, p. 130
3 Disraeli, *Bentinck*, p. 350
4 T.H. Bird, *Admiral Rous and the English Turf 1795–1877*, p. 75
5 Disraeli, *Bentinck*, p. 350

Chapter 1: The Blue Ribbon of the Turf

1 Benjamin Disraeli, *Sybil: or, the Two Nations*, p. 8
2 Palmerston quoted in Alastair Burnet, *The Derby: The Official Book of the World's Greatest Race*, p. 132
3 Palmerston quoted in Greville, *The Greville Memoirs*, ed. Strachey & Fulford, vol. VII, p. 478
4 Bird, *Admiral Rous*, p. 144
5 *The Times*, 23 May 1844
6 Sylvanus, *The Bye Lanes and Downs of England*, pp. 269, 271
7 Quoted in Patricia Connor and Lionel Lambourne, *Derby Day 200*, p. 8
8 Henry Pownall, *Some Particulars Relating to the History of Epsom*, p. 62
9 Quoted in Bird, *Admiral Rous*, p. 12
10 Quoted in Michael Wynn Jones, *The Derby*, p. 35
11 *The Times*, May 1795, quoted in Wynn Jones, *The Derby*, p. 35
12 Anonymous contemporary source quoted in Roger Mortimer, *The History of the Derby Stakes*, p. 34

Chapter 2: Lord George

1 Greville, _Memoirs_, vol. VI, p. 106
2 Kent, _Bentinck_, p. 16
3 Ibid., pp. 311–12
4 Sylvanus, _Bye Lanes_, pp. 92–3
5 Greville, _Memoirs_, vol. VI, p. 106
6 Michael Seth-Smith, _Lord Paramount of the Turf: Lord George Bentinck 1802–1848_, p. 19
7 Disraeli, _Bentinck_, p. 25
8 Portland Archives, correspondence PwH 92–106, Letter from Captain Ker copied by Bentinck to his father William Bentinck, Duke of Portland, 5 February 1821
9 Ibid., Bentinck to his father, 21 May 1821
10 Greville, _Memoirs_, vol. VI, p. 106
11 Kent, _Bentinck_, p. 53
12 Ibid., p. 53
13 Mike Huggins, _Flat Racing and British Society_, p. 21
14 Roger Longrigg, _The History of Horse Racing_, p. 93
15 Quoted in ibid., p. 94
16 Quoted in Kent, _Bentinck_, pp. 381–2
17 Bird, _Admiral Rous_, p. 115
18 Sylvanus, _Bye Lanes_, pp. 210, 195
19 Kent, _Bentinck_, p. 54, 55
20 Greville, _Memoirs_, vol. VI, p. 109
21 Kent, _Bentinck_, p. 55
22 Greville, _Memoirs_, vol. VI, p. 110
23 William Day, _Reminiscences of the Turf_, p. 54
24 Greville, _Memoirs_, vol. VI, p. 106
25 Kent, _Bentinck_, p. 74
26 Day, _Reminiscences_, pp. 86, 103, 101
27 Kent, _Bentinck_, p. 246
28 Ibid., p. 317
29 Bird, _Admiral Rous_, p. 42
30 Kent, _Bentinck_, pp. 102, 103
31 Ibid., pp. 152, 106, 112
32 Bird, _Admiral Rous_, p. 44
33 Kent, _Bentinck_, p. 112
34 Greville, _Memoirs_, vol. VI, p. 117
35 Kent, _Bentinck_, p. 62
36 Ibid., pp. 65, 71

Chapter 3: Racing Magnate

1 Greville, *Memoirs*, vol. VI, p. 111
2 Kent, *Bentinck*, p. 129
3 Ibid., p. 316
4 The Druid, *Post and Paddock*, p. 49
5 Day, *Reminiscences*, p. 119
6 Hermann Puckler-Muskau, *Tour in England, Ireland and France in the Years 1828 and 1829*, Letter XLVI, 31 December 1828, p. 474
7 Day, *Reminiscences*, pp. 105–6
8 Greville, *Memoirs*, vol. VI, p. 113
9 Day, *Reminiscences*, p. 87
10 Kent, *Bentinck*, p. 452
11 Day, *Reminiscences*, pp. 126, 124, 125
12 Kent, *Bentinck*, p. 179
13 Ibid., p. 179
14 Greville, *Memoirs*, vol. VI, p. 117
15 Ibid., p. 109
16 Mortimer, *Jockey Club*, p. 64
17 Quoted in Kent, *Bentinck*, p. 402
18 Thomas Creevey quoted in Introduction to George Osbaldeston and E.D. Cummings, *Squire Osbaldeston: His Autobiography*, John Lane, London (1926), p. xii
19 George Payne quoted in Osbaldeston and Cummings, *Autobiography*, p. 186
20 Ibid., p. 187
21 Ibid., pp. vii, 189
22 Ibid., p. 190
23 Portland Archives, correspondence on Bentinck's dispute with Squire Osbaldeston, PwL 30, Welbeck, 15 April 1836

Chapter 4: Victorian Dawn

1 'England's Trust' by Lord John Manners, quoted in Dodds, *Paradox*, p. 183
2 Kent, *Bentinck*, p. 373
3 Greville, *Memoirs*, vol. VI, pp. 116–17
4 Quoted in Dodds, *Paradox*, p. 25
5 Quoted in A.L. Humphreys, *Crockford's*, p. 152
6 Quoted in C. Brad Faught, *The Oxford Movement*, pp. 46, 84

7 'England's Trust', quoted in Dodds, *Paradox*, p. 183

8 Quoted in Disraeli, *Bentinck*, p. 373

9 Newspaper report quoted in Wynn Jones, *The Derby*, p. 77

10 Ibid., p. 77

11 *Bell's Life in London, and Sporting Chronicle* (hereafter *Bell's Life*), quoted in ibid., p. 78

12 Evidence given before the Select Committee on Gaming, House of Commons, 1844, lines 1546/7

13 *Fraser's Magazine*, August 1833, p. 200

14 House of Commons Select Committee, line 2499

15 Charles Dickens, *Martin Chuzzlewit*, p. 407

16 Henry Luttrell, *Crockford's, or Life in the West*, vol. II, p. 13

17 Ibid., vol. II, p. 12

18 Pierce Egan, *Boxiana, or Sketches of Ancient and Modern Pugilism*, pp. 87, 88

19 Day, *Reminiscences*, p. 54

20 Downes Miles, *Pugilistica*, p. 172

21 Day, *Reminiscences*, p. 55

22 Downes Miles, *Pugilistica*, p. 173

23 Egan, *Boxiana*, p. 175

24 Downes Miles, *Pugilistica*, p. 175

25 Egan, *Boxiana*, p. 78

26 Downes Miles, *Pugilistica*, p. 174

27 Egan, *Boxiana*, pp. 78, 79, 80

28 Hen Pearce, quoted in Downes Miles, *Pugilistica*, p. 175

29 Bernard Darwin, *John Gully and His Times*, p. 17

30 Downes Miles, *Pugilistica*, p. 184

31 *Bell's* Weekly Dispatch, quoted in Downes Miles, *Pugilistica*, p. 189

32 Quoted in Darwin, *John Gully*, p. 34

33 Day, *Reminiscences*, p. 65

34 Ibid., pp. 56–7

35 Huggins, *Flat Racing*, p. 20

36 'Gallery of Celebrated Sporting Characters, No. IX, John Gully esq., MP', *Sporting Magazine*, 1835

37 Druid, *Post and Paddock*, p. 55

38 *Monthly Magazine*, vol. XXIV (July–December 1837), Craven, *Tableaux from Sporting Life*

39 Luttrell, *Crockford's*, vol. I, p. 43

40 Hen Pearce, quoted in Downes Miles, *Pugilistica*, p. 175

41 Greville, *The Diaries of Charles Greville*, ed. Pearce, p. 110

42 Day, *Reminiscences*, p. 71

43 House of Commons Select Committee, line 1048

44 Quoted in Day, *Reminiscences*, pp. 72, 74

45 Sylvanus, *Bye Lanes*, p. 118

46 Druid, *Post and Paddock*, p. 47

47 Sylvanus, *Bye Lanes*, p. 176

48 *Monthly Magazine*, vol. XXIV (July–December 1837), Craven, *Tableaux from Sporting Life*

49 Druid, *Post and Paddock*, p. 56

50 House of Commons Select Committee, line 1425

51 *New Sporting Magazine*, August 1844, pp. 83–4

52 Sylvanus, *Bye Lanes*, p. 307

53 James Christie Whyte, *History of the British Turf*, vol. I, pp. 187, 188, 189

54 House of Commons Select Committee, line 410

55 Sylvanus, *Bye Lanes*, p. 307

Chapter 5: Sporting Paladin

1 Quoted in Huggins, *Flat Racing*, p. 187

2 Kent, *Bentinck*, p. 296

3 *New Sporting Magazine*, 1841, p. 379

4 Quoted in Kent, *Bentinck*, p. 297

5 House of Lords Select Committee on Gaming, line 435

6 Quoted in Kent, *Bentinck*, pp. 298–9

7 Quoted by Lord George Bentinck in a letter to the *Morning Post*, 14 February 1842

8 Quoted in Patrick Polden, 'A Day at the Races: Wood v Leadbitter in Context', *Journal of Legal History*, vol. 14, April 1993

9 *Morning Post*, 14 February 1842

10 Quoted in Seth-Smith, *Lord Paramount*, p. 62

11 *Morning Post*, 14 February 1842

12 Grantley Berkeley, *My Life and Recollections*, quoted in Humphreys, *Crockford's*, pp. 131–2

Chapter 6: The Gambling Fishmonger

1 Rhys Howell Gronow, *The Reminiscences and Recollections of Captain Gronow*, abridged by John Raymond, p. 255

2 Ibid., p. 256

3 Greville, *Memoirs*, vol. I, pp. 79–80
4 Sylvanus, *Bye Lanes*, p. 62
5 Quoted in Alan Wykes, *Gambling*, p. 170
6 Gronow, *Reminiscences and Recollections*, p. 255
7 Luttrell, *Crockford's*, vol. I, p. 229
8 Ibid., pp. 231–2, 233
9 Sylvanus, *Bye Lanes*, p. 192
10 Luttrell, *Crockford's*, vol. I, pp. 77, 79
11 Letter to *The Times* from Expositor, 23 July 1824
12 Letter to newspaper quoted in Humphreys, *Crockford's*, p. 42
13 Sylvanus, *Bye Lanes*, p. 63
14 Expositor to *The Times*, 14 October 1824
15 Gronow, *Reminiscences and Recollections*, p. 255
16 *The Times*, 28 October 1822
17 Ibid., 28 October, 24 October 1822
18 *Bailey's*, vol. 50, p. 93, quoted in Humphreys, *Crockford's*, p. 222
19 *The Times*, 1 March, 13 February 1823
20 Ibid., 13 February 1823
21 Ibid., 24 October 1822
22 Ibid., 23 July 1824
23 Ibid., 17 August 1824
24 *Fraser's Magazine*, August 1833
25 Expositor to *The Times*, 23 July 1824
26 *Bentley's Miscellany*, vol. XVII
27 Luttrell, *Crockford's*, vol. I, p. 83; vol. I, p. 137
28 *The Times*, 11 June 1829
29 *Bentley's Miscellany*, quoted in H.T. Waddy, *The Devonshire Club – and Crockford's*, E. Nash, London (1919), pp. 120–1
30 *Bentley's Miscellany*, vol. XVII, quoted in Humphreys, *Crockford's*, pp. 49–50
31 Ibid., quoted in Humphreys, *Crockford's*, p. 51
32 *Bentley's Miscellany*, quoted in Waddy, *Crockford's*, pp. 122–3
33 James Grant, *The Great Metropolis*, vol. I, p. 160
34 *Bentley's Miscellany*, quoted in Waddy, *Crockford's*, p. 127
35 Grant, *Metropolis*, vol. I, p. 166
36 Quoted in Ralph Nevill, *London Clubs: Their History and Treasures*, p. 232
37 Gronow, *Recollections*, p. 256
38 Grant, *Metropolis*, vol. I, p. 163
39 *Bentley's Miscellany*, quoted in Waddy, *Crockford's*, p. 124
40 Ibid., p. 132
41 Grant, *Metropolis*, vol. I, pp. 172, 169–70, 162, 167–8

42 *Fraser's Magazine*, May 1838

Chapter 7: Legal Matters

1   Disraeli, *Bentinck*, pp. 23, 24, 1, 24
2   Richard Tattersall before the House of Lords Select Committee, line 407
3   *Bell's Life*, Sunday 30 June 1844
4   Bentinck quoted in ibid.
5   Bentinck quoted in ibid.
6   *Bell's Life*, Sunday 30 June 1844
7   Richard Tattersall before the House of Lords Select Committee, line 406
8   House of Lords Select Committee, question ref. 1112
9   *Hansard*, Lords sitting, 5 February 1844
10 Letter from Bentinck to John Bowes, 8 November 1843, Durham County Record Office (DCRO) D/St/C5/49/8
11 Ibid., D/St/C5/49/8
12 House of Lords Select Committee, question refs 1120, 1112, 1042, 1121, 1123–6
13 *Hansard*, 10 July 1844
14 Letter from Bentinck to Bowes, 9 November 1843, DCRO, D/St/C5/49/9
15 Ibid., 8 November 1843, D/St/C5/49/8
16 Letter to Sir William Gregory, 17 November 1843, quoted in Kent, *Bentinck*, pp. 414, 415
17 Bird, *Admiral Rous*, p. 33
18 Letter from Sir William Gregory to Bowes, 15 November 1843, DCRO, D/St/C5/49/16
19 Letters from Vane to Bowes, 24 November 1843, DCRO, D/St/C5/49/19; 5 December 1843, D/St/C5/49/26
20 Letter from H.H. Dixon to Bowes, 6 December 1843, DCRO, D/St/C5/49/27
21 Letter from Sir William Gregory to Bowes, 30 November 1843, DCRO, D/St/C5/49/22
22 Letter from Bentinck to Bowes, 3 December 1843, DCRO, D/St/C5/49/24
23 *Hansard*, 21 February 1844, Commons sitting
24 House of Commons Select Committee, lines 1913, 1447, 1937
25 Letter from Vane to Bowes, 5 December 1843, DCRO, D/St/C5/49/26
26 Disraeli, *Bentinck*, p. 25
27 Letters from Bentinck to Bowes, 14 November 1843, DCRO, D/St/C5/49/14(i); 8 November 1843, D/St/C5/49/8(ii); 9 November 1843, D/St/C5/49/9(i); 15 December 1843, D/St/C5/49/35

28 Letter from Hutt to Bowes, 21 December 1843, DCRO, D/St/C5/49/37
29 Letter from Bentinck to Bowes, 30 December 1843, DCRO, D/St/C5/53/1
30 Ibid., 10 January 1844, D/St/C5/53/9
31 Letter from Hutt to Bowes, 10 January 1844, DCRO, D/St/C5/53/10
32 Letter to Sir William Gregory, quoted in Kent, *Bentinck*, p. 416
33 Bentinck's speech in the House of Commons, Thursday 27 February 1846, from the *Morning Post*, 23 March 1846
34 Letter from Bentinck to Bowes, 11 December 1843, DCRO, D/St/C5/49/31

Chapter 8: Parliamentary Hypocrites

1   *Hansard*, Commons sitting
2   Greville, *Memoirs*, vol. VI, p. 107
3   *Hansard*, 5 February 1844, Lords sitting
4   Ibid., 8 February 1844, Lords sitting
5   Ibid., 14 February 1844, Commons sitting
6   *The Times*, 15 February 1844
7   *Hansard*, 14 February 1844, Commons sitting
8   *The Times*, 15 February 1844
9   *Hansard*, 14 February 1844, Commons sitting
10 *The Times*, 15 February 1844
11 *Hansard*, 14 February 1844, Commons sitting
12 Sylvanus, *Bye Lanes*, p. 287
13 *Hansard*, 21 February 1844, Commons sitting
14 Ibid., 14 February 1844, Commons sitting
15 Ibid., 21 February 1844, Commons sitting

Chapter 9: The Giant Evil

1   Revd T. Archer, *Gaming and Its Consequences*, pp. 123, 122, 113, 114, 120, 123, 118
2   Greville, *Memoirs*, vol. III, p. 291
3   Sylvanus, *Bye Lanes*, p. 288
4   Greville, Ed Pearce, p. 156
5   Annual Register for 1837
6   *The Times*, 5 November 1823, 31 October 1823, 1 November 1823, 4 November 1823, 1 November 1823, 4 November 1823, 14 November 1823
7   Luttrell, *Crockford's*, vol. II, p. 194
8   Grant, *Metropolis*, vol. I, pp. 215, 207, 208

9 F. Byng before the House of Commons Select Committee, lines 1010, 1008, 1013
10 Grant, *Metropolis*, vol. I, p. 209
11 Ibid., pp. 174, 172
12 *Fraser's Magazine*, 1834
13 *Morning Chronicle*, quoted in ibid., October 1834
14 Luttrell, *Crockford's*, vol. II, p. 97

Chapter 10: Gambling in the Dock

1 House of Commons Select Committee, line 3152
2 *Hansard*, 19 February 1844, Lords sitting
3 Ibid.
4 *New Sporting Magazine*, September 1844, p. 192
5 The quotations on pp. 131–133 are from the evidence brought before the House of Commons Select Committee, p. v; lines 889, 883, 485, 64, 154
6 The quotations on pp. 133–137 are from the evidence brought before the House of Lords Select Committee, lines 58, 156, 163, 356, 363, 888, 2868, 2602–3, 2606, 2609, 2611, 2622, 2620, 2717, 2707, 2776, 2836, 3098, 3152
7 Bird, *Admiral Rous*, p. 111
8 Preface to *The Laws and Practice of the Turf*, quoted in ibid., p. 112
9 Quotations on pp. 137–40, House of Commons Select Committee, lines 3088, 3090, 3091, 859, 1019, 1389
10 *Fraser's Magazine*, August 1833
11 Luttrell, *Crockford's*, pp. 201–2
12 *The Times*, 11 June 1829
13 House of Commons Select Committee, lines 1158, 1182–3, 1303
14 Charles Dickens, *Nicholas Nickleby*, vol. IV, Ch L, p. 51
15 Ibid., p. 49
16 House of Commons Select Committee, lines 1333, 1359, 1360

Chapter 11: Raid

1 House of Lords Select Committee, line 32
2 *The Satirist*, May 12, 1844

Chapter 12: Tension Mounts

1 Quoted in Stella Margetson, *Leisure and Pleasure in the Nineteenth Century*, p. 177
2 Portland Archives correspondence, letter to John Kent, Welbeck and Worksop, 7 May 1844
3 Quoted in Huggins, *Flat Racing*, p. 91
4 *Bell's Life*, 19 May 1844
5 Letters from Bentinck to Kent, Welbeck and Worksop, 16 December 1843
6 Kent, *Bentinck*, p. 201
7 Letter from Gregory to Bowes, 30 November 1843, DCRO, D/SE/C5/49/22
8 Sylvanus, *Bye Lanes*, pp. 67–8
9 Kent, *Bentinck*, p. 156
10 *Bailey's*, December 1860
11 *Hansard*, Lords sitting
12 Anon., *Horse-Racing, its history and early records of the principal race meetings, with anecdotes, etc.*, p. 411
13 Jockey Club case papers on Running Rein, JC/DC1/50 (ii) p. 1
14 *The Times*, 9 July 1828
15 Ibid., 9 July 1828
16 Ibid., 9 December 1836, 27 January 1840
17 Maidstone to the Epsom stewards, 20 May 1844
18 Noted in *The Times*, 22 May 1844
19 Anon., *Horse-Racing*, p. 411
20 *Bell's Life*, 19 May 1844
21 Sylvanus, *Bye Lanes*, pp. 181, 182
22 Kent, *Bentinck*, p. 158
23 Sylvanus, *Bye Lanes*, p. 168
24 Quotations on pp. 162–3 from House of Commons Select Committee, pp. v, viii, iii, vi, viii
25 Quoted in Margetson, *Leisure and Pleasure*, p. 177
26 *The Times*, 22 May 1844
27 Ibid., 23 May 1844
28 *Bell's Life*, 26 May 1844
29 *The Times*, 23 May 1844
30 Quoted in ibid., 23 May 1844
31 Ibid., 23 May 1844
32 *Lloyd's Weekly London Newspaper*, Sunday 26 May 1844

Chapter 13: Derby Day

1   *Bell's Life*, 19 May 1844
2   *The Times*, 22 May 1844
3   Sylvanus, *Bye Lanes*, p. 155
4   Charles Dickens, Letter XXXI, *American Notes for General Circulation*, p. 70
5   *Bell's Life*, 26 May 1844
6   Dickens, *Household Words*, 7 June 1851
7   *Bell's Life*, 26 May 1844
8   *The Times*, 23 May 1844
9   *Bell's Life*, 26 May 1844
10 House of Lords Select Committee, line 200
11 Ibid., line 446
12 *Bell's Life*, 26 May 1844
13 Ibid., 19 May, 26 May 1844
14 Sylvanus, *Bye Lanes*, p. 64
15 Quoted in Seth-Smith, *Lord Paramount of the Turf*, p. 97
16 Sylvanus, *Bye Lanes*, p. 118
17 *Bell's Life*, 26 May 1844
18 Ibid., 26 May 1844
19 *Bell's Life*, 19 May, 26 May 1844
20 The stewards of Epsom to Messrs Weatherby, 22 May 1844

Chapter 14: The Stock Exchange of Betting

1   Whyte, *British Turf*, vol. II, p. 624
2   Egan, *Book of Sports*, p. 179
3   Speech given by Richard Tattersall, son of Old Dick, in 1866, reproduced in Vincent Orchard, *Tattersall's: Two Hundred Years of Sporting History*, p. 217
4   Ibid., p. 161
5   Druid, *Post and Paddock*, p. 46
6   Ibid.
7   *Tattersall's New Rules and Regulations*, 9 February 1843
8   *New Sporting Magazine*, August 1844, p. 85
9   Druid, *Post and Paddock*, p. 45
10 Egan, *Book of Sports*, p. 179
11 *Monthly Magazine*, vol. XXIV (July–December 1837) Craven, *Tableaux from Sporting Life*

12 *Illustrated London News*, 25 March 1843, quoted in Orchard, *Tattersall's*
13 *Monthly Magazine*, vol. XXIV (July–December 1837) Craven, *Tableaux from Sporting Life*
14 *The Times*, 28 May 1844
15 Quoted in ibid., 28 May 1844
16 Sylvanus, *Bye Lanes*, p. 69
17 Letter from Sarah Crockford to Tattersall
18 *The Times*, 28 May 1844
19 *Bell's Life*, 2 June 1844
20 Ibid., 2 June 1844
21 Ibid., 7 July 1844
22 John Norman, evidence given before the House of Lords Select Committee, line 506
23 Select Committee, line 818
24 *New Tom Spring's Life in London*, Saturday 13 July 1844
25 Letter to the *Morning Post*, in *Bell's Life*, 2 June 1844
26 Jockey Club resolutions published in the House of Lords Select Committee, p. 180

Chapter 15: A Game of Musical Stables

 1 Jockey Club Inquiry, p. 30
 2 Ibid., evidence given by George Worley, p. 6
 3 Ibid., p. 7
 4 *Bell's Life*, trial report, Sunday 7 July
 5 Quoted in John Welcome, *Irish Horseracing: An Illustrated History*, pp. 23, 26–7
 6 Ibid., p. 27
 7 Jockey Club Inquiry, evidence given by Thomas Ferguson
 8 Ibid., evidence given by William Carlin, p. 31
 9 Ibid., evidence given by Thomas Ferguson, pp. 27, 28
10 Ibid., evidence given by Dominick Holland, pp. 34, 35
11 Ibid., evidence given by the Earl of Stradbroke, p. 50
12 Ibid., evidence given by George Worley, p. 7
13 Evidence given by Thomas Ferguson, pp. 29, 30
14 C.M. Prior, *The History of the Racing Calendar and Stud-Book*, p. 203
15 Quoted in James Rice, *The History of the British Turf*, p. 212
16 Jockey Club Inquiry, evidence given by the Earl of Stradbroke, p. 50
17 Ibid., evidence given by Mr Drage, p. 20
18 Ibid., evidence given by George Worley, p. 7

19 Ibid., evidence given by William Butt, p. 21
20 Ibid., evidence given by John Bartlett, pp. 22, 24, 25, 26

Chapter 16: The Full Majesty of the Law

1   Osbaldeston and Cummings, *Autobiography*, p. 196
2   Quoted in Prior, *Racing Calendar*, p. 203
3   Anonymous letter quoted in Kent, *Bentinck*, pp. 409–10
4   *The Era*, Sunday 7 July 1844
5   Quoted in *Bailey's Magazine*, January 1864
6   Letter from Wood's solicitor published in *Bell's Life*, Sunday 7 July 1844
7   Osbaldeston and Cummings, *Autobiography*, p. 196
8   Greville, *Memoirs*, vol. V, pp. 182, 184
9   House of Commons Select Committee, p. 146, line 2144; p. 150, line 2239
10 Mike Huggins, 'Lord Bentinck, the Jockey Club and Racing Morality in Mid-nineteenth-century England: The "Running Rein" Derby Revisited', p. 434
11 *Bell's Life*, Sunday 7 July 1844
12 Osbaldeston and Cummings, *Autobiography*, p. 196
13 John Timbs, *The Curiosities of London*, p. 502
14 *The Penny Cyclopaedia of the Society for the Diffusion of Useful Knowledge*, p. 110
15 Greville, *Memoirs*, vol. VI, p. 14
16 *Bell's Life*, 9 June 1844

Chapter 17: Their Day in Court

1   *Bell's Life*, 7 July 1844
2   Osbaldeston and Cummings, *Autobiography*, p. 196
3   Quotations on pp. 217–28 from *Bell's Life*, 7 July 1844
4   Osbaldeston and Cummings, *Autobiography*, p. 196
5   Luttrell, *Crockford's*, p. 43
6   *Bell's Life*, 7 July 1844
7   Jockey Club Inquiry, evidence given by John Bartlett, p. 26

Chapter 18: An Eventful Evening

1   House of Lords Select Committee, line 1295

2 *The Times*, 3 July 1844
3 Ibid., 4 June 1931
4 Ibid., 4 June 1931
5 House of Lords Select Committee, line 1287
6 Ibid. lines 1282, 1301; cover page
7 Ibid., lines 1295, 1435

Chapter 19: The Verdict

1 *The Times* 3 July 1844
2 *Bell's Life*, 7 July 1844
3 *The Era*, 7 July 1844
4 *Bell's Life*, 7 July 1844
5 Baron Alderson quoted in *Bell's Life*, 7 July 1844

Chapter 20: Gentlemen Triumphant

1 *Bell's Life*, Sunday 7 July 1844
2 Ibid., 14 July 1844
3 Ibid., 7 July 1844
4 *The Era*, 27 April 1845
5 *Bell's Life*, 7 July 1844
6 Prior, *Racing Calendar*, p. 209
7 *The Era*, Sunday 7 July 1844
8 Quoted in Prior, *Racing Calendar*, p. 209
9 *Bell's Life*, Sunday 25 August 1844
10 *The Times*, 4 November 1844
11 *Bell's Life*, Sunday, 28 July 1844
12 *Hansard*, 10 July 1844
13 *The Times*, 12 July 1844
14 *Hansard*, 10 July 1844
15 *The Times*, Friday 12 July 1844
16 *Hansard*, 10 July 1844
17 *The Times*, 12 July 1844
18 *Bell's Life*, Sunday 11 August 1844
19 Rice, *British Turf*, p. 227
20 *Bell's Life*, Sunday 11 August 1844

Epilogue

1 Kent, *Bentinck*, pp. 241–2, 241
2 Disraeli, *Bentinck*, p. 23
3 Kent, *Bentinck*, p. 242
4 Portland Archives, correspondence PwK 442 Bentinck to his brother the Marquis of Titchfield 5th Duke of Portland, on the sale of his stud, 11 September 1846
5 Portland Archives, correspondence PwL 425 Letter from Lord John Manners to his father, Dunblane, 27 September 1848
6 Greville, *Memoirs*, vol. VI, p. 122
7 Portland Archives, PwL 415
8 *Sportsman's Magazine*, 26 April 1845
9 Letter to Duncombe, in T.H. Duncombe, *The Life and Correspondence of Thomas Slingsby Duncombe*, p. 61
10 Weatherby and Weatherby, *Racing Calendar*, vol. 75, p. XXXV
11 *Morning Chronicle*, 16 July 1857
12 *Examiner*, Saturday 2 May 1857
13 *Bailey's Magazine*, January 1864
14 *The Sporting Magazine*, June 1845, p. 436
15 Prior, *Racing Calendar*, p. 204
16 Boulton, *Amusements of Old London*, p. 129
17 Ibid., p. 164
18 *Bell's Life*, 13 February 1886

Bibliography

Abdy, Charles, *Epsom Past*, Phillimore, UK (2001)

Anon., *Full Account of the Atrocious Murder of the late Mr W Weare*, Sherwood, Jones & Co., London (1823)

Anon., *Horse-Racing, its history and early records of the principal race meetings, with anecdotes etc*, Saunders, Otley & Co., London (1863)

Anon., *Pennycyclopaedia for the Society for the Diffusion of Useful Knowledge* (1858), Knight & Co., London (1958)

Apperley, Charles James, 'Nimrod', 'The Anatomy of Gaming' from *Fraser's Magazine* (1837–8)

——*The Chase, the Turf and the Road*, John Murray, London (1837)

Archer, Revd. T., 'Gaming and its Consequences', published in *Christian Instruction Society Lectures, 1837–1838*, James Paul, London (1838)

Ashton, John, *The History of Gambling in England*, Duckworth & Co., London (1898)

Baker, Rowland G.M., *Boyle Farm – Thames Ditton*, from molesey-history.co.uk (1987)

Bird, T.H., *Admiral Rous and the English Turf*, Puttnam, London (1939)

Birley, Derek, *Sport and the Making of Britain*, Manchester University Press, (1993)

Black, Robert, *The Jockey Club and Its Founders*, Smith, Elder & Co., London (1891)

Blyth, Henry, *Hell and Hazard*, Weidenfeld & Nicolson, London (1969)

Booth, J.B., *Bits of Character: A Life of Henry Hall Dixon*, Hutchinson, London (1936)

Boulton, William B., *Amusements of Old London*, vols 1 and 2, John C. Nimmo, London (1901)

Bourke, Algernon, *The History of Whites, with the White's Betting Book*, Waterlow & Sons, London (1892)

Brady, James, *Strange Encounters*, Hutchinson, London (1946)

Burnet, Alastair, *The Derby: The Official Book of the World's Greatest Race*, Michael O'Mara Books, London (1993)

Church, Michael, 'Derby Stakes 1780–1997', *Racing Post*, London (1997)

Clapson, Mark, *A Bit of a Flutter: Popular Gambling and English Society*, Manchester University Press, (1992)

Connor, Patricia and Lionel Lambourne, *Derby Day 200*, Westerham Press Ltd, p. 8

Cruikshank, George, *The Betting Book*, 2nd edition, W. & F.G. Cash, London (1852)

Custance, Henry, *Riding Recollections and Turf Stories*, Edward Arnold, London (1894)

Darwin, Bernard, *John Gully and His Times*, Cassell & Co., London (1935)

Day, William, *Reminiscences of the Turf*, Richard Bentley & Sons; London (1886)

Dickens, Charles, *American Notes for General Circulation*, Harper & Brothers, New York (1842)

——*Nicholas Nickleby*, Hurd & Houghton, New York (1867)

——*The Life and Adventures of Martin Chuzzlewit*, Penguin Classics, London (1999)

——*Selected Journalism 1850–1870*, Penguin Books, London (1997)

Disraeli, Benjamin, *Sybil: or, the Two Nations*, Bernh. Tauchnitz Jun., Leipzig (1845)

——*Lord George Bentinck: a political biography*, Colburn & Co., London (1852)

——*Letters 1852–1856*, University of Toronto Press, Canada (1989)

Dixon, H.H. 'The Druid', *The Post and the Paddock*, Rogerson and Tuxford, London (1862)

Dodds, John W., *The Age of Paradox*, Victor Gollancz, London (1953)

Downes Miles, Henry, *Pugilistica*, Weldon, London (1880)

Duncombe, T.H., *The Life and Correspondence of Thomas Slingsby Duncombe*, Horst & Blackett, London (1868)

Edwards, Frederic, *Brief Treatise on the Law of Gaming, Horse-Racing & Wagers*, H. Butterworth, London (1839)

Egan, Pierce, *Boxiana, or sketches of Ancient and Modern Pugilism*, The Folio Society, London (1813)

——*Pierce Egan's Book of Sports, and Mirror of Life*, William Tegg & Co., London (1847)

Faught, C.B., *The Oxford Movement*, The Pennysylvania State University Press, US (2003)

Flavin, Michael, *Gambling in the Nineteenth-Century English Novel*, Sussex University Press, Brighton (2003)

Foster, Theodore, *Foster's Cabinet Miscellany*, New York (1836)

Francis, George Henry, *Orators of the Age: Comprising Portraits, Critical, Biographical and Descriptive*, Harper & Brothers, New York (1854)

Grant, James, *The Great Metropolis*, London (1838)

Greville, C.F., *The Greville Memoirs 1814–1860*, ed. Lytton Strachey and Roger Fulford, Macmillan & Co., London (1938)

——*The Diaries of Charles Greville*, edited by Edward Pearce, Pimlico, London (2006)

Gronow, Rhys Howell, *The Reminiscences and Recollections of Captain Gronow*, abridged by John Raymond, Bodley Head, London (1964)

Huggins, Mike, *Flat Racing and British Society 1790–1914*, Frank Cass Publishers, London (2000)

——'Lord Bentinck, the Jockey Club and Racing Morality in Mid-nineteenth-century England: The "Running Rein" Derby Revisited', from *The International Journal of the History of Sport*, vol. 13, no. 3, pp. 432–44; Frank Cass Publishers, London (1996)

Hughson, David, *London, being an accurate History and Description of the Metropolis and its Neighbourhood*, J. Stratford, London (1808)

Humphreys, A.L., *Crockford's, or The Goddess of Chance in St James's Street*, Hutchinson, London (1953)

Hunn, David, *Goodwood*, Davis Poynter, London (1975)

Kent, John, *The Racing Life of Lord George Cavendish Bentinck MP, and other Reminiscences*, William Blackwood & Sons, Edinburgh and London (1892)

Latane, David E., 'Charles Molloy Westmacott and the Spirit of the Age', from *Victorian Periodicals Review*, vol. 40, no. 1 (Spring 2007) pp. 44–72

Longrigg, Roger, *The History of Horse Racing*, Macmillan, London (1972)

Luttrell, Henry, *Crockfords, or Life in the West*, Saunders & Otley, London (1828)

MacDonald Fraser, George, *Royal Flash*, Penguin Books Ltd, England (1970)

Margetson, Stella, *Leisure and Pleasure in the Nineteenth Century*, Cassell & Co., London (1969)

Monypenny, William Flavelle & George Earle Buckle, *The Life of Benjamin Disraeli Earl of Beaconsfield*, John Murray, London (1929)

Moorhouse, Edward, *The Romance of The Derby*, The Biographical Press, London (1908)

Mortimer, Roger, *The Jockey Club*, Cassell, London (1958)

——*The History of the Derby Stakes*, Cassell, London (1962)

Nevill, Ralph, *London Clubs. Their History and Treasures*, Chatto & Windus, London (1911)

Newmarket (pseudonym), *Chapters From Turf History*, National Review, London (1922)

Oliphant, G.H.H., *The Law Concerning Horses, Racing, Wagers and Gaming*, S. Sweet, London (1847)

Onslow, Richard (ed.) *Great Racing Gambles and Frauds*, vol. 2, Marlborough Books, Swindon (1992)

Osbaldeston, George, and E.D. Cummings, *Squire Osbaldeston: His Autobiography*, John Lane, London (1926)

Parker, C.S., *Life and Letters of Sir James Graham*, John Murray, London (1907)

Polden, Patrick, 'A Day at the Races: Wood v Leadbitter in Context', from the *Journal of Legal History:* vol. 14 (April 1993), Frank Cass, London

Pownall, Henry, *Some Particulars Relating to the History of Epsom*, W. Dorling, London (1825)

Prior, C.M., *The History of the Racing Calendar and Stud-Book*, Lewsey, London (1926)

Puckler-Muskau, Hermann, *Tour In England, Ireland, and France*, Effingham Wilson, London (1832)

Rice, James, *The History of the British Turf*, Sampson Low, Marston, Searle & Rivington, London (1879)

Rous, H.J., *On The Laws and Practice of Horse Racing, etc*, A.H. Baily & Co., London (1866)

Seth-Smith, Michael, *John Gully*, in *Stud & Stable*, vol. 4 no. 1 (January 1965) Stud & Stable Ltd, London

——*Lord Paramount of the Turf*, Faber & Faber, London (1971)

Seth-Smith, Michael, and Roger Mortimer, *Derby 200*, Guinness, Middlesex (1984)

Sheppard, F.H.W. (ed.), *Survey of London; Vols. 29 & 30*, English Heritage, London (1960)

Siltzer, Frank, *Newmarket: Its Sport and Personalities*, Cassell & Co., London (1923)

Steinmetz, Andrew, *The Gaming Table*, Tinsley Brothers, London (1870)

Sylvanus, *The Bye Lanes and Downs of England*, Richard Bentley, London (1859)

Tibballs, Geoff, *Great Sporting Scandals*, Robson Publishing, UK (2003)

Timbs, John, *The Curiosities of London*, David Bogue, London (1855)

Todd, Alpheus, *Parliamentary Government in England*, vol. 1; Longmans Green & Co., London (1887)

Vamplew, Wray, 'Reduced Horse Power: The Jockey Club & the Regulation of British Horseracing', from *Entertainment and Sports Law Journal*, vol. 2, no. 3, University of Warwick (2003)

——*The Turf*, Penguin Books, London (1976)

Wall, C.H., 'Hells in London', from *Fraser's Magazine* (August 1833)

Weatherby, Charles and James, *The Racing Calendar* (1844)

——*The Racing Calendar*, (1847)

Welcome, John, *Cheating at Cards: The Cases in Court*, Faber & Faber; London (1963)

——*Irish Horseracing: An Illustrated History*, Macmillan, London (1982)

Whyte, James Christie, *History of the British Turf,* 2 vols, Henry Colburn, London (1840)

Wykes, Alan, *Gambling,* Aldus Books Ltd, London (1964)

Wynn Jones, Michael, *The Derby,* Croom Helm Ltd, London (1979)

Newspapers & Magazines

Bailey's Magazine of Sports and Pastimes

Bell's Life in London and Sporting Chronicle

Bentley's Miscellany

Fraser's Magazine

The Illustrated London News

John Bull

Lloyds Weekly London Newspaper

Monthly Magazine

Morning Chronicle

Morning Post

New Sporting Magazine

Otago Witness

Sportsman's Magazine

Sportsman's Gazette

The Era

The Times

Official sources and documents

Annual Register for 1837

Strathmore Archives, Durham County Record Office (DCRO)

Goodwood Archives, West Sussex Record Office

Hansard debates

House of Commons Select Committee Report on the Laws Respecting Gaming, 1844, from Parliamentary Archives

House of Lords Select Committee Report on the Laws Respecting
    Gaming, 1844, from Parliamentary Archives
Portland Papers, University of Nottingham
Running Rein Case Papers from The Jockey Club Archives

Index